Veil Obsessed

Veil Obsessed

Representations in Literature, Art, and Media

Edited by
Umme Al-wazedi
and **Afrin Zeenat**

Syracuse University Press

For a listing of books published and distributed by Syracuse University Press,
visit https://press.syr.edu.

ISBN: 9780815638421 (hardcover)
         9780815638414 (paperback)
         9780815657118 (e-book)

Library of Congress Control Number: 2024903225

Manufactured in the United States of America

In memory of our fathers,
who gave us a good education,
which gave us the wings to fly.

Mohammad Siddique (1935–2014)
Dr. Wazed Ali (1936–2020)

Contents

Acknowledgments

This project began with a panel that we had organized for the Modern Language Association's annual conference. Seeing the number of interested participants and the many standing in the audience, we decided to write a book proposal, and here is that book now. We want to give our heartiest thanks to Deborah M. Manion, who was our first acquisition editor for Syracuse University Press. The COVID-19 pandemic and the death of one of our fathers in 2020 halted this project. Deborah was very kind and kept follow-up conversations with us. She also showed immense patience when waiting for the reviewers' comments as many of the faculty were struggling with teaching online, caring for people in their own families, and handling their students' mental health. We thank the anonymous reviewers, who took the time to read the manuscript during the pandemic and made constructive comments.

Our children are our most significant supports and were OK with sometimes having to heat up their food and go along their ways. Thank you, Filza and Zaria, Abhik and Ila. In addition, we cannot think of our academic careers without mentioning our spouses. Thank you, Iqbal Ahmed and Dr. Abdur Razzaque, for showing grace to us.

We thank our institutions, Augustana College and Dallas College, for their support. Augustana College provided a generous grant from the Academic Initiative Funds.

Finally, our contributors deserve all our gratitude. You have been with us through these past years. You have revised your chapters multiple times according to the reviewers' comments. This book would not have seen the light of day without your patience and support. So, thank you!

Veil Obsessed

Introduction

The Hijab

Umme Al-wazedi and Afrin Zeenat

The ancient and modern history of hijab and its resurgence in our time form an important aspect of the representation of women and Islam in literature, film and television, and the fine arts. Veiling, or hijab, as a practice has existed for thousands of years. Yet in Europe, the United States, and some countries in South Asia, the hijab is often presented through misconceptualizations. The discussions on hijab recurrently run along essentialist and ahistorical lines, associating Islam with ideologies of oppression, shame, and honor. The media in both the East and the West obsessively condemn or valorize practices of hijab. Moreover, the Muslim immigrant issue in Europe and the fear of Islam and Muslims in connection with terrorism in the United States have heightened the controversy over uses of the hijab. In France, the subjects of women and Islam—the veil in particular—have become highly politicized. In Denmark, the hijab is associated with the position of Muslim women as marginalized and subjugated. The rise of Islamic fundamentalism and Hindutva in South Asia, particularly in India, Pakistan, and Bangladesh, influence how Muslim women see and accept the practice of wearing the hijab as they negotiate their status in the nation-state. In *What Is Veiling?* (2014), Sahar Amer establishes the controversy surrounding the hijab by arguing, "The veil may symbolize any number of perceived threats. For some, the veil represents the rise of fundamentalist Islam worldwide, a constant reminder of the Iranian Revolution, and the plight of women in Afghanistan. For others, it demonstrates

1

Muslim women's subordination to Muslim men and the impossibility of assimilating Muslim immigrants into Euro-American secular societies. Others still view the veil as a threat to national security, a potential cover-up for suicide bombers, and a troublesome reminder that the world is not safe at the turn of the new millennium" (2–3). Considering these multiple perceptions of the hijab, we argue that the meaning of hijab can be natural or constructed, real or metaphorical, and religious or political when it is presented through the media, in the teachings of Islam, and as a national symbol of a nation-state. However, simply creating binaries does not adequately describe the situation. There are inherent tensions among the ideas concerning the power of the hijab. Does wearing it give agency to women, or does it represent oppression, thereby creating and perpetuating stereotypes? Such questions do not represent the whole spectrum of women's choices and experiences. Leila Abu-Lughod argues, "Not only are there many forms of covering, which themselves have different meanings in the communities where they are used, but veiling has become caught up almost everywhere now in a politics of representation—of class, of piety, and of political affiliation" (2013, 39). How an individual sees their relationship with the self, family, and community and the nation-state dictates their choice of whether to wear the hijab. Thus, multiple tensions are present in discussing the role of the hijab because we may not have answers to all the complexities. The chapters in this volume identify and address different types of tensions, investigating the history of the hijab, the political standpoint of a nation-state and its relationship to the hijab, and the representation of the hijab in television, artwork, and film. The contributors to this book not only challenge the stereotypes of the representation of the hijab but also go beyond those stereotypes to create complex readings of the hijab in the lives of Muslim women. Bearing in mind Fatima Amrani Zerrifi's argument that the veil "may be a political, religious or cultural taboo that women are trying to dismantle, as it may be a mask, a site of resistance, a third space that women hide behind" (2001, 2), the chapters in this book present multilayered stories of the representation of hijab to problematize the danger of believing in a single story.

Before describing the chapters, we first review some important controversies regarding the existing explanation of the use of hijab in the Quran and the application of that explanation in our societies, particularly in South Asia. Second, we analyze our observation of the controversies over hijab during the Women's March in Washington, DC, in 2017, thus situating ourselves as well as our contributors in a global context. As diasporic Muslim women, we feel that the Women's March is an important topic that should be discussed in this introduction as part of Muslim women's representation in the public (Joseph L. V. Donica further discusses this topic in chapter 9). Finally, we introduce the chapters of the book and their contribution in explaining the multilayered stories of the representation of hijab.

The Discourse on Hijab and the Tension in South Asia

Fatima Mernissi, Sahar Amer, and Asma Barlas have analyzed the verses pertaining to hijab in the Quran, demonstrating their understanding of the veil. Without exception, they found that the word *hijab* is not used to refer to women's clothing because there are other terms that describe women's attire. They also show that verse 33:59, Sura al-Ahzab, is contextual because it was addressed to the women of the Prophet's family: it was used in a particular time to tackle certain social misbehavior, especially on the part of men (Amer 2014, 26; Barlas 2002, 55). Women were not asked to wear an extra item of clothing, "Instead, the Qur'an recommends to adapt clothing already in use to changing circumstances to distinguish Muslim women from slaves and to protect them from harassment in public" (Amer 2014, 26–27), "at a time when women had no legal recourse against such abuse and had to rely on themselves for their own protection" (Barlas 2002, 56). Looking at the hijab from this historical standpoint certainly shows that the hijab gave power to women at this time.

In her book *The Veil and the Male Elite: A Feminist Interpretation of Women's Rights in Islam* (1991), Fatima Mernissi elaborates on the emergence of the veil in the Quran in a chapter titled "The Hijab, the Veil." Here she argues that "the Prophet, during a troubled period at the beginning of Islam, pronounced a verse that was so exceptional and determining for the Muslim religion that it introduced a breach in space that can be understood to be a separation of the public from the private, or indeed the profane from the sacred, but which was to turn into a segregation of the sexes. The veil that descended from Heaven was going to cover up women, separate them from men, from the Prophet, and so from God" (101). She further expounds that after his marriage to Zaynab Binte Jahsh, the Prophet noticed that the male relatives were not leaving his home. This upset him. At this point, "the verse of the *hijab* 'descended' in the bedroom of the wedded pair to protect their intimacy and exclude a third person" (85). According to Mernissi, the first practice of hijab was thus meant only for the women of the Prophet's family. Amer concurs. In verse 33:53, hijab is a special marker, a practice intended for men. Amer states, "It is important to note that the responsibility of observing *hijab* as a spatial curtain is placed here on men, not women" (2014, 24). Barlas argues along these same lines: "Conservatives read these Āyāt as giving Muslim males the right to force women to don everything from the *hijab* (a head veil that leaves the face uncovered) to the burqa (a head-to-toe shroud that hides even the feet; some models even mandate wearing gloves so as to hide the hands). They justify such forms of veiling on the grounds that women's bodies are pudendal, hence sexually corrupting to those who see them; it thus is necessary to shield Muslim men from viewing women's bodies by concealing them" (2002, 54). The important note from Barlas is how the meaning of the hijab and how it is worn and for what purpose have changed in many parts of the world. This tension has created a divide between secular and religious people. Amina Jamal argues that the Islamist movements often use "universal notions of rights," and secular progressive people invoke flexible Islamic traditions (2012, 55). And these shifting meanings are nowhere more controversial than in South Asia.

We feel that the controversy regarding hijab practices is more prominent in South Asia (Afrin Zeenat's chapter reflects some of those controversies). Having grown up in the 1980s and 1990s in South Asia, particularly in Bangladesh and India, we shared some common experiences despite living in different cities. We are surprised by the sudden increase in the number of South Asian women, young and old, wearing the hijab. But this could be happening because, as Jamal argues, the Islamic universalist notions of women's rights are becoming more important than the salient flexible Islamic traditions that have been historically practiced in South Asia. In Bangladesh, national identity does not necessitate Muslim identity, yet there have been some recent tensions about the conflict between Bengali nationalism and what it means to be a Muslim in celebrating the Bengali culture. Dina M. Siddiqi argues that "migration (especially to Arab countries) and access to mass media [have] shifted the public practice and understandings of 'authentic' Islam, which for many people is associated with the Arab/Saudi world" (2020, 67–68).

Our surprise does not stem from an unfamiliarity with purdah, which has always been an important aspect of South Asian Muslim families. We saw our mothers, elderly aunts, and grandmothers use the *achal* (end) of the sari or a *dupatta* to cover their heads, but the recent trend is different. The word *purdah*, an anglicized form of *parda* in Bengali, Hindi, and Urdu, simply means "curtain." Hanah Papanek writes, "To cite only a few selected meanings from a great dictionary of Urdu and Hindi: parda . . . [a] curtain, screen, cover, veil" (1988, 63, ellipses in original). Nishat Haider's chapter continues this discussion about the historical change in South Asians' gaze toward the hijab. We grew up listening to stories about hijab and the oppression of Muslim women in Bengal during British rule. Our grandmothers told us the stories written by Rokeya Sakhawat Hossain, the first Muslim feminist of South Asia. Chapter 7 discusses Hossain's feminist science fiction and utopia, focusing on the avant-garde short story "Sultana's Dream," written and published in 1905. We remember Hossain's story of the woman who fell on the rail lines and died because her maid would not let anyone touch her, not wanting any man to see her face, and thus "the Begum's body was smashed—the burqa torn" (Hossain 1988, 27). This story was written by Hossain in the early 1900s as she reflected on the lives of women caught between the aggression of British colonialism and that of Muslim men.

The notion of hijab in the way it is now celebrated in South Asia, particularly in Bangladesh, has attracted our attention because it is new to the culture that we grew up in. We think there is some truth to what Barlas writes that it is troubling to see "the veil's persistence in its most un-Qur'anic forms (the covering of the face, hands, and feet)" in many parts of the world (2002, 57). We can see how globalization and advancements in technology that collapse spatial and temporal boundaries have contributed to this new form of veiling in South Asia. Unlike the black, two-piece burka traditionally worn in South Asia following independence from Britain, the new colorful and embroidered headpieces that are often color-coordinated with matching outfits puzzle many like us. Instead of deflecting attention, appearing modest, and covering the wearer's curves, which was the main goal behind veiling in the early twentieth century, the new hijab practices call for attention, especially when the wearer supplements a color-coordinated hijab with bright makeup.

Scholars such as Elora Shehabuddin and Naila Kabeer point out that even though the rise of Islamic fundamentalism and geopolitical tensions are causes for new hijab practices, some women also decide to wear the hijab for very personal reasons. Many young girls and women start veiling as a bargaining chip to gain greater access to the outside world, especially in professional contexts in Bangladesh. Shehabuddin notes: "Defining purdah as a state of mind, a purity of thought, something that they carry inside them rather than an expensive outer garment, permits these women to remain in line with religion and tradition, yet free to meet the basic needs of survival. Contrary both to the charges of Islamists and the wishful expectations of secularists, such women do not see themselves as either rejecting religion or embracing a secular modernity" (2012, 9). These young women try to stay abreast of the needs of changing times and realize the need for a good education but also do not want to rebel against parents who are not aware of or have not accepted the new challenges of the changing times. Not only does wearing the hijab alleviate parental fears pertaining to their daughter's security, but it opens possibilities for the wearers, providing them access to the outside world and allowing them to achieve goals beyond their mothers' and grandmothers' wildest dreams.

Although considering this freedom to study and work outside the home that wearing the hijab affords women, we also observe and critique the capitalism that exploits the hijab (there is more discussion of this point in chapter 8). We also see the complexity that pervades this industry—in one way the fashion industry is trying to "educate" communities, and in another it is profiting from the practice of hijab. Amer gives us the history of the rise of the Islamic fashion industry. It began in the 1970s, alongside revivalist Islamic movements throughout Muslim-majority countries such as Saudi Arabia and the United Arab Emirates and in the Persian/Arab

Gulf region generally (2014, 151). Could these countries' fashion have traveled to countries such as Bangladesh? In contrast, Emma Tarlo, in *Visibly Muslim: Fashion, Politics, Faith* (2010), studies fashion in creating a distinct and visible Muslim woman's identity in Britain. She argues that the Muslim owners of these clothing companies, both men and women, are trying to create a counterdiscourse to the idea that "in the case of images of women, hijabs, jilbabs and niqabs function both to indicate (and by implication, confirm) the idea that Muslim cultural and religious values and behavior are somehow alien and different" (9–10). Tarlo sees this industry as instead contributing to Britain's awareness that Muslim women can and wish to look beautiful. The coexistence of beauty with Islamic fashion trends is the subject of Elizabeth Bucar's book *Pious Fashion: How Muslim Women Dress* (2017). She argues that many women use "clothing and adornment to cultivate their own characters, to build community, and to make social critiques" (190). Although this trend in fashion can help to fight Islamophobia, Sahar Amer and Martine Antle's chapter shows us that it can also create tensions within a nation-state such as France.

This discussion and criticism about hijab practices and the exploitation by the free-market economy are not new. Critics such as Amer and Bucar have already analyzed this issue, but here we address its relevance to the new surge in hijab practices. What is the market analysis for hijab and Muslim clothing as a whole? According to *State of the Global Islamic Economy Report 2015/16* (2015), Muslim consumers spend an estimated US$230 billion on clothing, a figure that is projected to grow to US$327 billion by 2019 (6). This amount is larger than the current combined clothing markets of the United Kingdom ($107 billion), Germany ($99 billion), and India ($96 billion). Fashion shows in the United States add to that market (potentially including clothing brands such as OBEY in the future). In discussing Euro-American designers and how they adapt to Islamic fashions, Amer notes that some fashion designers sell only to affluent women (2014, 156). Thus, we raise this question about the exploitation of the hijab in the fashion industry in light of the analysis by Hoda Katebi, a Chicago-based Iranian American fashion blogger who focuses on ethical fashion production. Katebi argues that "our [Muslim women's] representation stops at the cash registers. And fighting for inclusion in the very systems that require exploitation and even violence against our own communities is not a step forward, but a step back" (2019). We do see some connections between the rise in the use of fashionable hijabs in Bangladesh and India and the fashion industry's marketing.

Tension in the Women's March, 2017

One more example illustrates the controversy surrounding the hijab that we focus on in this book. The picture of a woman wearing a US flag hijab, widely advertised during and after the Women's March in 2017, was meant to show the power of the Muslim woman as a US citizen at a moment when Muslims were being targeted by Donald Trump and his administration. However, we argue that through this image the woman performs a gendered citizenship. Muslim women are being asked to prove their citizenship by showing that they are patriots who can wear the flag as their hijab. This is a nationalistic approach, like President Trump's rhetoric: America first and the American flag first, even in the guise of a hijab. This image alienates Muslim women who do not wear the hijab and questions the diversity of Muslim women. Furthermore, it creates the same fear that President Trump's rhetoric provoked among white, Christian Americans: Muslims are wearing the flag and thus have captured "our" country. Such fear can easily drive this propaganda: all Muslims are terrorists; they need either to be banned from coming to the United States or to be under surveillance. Jonathan F. Keiler explains what a Muslim woman wearing a hijab comes to mean as a result of this kind of representation: "If there were any doubt as to whether the woman depicted [wearing the US flag hijab] is a 'patriotic American Muslim' one need only examine her face to dispense with that idea. [She] is not smiling, nor seemingly proud of her Stars and Stripes covering. Rather her visage is at once seductive and defiant. . . . The intention is to seduce and intimidate at the same time. If there were any doubt about the latter, the caption of the image itself invokes the word 'fear[,]' subliminally reinforcing the idea" (2017). The photo creates fear more than it portrays a patriot, and that is exactly our point as well: Does the photo mean well for Muslim people, or is it simply appropriating a stereotype? Many people don't know that this was not a new photo in 2017; the woman in the photo is Munira Ahmed, a Bangladeshi American.

Her photo was taken by a Muslim photographer, Ridwan Adhami, to fight Islamophobia in the United States after September 11, 2001. However, the most distributed image of her was made by Shepard Fairey, the white male founder of the clothing brand OBEY. Such out-of-context representation creates tensions, as seen in Keiler's argument. Katebi writes about such tensions:

> Know that patriotism is not a form of liberation, but is inherently op-
> pressive. . . . Know that Muslims are tired of having to "prove" they are
> American. . . . An over-emphasis on being American as a prerequisite
> of deserving respect is harmful for immigrants and refugees. Especially
> under the new administration that already has plans of "extreme vet-
> ting" to prove American-ness. This is only pushing their agenda fur-
> ther. . . . Know that if the only time you are comfortable uplifting [a]
> Muslim woman is when her image has been crafted by a white man and
> is draped in the American flag, I cannot call you my ally. (2017)

We read Katebi's argument to mean that in this image only the reductive meaning of the hijab is being advertised. In chapter 9, Joseph L. V. Donica discusses the role of the hijab as a political critique, which "allows space for difference while allowing [Muslim women] to lead autonomous lives." He argues that "concepts such as critique, participation, and citizenship are al-ways in flux, but the veiled woman . . . seems to be at the center of what those concepts are coming mean." Thus, Shehabuddin's argument makes perfect sense: "The greater visibility of Muslim women in the United States—for example, at the Women's March, in Congress, in corporate fashion lines, and on TV and cinema screens—does not necessarily indicate that those Muslim women are fighting stereotypes" (2021, 284–85).

Multiple Global Tensions

The book's chapters are organized into five broad categories. Chapters 1, 2, and 3 are in part 1, "Beyond Orientalism and Colonialism: The Lasting Influence of the Colonial Gaze," addressing questions such as: How has the colonial gaze re-created/rephrased the notion of veiling? What are the lasting influences of this gaze? Why is it important to examine the colonial gaze? Both historically and politically, veiling in Islam is supposed to have its origins in the Quran, although the surah or verse where it is mentioned can be interpreted literally or metaphorically. Muslim religious leaders have invariably understood the Quranic injunction in a literal sense and have enjoined female believers to don the hijab. More liberal readings of the verse interpret "hijab" as symbolic veiling, simply practicing general modesty in clothing. Thus, veiling has been variously interpreted, reflecting how women's bodies are variously contested, and it has been manipulated according to its numerous interpretations.

In chapter 1, "Manipulations of the Veil in Victorian Imaginings of *The 1001 Nights*," Michael James Lundell examines two major versions of *The 1001 Nights*: Edward William Lane's *Arabian Nights Entertainments* (1838–40) and Richard F. Burton's *Alf Layla wa Layla* (1885–88). He argues that these two versions forever changed perceptions of the *Nights* by insisting on the story collection's anthropological verisimilitude. Both Lane and Burton included extensive paratextual elements in the form of appended essays, footnotes, and endnotes that attempted to explain a variety of cultural practices in Islam and the Arabic-speaking world based on their own interpretations. Both Lane and Burton, however, problematically and misguidedly examined and highlighted throughout their works the veil as evidence of what they interpreted to be Islamic beliefs regarding women. Lundell contends that the importance of studying views of the veil through Burton and Lane's writings cannot be underestimated. Both authors and their works were extremely influential in the ways they reaffirmed and illuminated skewed European anthropological ideas about "the East." Their versions of the *Nights* were reproduced often, and so the authors' explanations were accepted as truths in textbooks, dictionaries, literary histories, and other important texts. Lane's and Burton's portrayals of Muslim women in particular were tied to European ideas about Muslims' treatment of women and the secondary role that women supposedly play in that culture. These portrayals and ideas have had lasting impacts, at times even outside of Europe, on the manipulation of ideological elements concerning gender and Islam. Lundell's chapter explores how these elements have prompted Western views of the veil. Lundell applies a contemporary postcolonial and semiotic analysis to representations of the veil in several stories from Lane and Burton. He concludes that the presentation of complex anthropological meanings via the *Nights* has more to do with the politicization of literature than with the tales themselves.

In chapter 2, "Unveiling the Colonial Blind Spot in *The Battle of Algiers*," Abdullah A. Hasan critically explores Gillo Pontecorvo's film *The Battle of Algiers* (1966), chronicling the conflict between North African and European gender roles during the eight-year Algerian revolution against French colonization. This movie shows France's manipulation of its self-produced image of "nurturing motherliness" and motherly "selflessness" and points out that the struggle was also about gendered ideological discourse: France was the cultivating, maternal altruist, and Algeria was the obstinate, "infantile receiver." This chapter examines how veiled Algerian women diverged from prescriptive criticisms of patriarchy. Hasan states, "While historicizing the ontogenesis of Algerian feminine agency as a colonially determined event, the film presents unsettling female roles that disrupt both Algerian and French androcentric codifications of the ['free' woman]" by engaging in modes of resistance unsanctioned by mainstream feminism. The chapter demonstrates how Algerian women, by employing their clothing as a resistance tool, were able to redefine veiling as an amorphous cultural phenomenon that evolves alongside changing social and historical contexts. Both fundamentalist and orientalist discourses, Hasan contends, fail to capture the complexity of veiling because they complement each other in creating a worn-out dichotomy. Threatened by "fallen" women, fundamentalists assume women's rebelliousness and demand veiling to quell it. Orientalist discourse typically assumes complete submission until women are freed by colonial intervention, military or otherwise. Hasan's postcolonial and feminist analysis historicizes veiling in the film, juxtaposing it with orientalist depictions of North African women in Malek Alloula's collected postcards in *The Colonial Harem* (1986).

In chapter 3, "Roots and Routes of the Veil in the Maghreb," Rachida Yassine describes veiling practices in the Maghreb. She reiterates that "women's bodies are used everywhere to symbolize and project collective ideals." In the Maghreb (Morocco, Algeria, and Tunisia), "women's bodies, women's dress, and women's presence in particular spaces have always been used as a way of characterizing a host of moral, political, and religious notions." Yassine explores some of the historical, sociopolitical, cultural, and religious factors that have influenced the perception and representation of the veil in the Maghreb by "consider[ing] the impact of colonial history and Western cultural discourses that disseminated detrimental stereotypes of Arab/Muslim women through literature, photography, film, television, and the media. These stereotypes continue to shape images of Arab women in the West."

Part 2, "Immigrant Women and the Veil in Fiction: Patriarchy, Negotiations, and Agency," poses questions such as: How does the immigrant woman negotiate whether to wear the veil or not? What kind of agency does the veil provide for women in the Diaspora? In chapter 4, "Fictionizing the Veil: Patriarchy, Matriarchy, and Jihad in Fadia Faqir's *Willow Trees Don't Weep*," Dallel Sarnou delves into the stigmatization of the headscarf, hijab, or veil. As a major aspect of the interiorization of women by Islam, the hijab has been subject to criticism in recent novels by women authors from the Middle East who write in English for an English audience located in the United States or the United Kingdom. Fadia Faqir, one of these Anglophone Arab writers, seeks to re-represent the Arab and/ or Muslim woman in the West. As Sarnou points out, "[She] is one of the most acclaimed Arab writers in the West" because she has written "consistently for and about Arabs in the Diaspora." Sarnou analyzes Faqir's latest novel, *Willow Trees Don't Weep* (2014), demonstrating how Faqir "negotiates meanings of" secularism versus fundamentalism, jihadis as subjects, fathering, women, and wars. This chapter provides a different insight into how the veil is perceived by a secular Arab woman.

Part 3, "Television and the Veil: Reinforcement of the Veil," focuses on the following questions: How do the media portray the veil? What role does it play in reinforcing veiling in certain communities? In chapter 5, "Veiling and Ideology: The Islamic State's Use of Iranian TV Series to Propagate Its Gender Ideals through Veiling," Cherie Taraghi argues that the imposition of the veil is crucial for the Iranian regime's identity as an Islamic nation and Islamic ideology. At the same time, veiling is one of the most openly contested aspects of the country's gender laws, with many women using creative means of dressing to subvert and challenge the imposition. She states that although the subject of veiling in Iran has been extensively studied to date, the regime's efforts at visualizing and defining its stance on the topic have not been explored. This chapter discusses how the veil is used to define female identity and agency in locally produced Iranian TV dramas. On a deeper level, it examines how the Iranian regime negotiates and imposes its political and ideological values and norms on its citizens by means of these dramas. Since local television is entirely state owned in Iran, all TV dramas are vetted to reflect the regime's political and ideological values and norms before they are allowed to be aired. Although the veiling portrayed on TV is not as varied as what one encounters on the streets in Iran, it is by no means homogeneous. The level and type of veil portrayed changes based on the character's age, class, education, religiosity, location, lifestyle, and so forth. Through analysis of three recent local TV dramas, *Miveye Mamnoo'e* (Forbidden Fruit, 2008), *Madine* (2015), and *Tanhai'ye Leyla* (Leyla's Loneliness, 2015), Taraghi contends that characters' agency and destiny are directly defined by the way they cover up to suit the regime's ideological requirements.

Chapters 6 and 7 fall under the fourth theme in part 4, "Cinema and the Veil: Dismantling the Master Narrative." They critique Bollywood's use of the veil by addressing these questions: How does cinema reinforce the stereotypical role of the veil? How does the nation-state appear to create a new narrative of the identity of the state (in this case India and the Hindu versus the Muslim) through cinema? In chapter 6, "Representations of Veiling in Bollywood Cinema," Nishat Haider contends that "the frames of veiled women in Bollywood cinema . . . dominate and seduce by investing power in the particular signifier, trope, and description of veiling/unveiling/reveiling in films. The trope of the veiled woman is so powerful in Bollywood that [the veil], . . . though often dialogized . . . as a signifier that silences Muslim women's sexuality, also represents a liberating force, a recovery of the female space, a reclamation of the female gaze, and ownership of both the scopic and haptic zones of the body." This chapter maps out the trajectory of Indian Muslim women's identities based on a "set of visual signifiers" (Karim 2000, 68), namely cultural habitation and the sartorial engagement of veiling. Haider includes "examples from four major shifts in Bollywood cinema" narrative genres: the Muslim historical, the Muslim courtesan, the Muslim social, and the Muslim trauma after September 11, 2001. The veil gathers different significations depending on the spectator and the location. Haider explains that through "concrete analysis of films," she "explores haptic images and their connections to representations of gender/cultural difference framed by means of both 'the skin of the film' . . . and the thin, evocative veil."

Chapter 7 focuses on a particular movie that created furor among Indian audiences and its representation of the Muslim woman's veil. In "Veiled Anxieties in Mani Ratnam's *Bombay*," Afrin Zeenat charts the trajectory of two cultural artifacts and their very different representations of Muslim women. According to Zeenat, utopian possibilities abound for colonial South Asian Muslim women in Hossain's "Sultana's Dream" (1905), "where the practice of purdah (veiling) enforced by Muslim patriarchs is questioned" and subverted through Hossain's portrayal of Ladyland. Infused with "revolutionary potential," Hossain's "avant-garde" vision presents a Muslim "society where women engage in public duties and various intellectual activities, while men remain confined in the *murdana* (male quarters), the inverse of the zenana (female quarters)." A century after Hossain narrated her vision, some South Asian Muslim women have fulfilled her dream, but countless others continue to be oppressed. Although the hijab has recently garnered much attention in global secular discourse, the practice of purdah was and continues to be a scourge in the empowerment of Muslim women. Prevalent among South Asian Muslim women, purdah usually entails wearing some form of outer covering, using a privacy screen in vehicles, and designating a zenana, or female quarters, in homes. The term *purdah* itself refers to a screen or curtain that deflects the male gaze.

Although purdah pervades the Bollywood film industry's century-long history, it has served multiple cinematic purposes in that industry. Used more often by men than women in films, states Zeenat, the burka has been "successfully deployed . . . as the quintessential garment of disguise or camouflage. . . . Once . . . donned, it offers men free access to the zenana quarters or exclusive female gatherings, clandestine meetings with their beloveds, and, most importantly, a getaway from a difficult situation." In *Bombay* (1995), "a neoliberal attempt at depicting Hindu–Muslim communal tensions in a post–Babri Masjid India," Mani Ratnam delineates a Muslim girl "wearing the burka as a religious Other." What happens to the

veiled Shaila reflects "the neoliberal Hindu male concern for her assimilation through a voluntary eschewing of the practice of veiling" as well as the
troubled nature of her exclusion from modern Indian society. To become a
part of that society through marriage to a Hindu, "Shaila must surrender
her burka." Hossain's beatific vision of Indian Muslim women's disavowal
of the "veil as a symbol of female empowerment becomes for Ratnam a
tool for their forced assimilation into the larger identity politics that define the Bollywood entertainment-industrial complex." In analyzing Hossain's "Sultana's Dream" and Mani Ratnam's *Bombay*, Zeenat argues that,
notwithstanding the intent of feminists such as Hossain to call for women
to display agency and unveil themselves, "the Hindu patriarch-savior"
Ratnam becomes the agent who "repurposes the Muslim woman's unveiling as expedient for social assimilation." In Ratnam's hands, the unveiled
Muslim woman becomes the representation of a free Muslim woman.

Finally, Sahar Amer and Martine Antle's essay "The Enduring Controversy over Veiling in Western Europe Today" (chapter 8) and Joseph L. V.
Donica's essay "The Veil in Public Space: Critique, Participation, Citizenship" (chapter 9) point to the theme of part 5, "Toward a New Discourse:
Who Creates the Image?" Together they address the following question:
What is the current position of the veil in the public sphere in the global
world? Amer and Antle argue that one of the biggest misunderstandings
of contemporary Muslim practices is undoubtedly Muslim women's dress.
Laws have been passed in France, Belgium, Germany, and across Europe
over the past ten years legislating what Muslim women can wear and
where. Behind these laws looms the fear of Islamism, the threat posed by
the Islamic State of Iraq and Syria, and the alarm over the radicalization of
Muslim youth—a fear camouflaged in a feminist rhetoric of women's and
human rights. This anxiety over Muslim women's dress appears system-
atically in the wake of bombings and terrorist attacks on European soil.
Most recently, it resurfaced following the killings in Paris in November
2015, the *Charlie Hebdo* massacres in January 2015, and the attacks in
Brussels in March 2016. Along the lines of Amer and Antle's discussion,
the recent criticism by Laurence Rossignol, France's minister for women's
rights, of the rising trend by Western designers to cater to Muslim wom-
en's conservative dress, calling those who encourage "the imprisonment

of women's bodies . . . irresponsible" (qtd. in Amer 2016), demonstrates a larger political desire to regulate what Muslim women wear.

This chapter demonstrates that the new horizons of piety in contemporary Islam are not the radical voices we hear about and see so often in the media. Rather, they consist also and especially of the growing worldwide movement of progressive Islam. This movement is calling for a revision of all conservative interpretations of Islam, peeling off the layers of exegesis that have been imposed on religious texts and that have effectively silenced women and other minorities (LGBTQ+ people, for instance). It is committed to a type of piety that allows these groups to participate in shaping the future of Islam in an egalitarian and inclusive way.

In the final chapter of this book, Joseph Donica explores how "the veil's role in public life has come under well-documented attacks about what exactly it symbolizes and who should be able to wear it." According to Donica, "there are both a political problem and a representative problem in attempts to make the veil cool or hip or just as Western as skinny jeans. These attempts remove not only the veil's religious significance but also its ability to have any critique on US conceptions of what it means to be a citizen and to participate in public life."

This chapter first addresses the role of the veil in public life in the United States and how it has conflicted with certain norms. It then asks "what role the veil might play in offering not only a political critique but also a form of representation for Muslim women that allows space for difference." Donica addresses these questions by analyzing "the role the veil has played in public art" in the #DamnILookGood project as well as in street art. He looks in particular at the controversial French artist Princess Hijab as well as other street artists such as Shepard Fairey, BR1, and Banksy, "all of whom have deployed representations of the veil as social commentary about its role in public life." Finally, the chapter turns to the exhibition *The Seen and the Hidden: (Dis)covering the Veil* at the Austrian Cultural Forum in New York in 2009. "In looking to the role of the veil in public art," states Donica, "we can begin to see how the veil can simultaneously critique certain norms while also offering Muslim women some form of representation that allows for a discussion of their autonomy . . . and what citizenship has come to mean in the United States and Europe."

The Veil! The Veil!

Fatima Mernissi writes, "Like [Scheherazade] I have to face the daily threat of political violence unarmed. Only words can save me. If the West has the power to control time by manipulating images, I thought, then who are we if we do not control our images? Who am I—and who makes my image?" (2001, 82). The various chapters in this book critique the many stereotypes of the hijab and dismantle the attempts to portray a monolithic narrative about the lives of women who wear it. Some of the chapters also point out both the East's and the West's exploitation of the use of the hijab. In conclusion, we must explain the title of our book. We used the anglophone word *veil* rather than *hijab* in the title for a reason. We want to have the "Achebe effect." Readers may recall that Chinua Achebe ends his novel *Things Fall Apart* (1958) from the British district officer's point of view. He seems to say that now that the readers know about the Igbo civilization, would they dare believe the words of the district officer that the Igbo were primitive? It is the same with our title. Now that readers know about the Oriental presentation of the hijab, the current controversy, would they dare to believe a single stereotyping story about the hijab?

Works Cited

Abu-Lughod, Lila. 2013. *Do Muslim Women Need Saving?* Cambridge, MA: Harvard Univ. Press.

Achebe, Chinua. 1958. *Things Fall Apart.* Portsmouth, NH: Heinemann.

Amer, Sahar. 2014. *What Is Veiling?* Chapel Hill: Univ. of North Carolina Press.

———. 2016. "Don't Judge a Muslim Woman's Dress Choice." *Straits Times*, Apr. 14. At https://www.straitstimes.com/opinion/dont-judge-a-muslim-womans-dress-choice.

Barlas, Asma. 2002. *"Believing Women" in Islam: Unreading Patriarchal Interpretations of the Qur'ān.* Austin: Univ. of Texas Press.

Bucar, Elizabeth. 2017. *Pious Fashion: How Muslim Women Dress.* Cambridge, MA: Harvard Univ. Press.

Hossain, Rokeya Sakhawat. 1988. *"Sultana's Dream: A Feminist Utopia" and Selections from "The Secluded Ones."* Edited and translated by Roushan Jahan. With an afterword by Hanna Papanek. New York: Feminist Press at the City Univ. of New York.

Jamal, Amina. 2012. "Global Discourses, Situated Traditions, and Muslim Women's Agency in Pakistan." In *South Asian Feminisms*, edited by Ania Loomba and Ritty A. Lukose, 54–74. Durham, NC: Duke Univ. Press.

Karim, Karim H. 2000. *Islamic Peril: Media and Global Violence*. Montreal: Black Rose.

Katebi, Hoda. 2017. "Please Keep Your American Flags off My Hijab." *Mondoweiss*, Jan. 25. At https://mondoweiss.net/2017/01/please-american-flags/.

———. 2019. "Muslims Have More Visibility Than Ever. But Can We Praise It?" *Washington Post*, June 2. At https://www.washingtonpost.com/opinions/2019/06/02/muslims-have-more-visibility-than-ever-can-we-praise-it/.

Keiler, Jonathan F. 2017. "American Flag Hijab." *American Thinker*, Jan. 22. At https://www.americanthinker.com/articles/2017/01/american_flag_hijab.html.

Mernissi, Fatima. 1991. *The Veil and the Male Elite: A Feminist Interpretation of Women's Rights in Islam*. Translated by Mary Jo Lakeland. New York: Perseus.

———. 2001. *Scheherazade Goes West: Different Cultures, Different Harems*. New York: Washington Square Press.

Papanek, Hanna. 1988. "Afterword. Caging the Lion: A Fable for Our Time." In Rokeya Sakhawat Hossain, *"Sultana's Dream: A Feminist Utopia" and Selections from "The Secluded Ones,"* edited and translated by Roushan Jahan, 58–86. New York: Feminist Press at the City Univ. of New York.

Shehabuddin, Elora. 2012. *Reshaping the Holy: Democracy, Development, and Muslim Women in Bangladesh*. New York: Columbia Univ. Press.

———. 2021. *Sisters in the Mirror: A History of Muslim Women and the Global Politics of Feminism*. Oakland: Univ. of California Press.

Siddiqi, Dina M. 2020. "Muslim Bodies, Imperial Politics and Feminist Frames." In *Women, Veiling and Politics*, edited by Imtiaz Ahmed, 53–73. Dhaka, Bangladesh: Univ. Press Limited.

State of the Global Islamic Economy Report 2015/16. 2015. At https://www.halalbalancing.com/Downloads/Events/2015/SGIEReport2015.pdf.

Tarlo, Emma. 2010. *Visibly Muslim: Fashion, Politics, Faith*. Oxford: Berg.

Zerrifi, Fatima Amrani. 2001. "Stripping Off the Veil: Women's Performance of the Veil from Street to Stage." PhD diss., Univ. of Surrey.

Part 1 Beyond Orientalism and Colonialism

The Lasting Influence of the Colonial Gaze

1

Manipulations of the Veil in Victorian Imaginings of *The 1001 Nights*

Michael James Lundell

> As I approached the shore, I felt like an Eastern bridegroom, about to lift up the veil of his bride, and to see, for the first time, the features which were to charm, or disappoint, or disgust him.
> —Edward William Lane,
> *Description of Egypt* ([1831] 2000)

Edward Lane's description of visiting Egypt for the first time in 1825 is a definitive example of generalized Western apprehensions about the veil. It is a covering for Lane and other Westerners to examine, remove, eroticize, fear, and possibly be charmed by. It is also a representation that can be and has been essentialized and generalized to represent entire countries, cultures, and religions through the lens of Western inspection, with as little input from the people being "studied" as possible. Edward Said's *Orientalism* (1978) refers to these methodologies as problematic in their "generalization about 'the Orient' [that] drew its power from the presumed representativeness of everything Oriental; each particle of the Orient told of its Orientalness" (231). The veil, therefore, became and continues to be a particle for not only Islam and the Muslim woman but also for the entirety of the region encompassing North Africa, Southwest Asia, and beyond. Nineteenth-century translators such as Edward Lane and Richard F. Burton, both of whom published extremely popular renditions of *The 1001 Nights* or *Arabian Nights*, inserted themselves into this essentialist

21

framework and insisted on its continuance. Their translations highlighted purportedly anthropologically true information on the veil that simplified understanding of the Muslim woman into two categories: the oppressed and/or the erotic. This chapter seeks to explore how this essentialist reading of the veil has continued to operate in uneasy and misinformed fashion through the *Nights*—coupling fictional literature with false and colonially related "truths" that have continued to be used as evidence by Western writers of the Muslim woman's "plight."

In her book *Do Muslim Women Need Saving?* (2013), Lila Abu-Lughod writes, "One cannot reduce the diverse situations and attitudes of millions of Muslim women to a single item of clothing" (40), and, indeed, one cannot. This statement seems obvious, and yet texts such as the *Nights* and their readers have continued to do just that: reduce the incredibly diverse physicality of the veil, not to mention the incalculable idiosyncratic reasons for wearing it, across perhaps the entirety of the planet to one simplistic (and easily digestible) yet highly problematic reading. Qasim Amin's book *The Liberation of Women* (1899), in which the author called for a complete ban on the veil in Egypt, highlighted early on the problems inherent in simplistic and misguided "solutions" to gender disparity in Egypt and the region. By focusing efforts so exclusively on a singular reading of the veil across Egypt's vast cultural socioeconomic landscape, Amin offered a one-dimensional "answer" to the state of women in Egypt while ignoring many arguably more important aspects of their lives. Abu-Lughod writes about this book and this generalized reading of the veil, suggesting that "there was a selective concern about the plight of Egyptian women that focused on the veil as a sign of their oppression but gave no support to women's education" (2013, 33). Leila Ahmed broadens the scope of the argument when she argues that "differences of class, ethnicity, and local culture critically qualify the experiences of women and give specificity to the particular ways in which they are affected by the broad discourses on gender within their societies" (1978, 7). There cannot be one simplistic rendering of any discourse on the veil because of the veil's incredibly diverse usage and long, multicultural, and, indeed, multireligious connotations. Texts such as *The 1001 Nights*, however, continue to insist on a singular reading of such cultural elements and to do so problematically from an outsider perspective. These texts sought to speak for the Orient and to transmit that information back to the West. "From the beginning of Western speculation about the Orient, the one thing the Orient could not do was to represent itself," Said suggests (1978, 283), and, indeed, with the *Nights* this silencing has been particularly awkward because the translated and anthropologized text has long also been misrepresented in the West as some kind of archetype of Eastern literature.

The 1001 Nights is still one of the world's most well-known pieces of literature. The story collection continues to be transformed and performed in new translations, stage performances, film, music, scholarship, and more. Its complicated and Eurocentric textual history has been eclipsed by this continued popularity. Despite being generally seen as a work with non-European origins, it is very much *only* a product of the eighteenth- and nineteenth-century European imagination. Antoine Galland purportedly "translated" the text from an Arabic manuscript in his twelve-volume *Les mille et une nuit* (1704–17), but most of the stories he included were not from this manuscript. Pre-eighteenth-century mentions of the *Nights* are scant, as are pre-eighteenth-century manuscripts of the *Nights*. The very few mentions of the work in Arabic are either cursory or dismissive: the tenth-century CE book *Kitab al-Fihrist* by Ibn al-Nadim (Abu'l Faraj Muhammed bin Is'haq al-Nadim) says the *Nights* is "truly a coarse book, without warmth in the telling" (Ibn al-Nadim 1871, 713–14; see also *The Fihrist* 1970). Most other writing and scholarship on pre-eighteenth-century Arabic manuscripts and influences on the *Nights* were written well after Galland's edition as well.

Muhsin Mahdi maps the history of the European manipulation of *Nights'* manuscripts in his edited Arabic version of the work. In the introduction, he shows that nineteenth-century Arabic manuscripts of the *Nights*—ones often pointed to as "originals" or supposedly based on authentic originals—were merely by-products of the European demand for Arabic sources of this hugely popular text (*Kitab Alf Layla wa Layla* 1984). It is curious, therefore, and worth further study as to why the Nights continues to be touted as a representative of Arabic literature and culture when there are so many more important texts that fill this bill. It is unfortunate that texts such as *Kitab al-aghani* (The Book of Songs) by Abu al-Faraj (published 1927–61) and *Muruj al-dhahab* (Meadows of Gold) by al-Masudi (translated into French in 1861)—both from the Abbasid Caliphate time frame in which the *Nights* is considered to have its Arabic genesis and both with scores of existing pre-eighteenth-century Arabic manuscripts, scholarship, and literary mentions—remain understudied and not adequately translated in any European language.

Despite its largely European origins, the *Nights* continues also to be a text that has been studied and received not only as an Eastern text but also as an anthropological work—one offering insight into Islamic customs, Arabic culture, and, more generally, life in the East. This particular manifestation of the *Nights* began in earnest in the nineteenth century, even though the story collection had been published and very popular in Europe since 1704. During the eighteenth century, most versions of the *Nights* and responses to those versions were situated in a much more generally fictional, largely fantastical—rather than truthful—framework. They consisted primarily of Galland's French edition and an anonymously translated English version of Galland titled *The Arabian Nights' Entertainments* that has been dated to 1706 (see *Arabian Nights' Entertainments* 1995; *Arabian Nights Entertainments* n.d.). Both versions vaguely mention that the stories are from the "East," and little writing from the eighteenth century suggests that anyone read the *Nights* then as truth. Paul Nurse writes at length of this reception of the *Nights*. He suggests that eighteenth-century European readers could assuage any anxiety about the *Nights* owing to its possibly *foreign* origins by the "comforting notion that they were perusing contes largely removed only in setting from their indigenous folklore" (2010, 75, emphasis in original)—tales that were basically European folk and fairytales set in non-European settings.

The nineteenth century saw a marked turn toward the anthropological and historical setting of the *Nights*, largely via "paratextual" amendments (which, according to Gérard Genette's [1980, 1997] elaboration, include footnotes and endnotes, prefaces, and additional essays "presenting" the text) by the translators and authors, changing its intentions and receptions from eighteenth-century children's fairytales to more adult literature featuring truthful information on such important features of Eastern culture as the veil. This information not only was presented as truth but also told the reader how to read the truth. Such orientalist texts, according to Said, "can *create* not only knowledge but also the very reality they appear to describe" (1978, 94, emphasis in original). These works and their creators compiled lists of idiosyncratic cultural data and then explained to the reader how to understand them as universalizing truths. Edward W. Lane's version, *The Thousand and One Nights* or *Arabian Nights Entertainments*, published between 1838 and 1840, contains explanatory endnotes and essays that account for almost a quarter of his text. Richard F. Burton's version, *Alf Layla wa Layla*—published around 1885–88 and written largely as a counterresponse to Lane—is still most widely known for its misogynistic, sexually explicit, and racialist footnotes, endnotes, and essays than it is for the narrative contents of the stories themselves. Lane writes that his notes are essential paratextual amendments to the narrative contents: "The original work being designed solely for the entertainment of Arabs, I add copious notes to the translation, to render it more intelligible and agreeable to the English reader" (*The Arabian Nights Entertainments* n.d., 1:xviii). Edward Said aptly points out that such a "voice" carries with it authority over the East. According to Said, Lane's "first-person pronoun moving through Egyptian customs, rituals, festivals, infancy, adulthood, and burial rites, is in reality both an Orientalist masquerade and an Orientalist device for capturing and conveying valuable, otherwise inaccessible information" (1978, 160).

Richard Burton assures his readers that his edition and his notes will educate them. He writes about his personal relationship with people from the region: "Arabs and other Mahommedans, and my familiarity not only with their idiom but with their turn of thought, and with that racial individuality which baffles description, have given me certain advantages over the average student, however deeply he may have studied" (*Alf Layla wa Layla* n.d., 1:xvi). Both Lane and Burton show anxiety about the information within the stories and certainly proclaim a level of understanding that they will offer to their uninformed readership. Both authors were also well-known for their related anthropological works, such as Lane's *An Account of the Manners and Customs of the Modern Egyptians* (1836; see Lane [1836] 1978) and *Arabian Society in the Middle Ages: Studies from The Thousand and One Nights* (1848)—a book based on and expanding his notes in his version of the story collection—and Burton's account of his hajj in disguise in *Personal Narrative of a Pilgrimage to al-Madinah and Meccah* (1855–56; see *Edinburgh Review* 1856). Both men in fact often dressed and tried to pass themselves off as natives, Lane in Egypt and Burton in India, Arabia, and Egypt. This claim to an anthropologically based background contributed to the European reception of the nineteenth-century *Nights* and its perceived truthful contents.

Lane and Burton's *Nights* also have contributed significantly to the European/Western—and then later to even the global—understanding of the veil in problematic and complicated ways. Although contemporary scholarship and writing by Leila Ahmed (1978, 1992, 2001), Lila Abu-Lughod (2003), Katherine Bullock (2002), and Rana Kabbani (1986)—among many others—have critically reevaluated Western (mis)understandings of the veil, and many scholars have mentioned the *Nights* as a related source for these (mis)understandings, no study has exclusively focused on the *Nights'* particular relationship to this issue, even though *The 1001 Nights* has been, since Lane and Burton, one of the cultural literary productions by the West most responsible for its misunderstandings of the veil. These misinterpretations carry with them many nuanced problems but are treated here via two of their most significant ones. First, the veil of the nineteenth-century *Nights* was defined as a symbol of oppression that restricted women of the East from living free lives. Related is the notion that this oppression was an anxious state of being that Lane and Burton presented as an opportunity to portray themselves as liberators from. As in Ruth Bernard Yeazell's "imagined harem" in *Harems of the Mind* (2000), Lane and Burton's veil is an imagined space of entrapment. It is, like the European vision of the harem Yeazell describes, the "Eastern palace" that Westerners imagined entire cultures to be "locked up" in (59). It is a space that is also fictionalized as a helpless and backward arena awaiting liberation, according to Deepa Kuma: "Birthed in the nineteenth century in the context of European colonialism, [the colonial framework of women] rests on the construction of a barbaric, misogynistic 'Muslim world' that must be civilized by a liberal, enlightened West; a rhetoric also known as gendered Orientalism" (2014). Leila Ahmed (1992, 2001) elaborates on this issue as "colonial feminism."

Second, the veil was presented as an object of sensual seduction—a romanticized East that was covered and forbidden to the Western male—hiding possible physical beauty that these men were unable to access. The veil also hid a non-Western fantastical sexuality that Burton and Lane romanticized. Said writes, "The Orient was a place where one could look for sexual experience unobtainable in Europe" (1978, 190). The veil was also similarly a device that could also be used as a weapon to seduce men and get them into trouble or strip them of their money, a common motif throughout many stories in the *Nights*. In addition, Lane and Burton suggest, the veil can also be viewed as a false cover that hides ugliness and can therefore also be seen as a threat because of the resulting anxiety it creates. If a Westerner travels to the East to catch a glimpse of exoticized beauty underneath the veil, it is stated, then they can be severely disappointed if what they see doesn't meet their expectations. This disappointment is seen not only in Lane and Burton's texts but also in accounts by Western travelers to the East who were inspired by those texts.

Lane describes a certain type of veil in great detail throughout his volumes of the *Nights*. He explains early in volume 1 of *The Arabian Nights Entertainments* that "a Mohammadan woman is not allowed to show her face to any man excepting certain near relations and others whom the law prohibits her from marrying" and that "respectable females consider it a great disgrace to be seen unveiled by any men but those above alluded to" (*The Arabian Nights Entertainments* n.d., 1:104). Again, Lane is engaging with what Said calls "representativeness of everything Oriental" through his highly generalized treatment of culture here. By incorporating notes like these into the stories, by associating them with the narrative contents of the *Nights*, Lane offers not only to guide his readers but also to explain how to understand the veil. In this instance, the notes correspond to the "Story of the Porter and the Three Ladies of Baghdad," in which a young, beautiful woman shows her face to a poor porter, asking him to carry an extensive amount of goods from the marketplace for her. She then brings him to a mansion, where she and two other young women invite him to a party, and they all get drunk and have sex. By manipulating her veil in a disrespectful way, the first woman of the story becomes a sort of enchantress to the porter and has her way with him. Lane's suggestion that "respectable females" would never engage in this type of activity characterizes the three women as acting immorally, and so Lane engages in what Gayatri Chakravorty Spivak calls "white men saving brown women" (1988, 297) by reprimanding these characters in his notes and in the narrative itself. Lane resituates our understanding of the text into his own high-handed morality that has little to do with the actual narrative contents of the story, which are less about the veil and more about a humorous, sexually based, light situation. Lane imbues a level of moral seriousness into the situation because of its Eastern setting, warning us to pay attention to this situation because the particular culture represented finds such sexual behavior immoral and antireligious. Lane defines for his readers the moral relevance of the veil early on in his *Nights*. It is an eroticization of this important piece of clothing, one misused here and in many other stories in his version.

Burton's later renditions of the veil continue Lane's colonial-based generalizing but also highlight his own additional misogynistic tendencies, many of which appear in anthropological guises. In the frame tale, musing on his older brother's misfortune, Shah Zaman says to himself, "His wife is in love with that filthiest of filthy slaves. But this only showeth that they all do it," to which Burton appends the footnote, "The very same words were lately spoken in England proving the eternal truth of *The Nights* which the ignorant call 'downright lies'" (*Alf Layla wa Layla* n.d., 2:7). Burton takes a certain authoritative delight in suggesting throughout his *Nights* that all women in the world are dishonest, sexually obsessed, and prone to immoral actions. His paratexts continue this rhetoric in all sixteen volumes of his work, *Alf Layla wa Layla* (n.d., ten volumes) and *Supplemental Nights* (n.d., six volumes), and include several instances of his own anxious interactions with the veil. The story "Women's Wiles" from volume 2 of *Supplemental Nights* is an apt representation of how women and the veil are portrayed throughout Burton. The story, according to *The Arabian Nights Encyclopedia* (2004, 2:768), is found only in an edition of the *Nights* known as the "Breslau" or "Habicht" edition (1825–38), an Arabic edition based on Galland and other unknown sources. A supposed *Nights* manuscript from Tunisia that the German orientalist Maximilian Habicht claimed to have found containing a large number of stories not appearing in any other variant of the text, this edition was later discovered to be a nineteenth-century forgery written by Habicht's assistant, Mordecai ibn al-Najjar. This version consists of, therefore, stories of a strictly European creation masking themselves as Arabic and as being part of the *Nights*. This forgery might seem unusual, but in fact almost every edition of the *Nights*—especially those in the nineteenth century and including even the oldest Arabic manuscript of the *Nights*—has some similar European-based interest behind it (see *Kitab Alf Layla wa Layla* 1984; Nurse 2010; and Reynolds 2006 for further reading on this problematic history).

In Burton's rendition of the story, a young woman, incensed at a shopkeeper's misogynistic sign, tricks him into marrying her by using her veil and keeping her face hidden. She knows he wouldn't marry her if he saw that she is not good-looking, so she shows him other body parts instead: "'Seest thou in me aught of default?' He replied, 'No, O my lady'; and she continued, 'Is it lawful in any one that he should slander me and say that I am humpbacked?' Then she discovered to him a part of her bosom, and when he saw her breasts his reason took flight from his head and his heart craved to her and he cried, 'Cover it up, so may Allah veil thee!'" Burton writes in the explanatory footnote to this scene, "'Ghattí,' [is] still the popular term said to a child showing its nakedness, or a lady of pleasure who insults a man by displaying any part of her person" (*Supplemental Nights* n.d., 2:100). Like Lane's treatment of the three ladies of Bagdad, Burton insists on a singular reading of this scene, reducing the complicated interaction of these characters into what Said calls "generalized Orientalness" for easy consumption. Burton's reading attempts to mask the inherent comedy of the actual text within a morally superior and somber (and ultimately incorrect) rendition. Burton sees the woman's tricks as an insult to the maleness of the shopkeeper and imbues the scene with a binary reading. The woman is being immoral and disrespectful, regardless of her reasons for doing so.

The shopkeeper falls in love with the woman when she promises him a large dowry because of her father's position as qadi. She does not remove the veil, however, until they are married, and it is then that he finds out his "mistake." On the evening of their wedding, "when he lifted the head gear from the bride's head and the veil from her face and looked, he saw a foul face and a favour right fulsome; indeed he beheld somewhat whereof may Allah never show thee the like!" (*Supplemental Nights* n.d., 2:102). The veil, in this instance, clearly was used as a symbol of exoticism—the shopkeeper thought that a beautiful face lay beneath it simply because of that exoticism. It is also seen here as a symbol of (men's) oppression through the shopkeeper's horror at the brashness of the woman unveiling parts of her body to him. Overexaggerating the seriousness of this woman "immorally" revealing her breasts to the shopkeeper, the translator guides us toward a reading wherein this behavior is especially scandalous in an oppressive society that would rather see their women covered up. Burton moralizes the actual humor of the situation to showcase his supposed knowledge of the oppressive society he is teaching us about.

Although these representative examples of the veil in Lane and Burton might seem as if they are confined to the contents of a fictional narrative, their reception in the West and incorporation into Western ideas of the "truth" behind the veil show that these texts did have a significant impact. It is in fact the stories' paratexts, not their narrative contents, that presented this information in such a manner. This impact can be seen in writing from the nineteenth century and beyond and even in personal travel narratives. The demand to know the secrets behind the veil was palpable, yet when those secrets were revealed, as the shopkeeper's wife in Burton's story eventually does, they were sometimes disappointing. English short story writer Annie Jane Harvey's travel narrative *Turkish Harems and Circassian Homes* (1871) has the author seeking out the *Nights* on her journey through the Ottoman Empire. She describes herself at a reception where "slaves and women were gorgeously apparelled" in a setting that "was very earnest a scene from the 'Arabian Nights'" (60). Her romantic ideation of her setting, however, is put at risk when she discovers that while the veiled "Oriental women almost always look pretty" in their native dress, when "the fair dames let the veil fall a little . . . the illusion is lost at once," and "the face ceases to be beautiful" (85). Harvey echoes both the exotic enchantment of the veil, something for Westerners to imagine in a sexualized context, and the disappointment over what is "actually" there. The vision of the *Nights*, seen as actually existing, was taken away from Westerners by the reality of the real people they sought to romanticize.

The concern for the oppression of women via the veil is seen not only throughout Burton and Lane's *Nights* but also in the Western popular press up through the twentieth century. A nineteenth-century *New York Times* travel account opines that the "ideas of the *Arabian Nights*" are literally being sought out on the writer's trip to Persia and include two particular things: "the veiled lady and the walled-up house into which no outside eye can penetrate." The article cautions Western travelers against romanticizing the veiled women because they "may be young or old, white or black, fair or ugly, on a mission of sin or upon an errand of charity" and argues that having such conditions as the veil constitutes a "despotism within a despotism" throughout the entire country. The writer insists that the cultural knowledge contained in the *Nights* must be found on this trip because the *Nights* provides a truthful coverage of women of the East being oppressed by the veil (*New York Times* 1876). In the more recent article "Beauty Queen to Veil Face as Princess," the *Gettysburg Times* (1961) bewails the upcoming marriage of Nawal Ramli, a Syrian model, to a Prince Abdul Rahman of Yemen because she will forever be veiled and kept inside. It suggests that her "marriage will be a journey into the middle ages [sic] and the not-very-exotic realm of the Arabian Nights," where she will wear "billowy, shapeless harem clothes." "Except on magic carpet trips abroad, only the other harem wives would see the jewels and finery the prince has given her." The *Spartanburg Herald* (1926) worries for and is in awe of Mulai Idriss of Morocco: "Idriss will marry [sic] a woman whose face he never saw. The bride's heavy veil, as in the case of all faithful Moslem women, will not be taken off even for the groom until the wedding night," "in a setting worthy of and rivalling the Arabian nights." The text continues, "The bride has not been consulted and this is not a love match." This front-page newspaper article is anxious both for the groom, who hasn't seen his bride-to-be's face, and the bride, who wasn't asked who she wants to marry. Seeing the situation this way and tying it suggestively to the *Nights* clearly shows a marked level of worry about the oppression and treatment of women via the veil and about the veil's trickery.

If the West was anxious about the veil, it became even more so about the possibility of its disappearance through modernization. This erasure would mean that the exotic other that was on display for the Westerner to muse and care about would be taken from them. It would be as if the *Nights* itself were taken away. A column called "Women Here and There" in the *New York Times* in 1899 laments the westernization of the East via capitalism, writing that "the marvelous tales of the East, and even our 'Arabian Nights' become meaningless when we know that America is shipping typewriters, rubber shoes and perfumery to Turkey." It is terrible "to imagine the possibility of veiled houris, with their lustrous dark eyes, wearing rubber shoes and manipulating the typewriter." Trade would strip from the stories the romantic visage of the East that the *Nights* presented for the West. The article worries that technological progress is a product only of the West that won't be understood by the East and that women will start working. The *St. Petersburg Times* (1926) goes so far as to complain that the "visions of Arabian Nights" will be gone forever due to the Westernization of Turkey by Mustapha Kemal Pasha (Kemal Atatürk). Atatürk's eventual Law Relating to Prohibited Garments of 1934 forbade the wearing of veils and turbans in Turkey. The *Times* writes about the movement toward such a law with sarcastic mourning, suggesting that "the veil covering feminine Turkey vanished as if by magic" and that "no longer is it necessary for the amorous adventurously inclined to scale walls in the moon-light . . . to see what is behind the veil of the irresistible beckoning eyes daring him to come and lift it." The exotic will no longer be exotic. The East, it is implied, will no longer be of worth to the West because its mysterious displays of culture will no longer tantalize or arouse Westerners. People there will become just people and no longer be "special," the article suggests.

Obviously, not all writing about the veil and the *Nights* from a Western perspective overly romanticizes, critiques, or approaches the topic with anxiety. The *Sydney Mail* suggests that the veil "derives rather from the idea of feminine privacy and modesty than of masculine possession" and is a symbol of "modesty and decency." The article "Arab Women and Modern Progress" states that women's clothing and customs vary throughout the region and that many women don't wear any sort of veil in public (Coke 1935). The problematic Saidian Orientalist and binary tone, however—"the very privilege, the very ground on which the Orientalist places himself so as to write about, legislate for, and reformulate Islam" (Said 1978, 282)—persists in much of the writing about the veil and even in this article. It writes that "Arabs" are "lewd and ribald," that "only a woman of the poorest coolie class would permit herself to be seen abroad with her whole face visible," and that "the Arab woman is no prude; she would not be a true Arab if she were. Few races of mankind take such a generally Rabelaisian view of life, as any student of an unexpurgated edition of 'The Arabian Nights' will soon find out" (Coke 1935).

The connection between Western views on the veil and the *Nights* has only cursorily been suggested here, but it is not incorrect to argue not only that it was a widespread phenomenon in newspapers and the popular press but also that it was evident in modes of study and scholarship as well. Edward Said's descriptions in *Orientalism* offer proof enough. Said spends a large part of his book focusing on Burton, Lane, Galland, and the *Nights*. It could be argued as well that these versions of the *Nights* were a reflection of Western misconceptions rather than the genesis of those misconceptions, and this is of course true. The persistent coupling of the *Nights* with the veil, with Arabic literature, with Islam, and with cultures of the East in general continues to pervade discourse in newspapers, scholarship, popular culture, and more. Scholarship by *Nights* researchers such as Robert Irwin (2004, 2006, 2011) and Muhsin al-Musawi (2009) and new translations such as *The Arabian Nights: Tales of 1001 Nights* (2008) by Malcolm Lyons and Ursula Lyons that suggest "reclamation" of a pre-Galland Arabic *Nights* are marred by the fact that the *Nights* was not that well received in its own time, was not really a reliable representation of pre-eighteenth-century life anywhere, and has a scarcity of extant manuscripts. Al-Musawi, for example, argues in his book *The Islamic Context of* The Thousand and One Nights (2009) that the story collection's "title and concerns are Arab-Islamic" and that it should be read as "a repository of popular memory, collective consciousness, and cultural dynamics" (1), despite its clearly European and postcolonial framework. Irwin's collection *The Penguin Anthology of Classical Arabic Literature* (2006) and other works include the *Nights* as an integral part of the Arabic literary tradition. Texts and approaches like this essentially continue the original intent of Western versions of the *Nights*—proposing that the text is indeed somehow a representative of its period and place of origin even though in fact it very much is *not*. The self-integration of the *Nights* even in the East is problematic as well. The Arabian Nights Village, a desert-themed hotel in Abu Dhabi, features "Royal Arabian banquets," camel rides, and a website with a picture of a man in traditional Emirati dress pouring coffee for people in Western clothing (American Nights Village n.d.). This luxury resort catering to Western guests and their (false) expectations stemming from the pervasiveness of the *Nights* offers a strong example of the complications of this issue. It is hardly the only example in the West Asian/North African region of this complicated reintegration of the *Nights* into its culture, but it showcases some of the binarisms that this integration brings with it.

As a vehicle of understanding the East, the *Nights* continues to be a challenging cultural product of European orientalism. This isn't to say that the *Nights* cannot tell us anything about the Abbasid Caliphate or pre-eighteenth-century Arabic, Persian, and Indian folktales, literature, history, or culture. Several of its original stories and many stories from other European translators do have Arabic and Eastern origins. It did exist in an Arabic and Persian form. It just wasn't much of a representative of literary interests at that time. The packaging of it into a repurposed *1001 Nights*, especially with Burton and Lane's paratextual additions, is a revisionist literary history that obscures the need to approach Arabic literature from a less essentialist perspective. Understanding the story collection through this complicated lens opens up new areas of future study, however. The origin of the nineteenth-century Arabic manuscripts and their resulting effects constitute one such area. The "Calcutta" manuscripts (Calcutta I, 1814–18, and Calcutta II, 1839–42), versions of the *Nights* created by the British East India Company to train its men to learn Arabic, have not been vetted much at all in *Nights'* scholarship, and yet everyone from Burton to Lyons based their "complete" translations on these manuscripts. This, of course, points to how Westerners have been insisting that the *Nights* have been a part of Arabic literature for centuries. Despite or perhaps because of this insistence, the story collection continues to be associated with mistruths and misperceptions about the veil and associated cultural elements. To study the *Nights*, however, as the West's insistent need to be the voice of the East would illuminate much more about the machinations at work within its culturally embedded existence. Like Lane, lifting "up the veil of his bride, and to see, for the first time, the features which were to charm, or disappoint, or disgust him" ([1831] 2000, x), this more complex understanding of the *Nights* would open up many new avenues of exploration to see the text as what it is, not what it has for too long been made to seem.

Works Cited

Abu al-Faraj al-Isfahani. 1927–61. *Kitab al-aghani*. 24 vols. Cairo: Dar al-Kutub al-Misriyya.

Abu-Lughod, Lila. 2013. *Do Muslim Women Need Saving?* Cambridge, MA: Harvard Univ. Press.

Ahmed, Leila. 1978. *Edward W. Lane: A Study of His Life and Works and of British Ideas of the Middle East in the Nineteenth Century*. London: Longman.

———. 1992. *Women and Gender in Islam: Historical Roots of a Modern Debate*. New Haven, CT: Yale Univ. Press.

———. 2001. *A Quiet Revolution: The Veil's Resurgence, from the Middle East to America*. New Haven, CT: Yale Univ. Press.

Alf Layla wa Layla: The Book of the Thousand Nights and a Night. N.d. 10 vols. Translated by Richard F. Burton. N.p.: Burton Club.

The Arabian Nights Encyclopedia. 2004. 2 vols. Edited by Ulrich Marzolph and Richard van Leeuwen. Santa Barbara, CA: ABC Clio.

Arabian Nights' Entertainments. 1995. Edited by Robert L. Mack. Oxford: Oxford Univ. Press.

The Arabian Nights Entertainments (c. 1706). N.d. 4 vols. Translated by Edward William Lane. Illustrated by S. L. Wood. New York: Bigelow, Brown.

The Arabian Nights: Tales of 1001 Nights. 2008. Translated by Malcolm C. Lyons with Ursula Lyons. London: Penguin.

Arabian Nights Village. N.d. Accessed 2016, 2023. https://visitabudhabi.ae/en/things-to-do/desert-and-outdoor-activities/arabian-nights-village.

Bullock, Katherine. 2002. *Rethinking Muslim Women and the Veil: Challenging Historical and Modern Stereotypes*. London: International Institute of Islamic Thought.

Coke, Richard. 1935. "Arab Women and Modern Progress." *Sydney Mail*, June 12.

Edinburgh Review, or Critical Journal. 1856. "Art. III, Rev. of *Personal Narrative of a Pilgrimage to El-Medinah and Meccah,* by Richard F. Burton." 104, no. 212 (Oct.): 390.

The Fihrist of Ibn an-Nadim. 1970. Translated by Bayard Dodge. New York: Columbia Univ. Press.

Genette, Gérard. 1980. *Narrative Discourse: An Essay in Method.* Translated by Jane E. Lewin. Ithaca, NY: Cornell Univ. Press.

———. 1997. *Paratexts: Thresholds of Interpretation.* Translated by Jane E. Lewin. Cambridge: Cambridge Univ. Press.

Gettysburg Times. 1961. "Beauty Queen to Veil Face as Princess." Apr. 12.

Harvey, Mrs. [Annie Jane]. 1871. *Turkish Harems & Circassian Homes.* London: Hurst & Blackett. At https://archive.org/details/turkishharemsand00harv.

Ibn al-Nadim. 1871. *Kitab al-Fihrist: Mit Anmerkungen Herausgegeben von Gustav Flugel.* Leipzig: F. C. W. Vogel.

Irwin, Robert. 2004. The Arabian Nights: *A Companion.* London: I. B. Taurus.

———, ed. 2006. *The Penguin Anthology of Classical Arabic Literature.* London: Penguin Classics.

———. 2011. *Visions of the Jinn: Illustrators of the Arabian Nights.* Oxford: Oxford Univ. Press.

Kabbani, Rana. 1986. *Europe's Myths of the Orient.* Bloomington: Indiana Univ. Press.

Kitab Alf Layla wa Layla. 1984. Edited by Muhsin Mahdi. Leiden: Brill.

Kumar, Deepa. 2014. "Imperialist Feminism and Liberalism." openDemocracy, Nov. 6. At https://www.opendemocracy.net/en/imperialist-feminism-and-liberalism/.

Lane, Edward William. [1836] 1978. *Manners and Customs of the Modern Egyptians.* The Hague: East–West Publications.

———. [1831] 2000. *Description of Egypt: Notes and Views in Egypt and Nubia.* Edited by Jason Thompson. Cairo: American Univ. of Cairo Press.

Al-Masudi. 1861. *Les praries d'or.* A translation of *Muruj adh-dhahab* by C. Barbier de Meynard. Paris: Imprimerie Impériale.

Al-Musawi, Muhsin J. 2009. *The Islamic Context of* The Thousand and One Nights. New York: Columbia Univ. Press.

New York Times. 1876. "Traveling in Persia." June 25.

———. 1899. "Women Here and There." Jan. 24.

Nurse, Paul McMichael. 2010. *Eastern Dreams: How* The Arabian Nights *Came to the World.* Toronto: Viking Canada.

Reynolds, Dwight F. 2006. "*A Thousand and One Nights*: A History of the Text and Its Reception." In *Arabic Literature in the Post-classical Period*, edited by Roger Allen and D. S. Richards, 270–92. Cambridge: Cambridge Univ. Press.

Said, Edward. 1978. *Orientalism*. New York: Vintage.

Spartanburg Herald. 1926. "Arabs Gather for Wedding of Son of Sultan." Oct. 25.

Spivak, Gayatri Chakravorty. 1988. "Can the Subaltern Speak?" In *Marxism and the Interpretation of Culture*, edited by Cary Nelson and Lawrence Grossberg, 271–313. Urbana: Univ. of Illinois Press.

St. Petersburg Times. 1926. "Modern Days Have Robbed Constantinople of Veils." June 4.

Supplemental Nights to the Book of The Thousand and One Nights *with Notes Anthropological and Explanatory*. N.d. 6 vols. Translated by Richard F. Burton. N.p.: Burton Club.

Yeazell, Ruth Bernard. 2000. *Harems of the Mind*. New Haven, CT: Yale Univ. Press.

2

Unveiling the Colonial Blind Spot in *The Battle of Algiers*

Abdullah A. Hasan

An Overview: *The Battle of Algiers* and Its Rendering of the Veil

The Battle of Algiers, a black-and-white docufiction film by the Italian director Gillo Pontecorvo, received much acclaim for being objective when it was released in 1966 (Solinas 1973, ix). However, despite avoiding explicit political statements, the film deserves acknowledgment for its profound treatment of social and cultural issues in the struggle of decolonization. One of the topics the film adds much needed complexity to is the veil, especially how the veil's unconventional utilization in the revolution transpires as symptom of the shifting role of women in a society that colonial discourse presents as obstinately backward. The extent to which the film represents a direct expression of Pontecorvo's Marxist worldview is debatable, but it has certainly threatened the image of France as a benevolent colonial power because of its candid portrayal of violence and human suffering on both sides of the war. In part because the film does not exclusively sympathize with European settlers, it received disapproving reviews despite winning the Golden Lion award at the Venice Film Festival, where it was initially screened. As Patricia Caillé explains, after the award, right-wing elements in France viewed the film as anti-French, and most critics were dissatisfied with what they considered the low standards of the award committee and attacked Pontecorvo's lack of political analysis (2007, 375). Before regaining critical acclaim later, the film's unabashed realism upset many viewers. It neither supports the French military nor

38

glamorizes the Algerian rebels. Its realism is evident in its cast of amateur Algerian actors, minimal narration, and unapologetic depiction of the atrocities committed by both sides. However, this does not mean that it lacks an ethical perspective. The suffering of Algerians in the film is more pronounced, and the scenes of poverty, torture, execution, and massacre that the French commit against the native population bring attention to the damaging effects of colonialism.

Equally important is the film's portrayal of Algerian women, who suffer under both colonialism and patriarchal restrictions but gradually claim a more active role in the independence struggle. Algerian women claim agency in the film, and this chapter argues that Pontecorvo demonstrates a sophisticated understanding not only of Islamic culture in Algeria but also of the demeaning image of Muslim women and the veil in orientalist and colonial discourses. The film does not offer a historical overview of orientalist stereotypes about women or the veil but implies their prevalence. It demonstrates this awareness through scenes that seem to present veiled Algerian women as passive and inept but that are later qualified by an unraveling of the underlying complexity of Algerian culture. Therefore, appreciating the film's cultural sophistication necessitates comparing it against its cultural backdrop. To this end, I juxtapose, on the one hand, orientalist perceptions about the veil and Muslim women's agency and, on the other, Pontecorvo's delineation of these issues and how it contributes to the debates that postcolonial and feminist intellectuals have about the issue of women's empowerment within patriarchal traditions.

Muslim Women's Agency: Whence and Whither?

Pontecorvo's treatment of the veil in his film raises important questions about Muslim women's agency: Where does it come from, and what does it lead to? The film's handling of the question of agency should be understood in light of how Muslim women are portrayed in colonial imagination and how North African feminists respond to orientalism. Colonial discourse operates from the assumption that Muslim women's agency is derived from and indebted to the French intervention through colonialism and the civilizing mission. An Algerian girls' school song from 1851 aptly captures this view:

Oh! Protective France: Oh! Hospitable France! . . .
Noble land, where I felt free
Under Christian skies to pray to our God: . . .
And you, adoptive mother, who taught us
That we have a share of this world,
We will cherish you forever!
                                    (Lazreg 1994, 68, 69)

According to the school song, France represents a nurturing mother and an enlightening father figure to westernized Algerian women, and the children sing with joy to express their gratefulness to colonialism for their education and newfound voice. Whatever agency they possess has been endowed by the French. In contrast, as my discussion of Malek Alloula's (1986) collected postcards demonstrates in the next section, nonwesternized women lack agency in colonial imagination. This is particularly the case for veiled women, presented in French colonial discourse as passive and homogeneous, traits for which the veil is a debate-ending symbol in the orientalist imagination. The French in *The Battle of Algiers* view veiled women as apolitical beings who are unlikely to espouse colonialism or rebel against it and so are unlikely to be involved in subversive activity.

The film's treatment of clothing and physical appearance brings attention to this assumption and challenges it. Whereas imperial discourse gives veiling and unveiling close-ended meanings, the film stresses how Algerian rebels, by repurposing veiling and unveiling as strategies of resistance, bestow new possibilities upon an article of clothing long held in contempt by the French. The film mocks the thread linking the veil to passivity as well as the expectation that Algerian women who unveil are indebted to the colonial authority. Pontecorvo shows that Algerian women, whether veiled or unveiled, do not necessarily disavow their native culture. Rather, they claim a place within the process of nation making and exhibit fierce opposition to the French rule.

In the Algerian colonial context, westernization and veiling manifest as markers of agency or the lack thereof, respectively. *The Battle of Algiers* exposes the volatility of this dichotomy by presenting the veil as a transient and fluid expression capable of transcending historicity and subverting colonial as well as conservative patriarchies. The deterministic dichotomy of grateful westernized Algerian women loyal to the French presence versus passive veiled women betrays a blind spot in colonial thought. It is within this knowledge gap that veiling and unveiling claim cultural and political functions unforeseen by the civilizing mission. Signifying this transience, the film shows how four male rebels, Kader, Mourad, Ramel, and Ali, take up the veil to elude surveillance, while three women, Djamila, Zohra, and Hassiba, abandon it and westernize their appearance for the same purpose. Because both cross-dressing and westernization violate conservative Islamic doctrine,[1] this malleability symbolizes the disruption of a history of categorical identities that the French took for granted. The French, as Frantz Fanon emphasizes, view Algerians as a "formal society in which outside appearances are paramount" ([1959] 2007, 37). In other words, according to the French, Algerians are very predictable, for they are conservative Muslims who resist change and would not cross the boundaries of their restrictive culture just to resist the French.

However, critics of the portrayal of the veil in the film have been cautious about giving credit to Pontecorvo for disrupting the idea of Algerian women's predictability—mainly because Algeria's record in the area of women's rights after independence has been disappointing. For example, Lindsey Moore implies that the film exaggerates the level of women's participation in the revolution, pointing out that Algerian nationalists have viewed the women's political activity as an unavoidable "temporary aberration" (2003, 62). In a similar vein, Katherine A. Roberts questions the film's feminization of the Algerian national birth as well as its exaggerated optimism about women's participation in political activity (2007, 381–82). These concerns are valid, especially when the larger historical trajectory of Algeria's situation after independence is considered. However, I maintain that the film's strength lies mainly in its ability to capture the signs of transition in colonized society and less in imagining a brighter future for Algerian women. The film wavers between showing the abjection of veiled Algerian women and demonstrating the potential for social

---

1. Islamic teachings forbid Muslims from losing their religious identity through the imitation of non-Muslims (al-Khudri n.d.; Ibn Umar n.d.). Similar prohibitions exist regarding men or women imitating the other gender in manners or clothing (Ibn Abbas n.d.).

transformation. It is this social dynamism that shocks the French imperial apparatus, which views Algerian culture as the antithesis of European progress, locking it behind the gates of geography and history. The contrast between modern Europeans and the backward, unchanging Algerians is a fundamental concept of colonialism, and the film brilliantly deconstructs it by bringing attention to the superficiality of colonial segregation.

Capturing the temporal and spatial segregation between France and Algeria, Pontecorvo's first scene begins with a striking visual contrast between the rundown Algerian Casbah and the modern, neatly maintained French quarters and thus provides a lens through which the rest of the film can be viewed. As the film progresses, the veil then becomes yet another visual pronouncement of the separation between two peoples, Europeans and natives, each representing a different geography, history, and value system. For the French authorities, this dissimilarity justifies colonialism. Algerians must act French to attain agency, count as civilized, and invalidate the claims of colonial rule, but the French consider the veil a testimony of the Algerians' inability to join modernity. The film deconstructs this flawed logic by unsettling the links between veiling and subservience and between westernization and agency or loyalty to the colonizer. In the film, agency is intrinsic to Algerian culture, but colonization creates urgent circumstances that allow it to manifest only in unpredictable ways, such as veiling and unveiling, which become rational choices in the struggle for decolonization. This depth in Pontecorvo's assessment of the question of agency qualifies *The Battle of Algiers* as a film before its time, resonating with later attempts by postcolonial and feminist intellectuals who endeavor to challenge the West's claim to be the exclusive source of Eastern women's empowerment.

To contextualize the issue of the impetus of women's agency in North Africa, a brief overview of how feminist and postcolonial intellectuals from the region approach it is in order. Stressing that they do not depend on Western intervention for empowerment and that their native cultures and histories offer adequate role models, feminist and postcolonial intellectuals revive symbolic yet empowering feminine genealogies. For example, postcolonial North African feminists such as Assia Djebar, Leila Abouzeid, Fatima Mernissi, and Nawal El Saadawi pursue feminine genealogies that predate the advent of Western colonialism in the region. Djebar (1991) highlights the power of the Prophet Muhammed's contemporary female relatives, especially his daughter, Fatima. Abouzeid (2009, 2010) highlights the voice of Aisha, the Prophet's powerful wife, known for leading wars from behind her partition. Seeking more secular alternatives, Mernissi (2001) invokes the figure of Scheherazade, while El Saadawi (2009) invokes the Egyptian goddess Isis to celebrate the prominence of the role of women in Middle Eastern imagination and history. Other feminists, such as the French-educated Algerian writer Ahlam Mosteghanemi (2015) and the Algerian-born French author Hélène Cixous (1998), offer a paradigm of multiple origins seemingly derived from the duality of their experience, whereby they locate agency in various sources complicated by the complex expressions of the colonized body. The common denominator among these views is how they consider alternative routes for women's empowerment that do not emanate from the authoritative values of the French civilizing mission, or at least they negotiate with those values, as in Cixous's and Mosteghanemi's cases. Pontecorvo's film is closer to this polygenetic model, for it acknowledges the role of Western imperialism in accelerating the social transformation in Algeria but also shows how the nature of this transformation undermines the interests of the French.

In this respect, the film's mockery of imperial arrogance and confidence about employing indigenous women as tools of colonialism is Fanonian in its perceptiveness. In a chapter aptly titled "Algeria Unveiled" in *A Dying Colonialism* ([1959] 2007), Fanon unravels the colonial interest in liberating Algerian women and the naïveté of the wishful idea of "unveiled women aiding and sheltering the occupier" (38). Both Fanon and the film ridicule the idea that the West sows its values and reaps gratefulness. The implication of this colonial ideology is that the decision to unveil cannot emerge organically in patriarchal Islamic cultures, let alone be embraced by individual women in defiance of established customs. Unveiling is agency, and any sign of agency is a form of westernization obtainable only under pressure from France. Unveiling, then, is evidence of France's success in winning the hearts and minds of Algerian women. This is an oversimplistic assessment of indigenous cultures, however, and the film lays bare this patronizing outlook. Women such as Djamila, Zohra, and Hassiba unveil to aid the rebels, without deliberating the degree to which their decision adheres to Islamic or French value systems. In fact, the unveiling scene is a slow, vivid, yet silent one, letting viewers witness feminine agency unmediated by direct patriarchal mandates. Even the National Liberation Front's (Front de libération nationale, FLN) secular patriarchal ideology of national liberation, albeit not completely ignored, is dimmed in the film. In one of the most iconic scenes, after the women unveil, Hassiba dyes her hair blond with peroxide to acquire European looks. The three women put on makeup and European clothing as they prepare to smuggle explosives and arms into the French quarters. Once they finish, they meet the Algerian leader, Kader, saluting him in impeccable French. Mastery of the French language is highlighted for its ability to act as a mask in place of the veil to allow the women to pass through the checkpoints overseen by the French military at the exits of the Algerian Casbah.

These westernized women pass easily through the checkpoints because in the imperial mindset they owe their freedom from oppressive indigenous traditions to France, so they would not rebel against France. But the film shows that Algerian women take advantage of this misconception to further the national struggle of liberation. By doing so, it presents a straightforward answer to the second half of the question I raised earlier about the implications of agency. It shows that culturally hybrid women, although potentially considered tools of imperialism, often assert their independence from the West. But the film's directness in handling this issue only reinforces its cultural foresight and feminist outlook. In fact, this issue continues to be an essential concern in postcolonial feminism today. It is worth noting that this refusal to feel obliged toward European or North American influence is common in feminist thought. It can be seen even in nationalistic North African feminist narratives that have made it onto the international stage using French or English as their interface to the world. For example, although Ahlam Mosteghanemi and Leila Abouzeid were educated in France and the United States, respectively, and rose to fame in their own countries in part due to Western recognition, they avoid giving the impression that they are influenced by the West, and they are cautious about identifying as Western or secular feminists

(Abouzeid 2014, 47; Baaqeel 2015, 149; Bakr 2015). More remarkably, when Clarisse Zimra, the American scholar of North African literature, asked the Francophone Algerian feminist Assia Djebar about her indebtedness to European influence, Djebar responded: "Who had time to wait for them? We were already there!" (Djebar and Zimra 2005, 203). These attitudes demonstrate the persistence of sensitivity about the notion that the female hybrid is dependent on or a tool of the West, a notion that is traceable to the civilizing mission's desire to focus on women as the backdoor to dominating indigenous culture. Like the implied national feminine collective in Djebar's "we," Pontecorvo's female protagonists do not wait for help from the outside. They are already there, fighting the battle of ideas as they physically strive for sovereignty. For an activist such as Djebar, who writes mostly in French about Algeria, such a statement then seems to be an aesthetic counterhegemonic gesture rather than a flat-out rejection of all outside influence. One explanation for this gesture is that North African feminists resist projecting their activism as a translation of Western achievements. Because Djebar's enthusiastic answer—taken at face value—ultimately effaces the monogenetic claim of indebtedness in favor of the possibility of a polygenetic native agency, it calls attention to the ways in which Algerian women, in history and in the film, diverge or derive from French and Algerian prescriptive criticisms of patriarchy. The film entertains the view that Algerian women are not indebted to French influence, but it does not employ Djebar's definitive tone. It is true that the way the Algerian Revolution developed was not in concert with the ideological ends of French indoctrination, but France's footprint on Algerian culture, language, and gender relations is unmistakable. Although France did not reap the fruits of its mission, Europe is now part of the story of the veil in contemporary Algerian history.

For this reason, the bodily paradigms offered by Cixous and Mosteghanemi can add much needed nuance to the relationship between the veiled body and imperialism in the film. Cixous applies the semiotics of resistant bodies to feminism as a whole, and Mosteghanemi applies it to colonized subjectivity. For example, when the Algerian-born French feminist Cixous calls upon the woman to "put herself into the text," what immediately comes to mind is the idea that the textualization (or detextualization, one might also argue) of the female body has for a long time been the product and prerogative of what she later describes as "the conventional man" (1976, 875). Dominant ideology manufactures and perpetuates the patriarchal semantics of the feminine body. Canonical texts are male-marked territories, and feminism undoes this textual hegemony. In the same vein, Mosteghanemi treats the colonized body as a territory branded by colonialism in her novel *Memory in the Flesh* ([1993] 2003). Algerian bodies and, by extension, Algerian national independence, are maimed by the French. The national memory of independence is asterisked by the very history it is striving to shed.

Women's contribution to the Algerian War of Independence, in this light, was not merely military. It was an act of marking and unmarking the body as well as of feminizing its semantics. Since the film dramatizes the symbolic role of evolving gender dynamics in an otherwise hypermasculine anticolonial struggle, Cixous's (1976) metaphor of gendered texts, "sexts," illuminates how the Algerian women in the film, by instrumentalizing their bodies and gendered attire (especially the veil), semantically and physically outmaneuver both orientalist and local modes of textualizing the female body. If Cixous's "sexts" bring together what is private (the body/sex) and what is public (text as a technology of negotiating with the masculine other), the tactics of westernizing one's body and degendering the veil's function as a form of subversive sexuality, so to speak, in the way they allow private bodies to evade the constrictive racialized gaze imposed from outside. Unveiling and westernizing one's body is a transaction in which the colonized female negotiates a compromise with a male other in pursuit of a new subjectivity. In the film, the women do not go back to the veil once unveiling has served its subversive purpose, but unveiling remains entangled with the conflict of patriarchies.

Cixous's theory of the body as language elucidates the symbolic nature of women's role in the Algerian War of Independence and sheds light on the film's treatment of the relation between the body and patriarchy. *The Battle of Algiers*, while historicizing the ontogenesis of Algerian feminine agency as a colonially determined event, presents unsettling female roles that disrupt both Algerian and French androcentric codifications of the feminine body. If "inscription of femininity"—to bestow a new context upon Cixous's theorization of the body as text—has customarily been the exclusive right of masculine ideologies and institutions, the fluidity of the veil in the film paradoxically constitutes the most effective counterinscriptive instrument in the process of Algerian women's liberation.

Instead of fixing the gendered attire as a continuation of a culturally and patriarchally predetermined social function, the tactics of the Algerian War of Independence, including cross-dressing, detach the meaning of the female body and attire from their historical rootedness, thus metamorphosing the indigenous body from natural/biological fixtures into ahistorical signifiers. By "ahistorical," I mean that the female body ceases to be historically inscribed and becomes historically inscriptive. The veil, no longer a natural extension of the colonized female body, writes its own history. Because Algerians repurpose and reinvent the veil, as many Muslims do today, imperial knowledge about Islam or Algeria does not help the French quell the revolution in the film.

The unveiling of Algerian women, therefore, is not a linear progression from oppression under the patriarchy of the colonized to liberty under the patriarchy of the colonizer. An unfamiliar mode of feminine agency appears that does not emanate from any particular masculine discourse. The emerging feminine agency defies categorization in spite of its entanglement in the macho values of essentialist, nationalist anticolonialism, the masculine purity of which has been contaminated by feminine participation. More than a decade before Cixous called for women to "explode" the "discourse of man" (1976, 887), Algerian women started to liberate themselves extradiscursively. Because feminine rebellion embraced noncodified forms, it epistemologically sabotaged the orientalist discourse of French colonialism. Therefore, the film also endeavors to show not only the disruptive transformation of the role of the veil but also that "the discourse of man" gives rise to unintended, unorthodox feminine roles.

Inscribing the Female Body under Imperial Patriarchy

Pontecorvo shows that the colonial view of the veil revolves around notions of incompetent motherhood and voiceless femininity. In the film, after the Algerians organize a peaceful strike to protest the colonial rule and embarrass France in front of the United Nations, the French authorities are compelled to release a few political prisoners. As the prisoners are forced back to the Algerian quarter under the supervision of French paratroopers, the film shows a veil-clad mother desperately searching for her released son, Muhammad. Immediately following this scene of faceless and oppressed womanhood that is devoid of motherly expressions, a French army general addresses the striking Algerians: "People of the Casbah, France is your motherland."[2] The next scene exemplifies the nurturing motherliness of France by showing jubilant soldiers giving away French bread to impoverished Algerian children. In one of his most piercing critiques of French colonialism, Fanon argues that when the empire is the provider, sustaining the indigenous body is secondary to advancing the colonizer's ideology: "Every kilo of semolina distributed was accompanied by a dose of indignation against the veil and the cloister" ([1959] 2007, 38). In light of this argument, the imperialist dogma of the French colonization, while flaunting with pride France's uncovered and educated women, is extremely ironic if one considers the gender-divisive language of the colonialist discourse.

Whereas France is a nurturing motherland when giving away bread, it is a cruel-for-your-own-good fatherland when imposing order and enlightened ideas at the hands of the male-dominated military. In other words, France's maternal selflessness is supplemented by a patriarchal mission where France is performing "the white man's burden," as Rudyard Kipling's popular poem put it. In the French colonies, the burden of the civilizing mission can be seen in school songs celebrating Imperial Day. One such song is Biokou Salomon's "Papa Pétain," the lyrics of which "highlight the figure of [Marshal Henri Philippe] Pétain as a loving father of his African children" (Ginio 2006, 42). In return, African children promise to be obedient: "To accomplish the mission that was started . . . we will work with zeal and confidence, and you will be proud of us, our Marshal Pétain, our Papa" (qtd. in Ginio 2006, 197). Likewise, Algerians in the film are, from the colonizers' perspective, the infantile receivers of not only motherly nurture but also fatherly enlightenment.

---

2. All quotes from the film are from the English subtitles.

Before French colonization, the Algerian society is orphaned because a veiled mother is not a competent one.

France's ideological cause, it should be added, was not merely a cover-up for economic interests or simply just rhetoric reiterated after the fact of colonization to silence outspoken critics of imperialism, such as Jean-Paul Sartre. France's ideological interests seemed genuine. Historically, even many leftists supported French colonialism. It is astounding that Albert Camus, the prominent French existentialist who often emphasized his love for his Arab "brothers," shared with Kipling and the "submissive" natives more than the fact of imperial birth.[3] Barbara Harlow notes how Camus looked at the conflict between France and Algeria as a "struggle of ideas" and preferred an "Algeria tied to France" lest their culture lead them to "misery" (1986, xii). Supporters of French colonialism essentially contended that the misery of the natives was why France was in Algeria in the first place, where it was playing a savior's role. The film does not deny the misery of Algerians, but it flips cause and effect. The suffering of Algerians saturates most scenes. However, colonial rule, instead of al-leviating abjection, is responsible for causing it or aggravating it where it already exists.

Locating the Veiled Feminine Body across Multiple Patriarchal Regimes

To accurately contextualize the disruptive thrust of veiling and unveiling, it helps to contrast the film's treatment of the veil with two relevant patriar-chal frameworks: Algerian patriarchy and French orientalism. In Algerian society, the function of the veil is to interrupt the male gaze and preserve social purity. The Moroccan feminist scholar Fatima Mernissi remarks in *Beyond the Veil* [1975] 1987) that veiling aims to achieve social cohesion: "The desegregation of the sexes violates Islam's ideology on women's po-sition in the social order. . . . Since women are considered by Allah to be destructive elements, they are to be spatially confined and excluded from

3. Both Kipling and Camus were born and raised in the European empire, India and Algeria, respectively.

matters other than those of the family" (19).[4] But this forbidden space becomes Algeria's most prominent marker of otherness under the imperial gaze. Although the veil supposedly interrupts the male gaze, it ironically plays a revelatory role, confirming and exposing Muslim backwardness in imperial eyes.

French colonialism perceives Algeria not as a cohesive society but rather as a broken one. Most veiled women in the film are voiceless, but when they speak, they mutter incomprehensible words of agony and suffering. Many small children, such as Petit Omar, roam the streets unaccompanied by their mothers or participate in terrorism. If Algerians march to protest the occupation, the camera zooms out and shows them as a desperate, chaotic mass of children, teenagers, and women. The age and gender expectations do not correlate with Western modernity. When the French bomb a densely populated area and the physical walls fall apart, burying civilians and exposing Algerian women's privacy, the women appear motionless in their veils, while the men recover the dead. It is a shocking scene where veiling takes priority over mourning. For colonial France, the helpless, passive women signify that the Algerian society is incapable of protecting women and that it denies them personalized human expression by concealing individuality under a white veil. The scene of veiled women watching passively is a stark re-creation of the clichéd orientalist trope that holds the veil as the ultimate instrument of the patriarchal oppression exercised by Muslim culture. But the trope does not go unchallenged in the film, and Pontecorvo does not spare the French from criticism.

---

4. In this context, "veiling" refers to the general practice of covering women, whether by means of clothing or walls. Veiling as a social, quasi-religious practice departs from the original theological justifications. The Quranic justification hinges on the presence of slavery ("Al-Ahzab" n.d.). The veil distinguishes free women from female slaves, whose 'awra (private area of the body) correlates, according to mainstream Islamic scholars, with that of men, navel to knees ("'Awrah of Female Slaves" 2008). Theologically, the veil is a marker of freedom—for some at the expense of others—the opposite of what it stands for in colonial discourse (Hoodfar 1993, 6). It is common for Muslims to justify discarding the veil by citing the fact that slavery has been abolished.

How, then, does the French colonial masculinity exert its influence in the presence of a local patriarchy? And are French colonial views of Muslim women egalitarian and disinterested? At least two mutually exclusive patriarchal regimes in this context are not equal in their force or tactics but at least similar in claiming the woman's body as their own. When approaching the question of women under colonization, one has to be aware of layers of masculinity at play, with power concentrated in the topmost stratum—the power domain of the colonizer. Therefore, Algerian women, veiled or not, are not spared the French male gaze: if veiled, they are disdained, dehumanized, and feared; if unveiled, they are desired and eroticized because they are the long-forbidden flesh now available for the sexual fantasies of French soldiers at checkpoints. When Hassiba is about to cross the blockade, with a bathing suit dangling from her bag, the soldiers change their mind about searching her and give her a free pass. They whistle at her. One of them asks her out: "Next Sunday I'm free. . . . Shall we go together [to the beach]?" (ellipses in subtitles). The soldiers do not request her identification documents, as they do with other Algerians. Her Western clothing is the only identification they need to define her as a safe supporter of French colonization.

In the context of the colonization of the Muslim-majority areas in general and of North Africa in particular, a stark double standard can be detected if one considers how competing patriarchal structures operate. On the one hand, in colonialist ideology the "Moor" represents the paradigm of male oppression. Therefore, the mission of the colonizer—to reassign Gayatry Chakravorty Spivak's famous sentence on the British approach to the Hindu practice of sati—is to "save brown women from brown men" (1988, 296). On the other hand, in traditional anticolonialist discourse, women are allocated the innermost core, where they are to be protected from the undressing gaze of the panoptical colonizing regime that cannot tolerate or comprehend the sight of covered femininity. Whereas nationalist and religious patriarchal doctrines call for interrupting the sexual gaze by means of gender segregation and modest clothing, the orientalist mindset has historically been extremely fascinated with interrupting this interruption.

The "scenes and types" genre that Alloula elaborately discusses in *The Colonial Harem* (1986) provides a rich historical context for this fascination. Most of the surviving photographs of this genre were staged and sent back to France by travelers touring Algeria in the early twentieth century. Many of them serve as examples of the orientalist fixation on Muslim women's covered bodies. For example, the postcard "'Uled-Nayl woman" shows a woman partly lifting her veil, squinting, and hanging the veil on both hands as if to imply that she will reveil momentarily (60). But rather than serving as fleeting moment of liberation for the woman, as the staging seems to imply, the photograph is privileging the gazing Europeans with a glimpse into the elaborately ornamented harem and a limited access to a forbidden space.[5] The gazing subject is seduced, but his desire is never fulfilled, the staging further implies. The veil hides treasures: beauty and jewels. The onlooker is called on to fantasize or act upon his desire: the exotic body waits to be uncovered.

Another postcard, "Arabian woman with the Yachmak," shows a woman with a less ornamental veil leaving her breasts uncovered (Alloula 1986, 126). This postcard reduces the woman to helpless eyes and naked breasts, suggesting the primitive motherhood of North African women. All she can offer as a mother is essential nourishment for the children of Algeria, but her mouth is covered, and therefore she cannot enlighten them with knowledge. In the orientalist imagination, the true enlightening role is left for the one true motherland, which is France, according to Alloula's commentary on the postcards (1986, xxi, 3, 129). Alternatively,

5. In European travel narratives about the Orient by writers such as Gustave Flaubert, Gerard de Nerval, Richard Burton, and Edward Lane, the East represents "sexual experience unobtainable in the West," for its pleasures are "libertine and less guilt-ridden" (Said 1978, 190). The harem is the epitome of this possible experience and a quintessential site of colonial fantasy and desire. But it remains an erotically charged enclave within the East because of the sense of frustration about its inaccessibility to European explorers. For a more detailed account of the portrayal of the harem in literature, consider Fatima Mernissi's books *Dreams of Trespass* (1994) and *Scheherazade Goes West* (2001), where she compares the erotic harem of orientalist imagination with the domestic harem of the twentieth century, a common household for extended Muslim families where segregation is meant to preserve women's privacy.

one might see the postcard as an expression of colonial fantasy about the potential but not yet actualized subjugation of native culture, which is feminized in this image. The voyeuristic colonial gaze is halted midway between satisfaction and rejection. The photographer's employment of the reveal-and-conceal technique produces an open-ended narrative where the limitless possibilities are left for the colonial gaze to imagine. The photographer calls upon the observer to proverbially undress the woman in order to gain full access to her body. This territorialization of the body into a virgin space (covered but obtainable) and a colonized space (uncovered and obtained) is akin to the spatial segregation in the film and the different treatment that veiled and unveiled women receive in it. From the colonizer's viewpoint, Algeria is halfway through the process of civilization. Unveiled women are already colonized—undergoing liberation. They are evidence of the success of the civilizing mission. Although not part of France proper due to their (supposedly) racial, national, and religious differences, they are an extension of the empire. Treating unveiled women with the same contempt as the native men or their veiled counterparts would amount to an admission of failure. It would undermine confidence in the success of Frenchification. In the film, soldiers search a veiled woman's handbag and drag a man for not having proper identification. Conversely, Djamila and Zohra, clad in European clothing and revealing their legs and arms, pass checkpoints with relatively the same ease as Hassiba.

Unintelligible Nativity: Unveiling in an Orderly Universe

Every outdoor space in *The Battle of Algiers* is immediately recognizable as either European or Algerian. These two spaces are kept strictly apart by means of fences, checkpoints, and surveillance cameras, which regulate the inbound and outbound flow of native workers and French settlers. This careful separation, however, is not purely physical. The segregation of the European quarter from the rebellious native enclaves is part of the epistemic housekeeping that operates along with the colonizing regime's exercise of ideological inscription over landscape and its paraphernalia— the natives. The natives are fossilized as the Other of the civilized French colonists by means of spatial delimitation.

This epistemic housekeeping is as geographic as it is racial and gendered. Early on, the film underscores this housekeeping visually through a bird's-eye view of the landscape and the stark scenic disjunction between the European locale and the Algerian one. The camera moves from a visually appealing European quarter that is vibrant with aspects of modern lifestyle—cars, clear lanes, and urban infrastructure—to an appalling Algerian quarter swamped with vagabonds, veiled women, beggars, prostitutes, and peddlers who travel noisily through messy alleys.

For the security of the European colonists and to detect any subversive activities, surveillance cameras supplement barbed wire in keeping Algerian terrorists from leaving the Casbah, particularly because members of the FLN have found their way around racial and gender profiling by recruiting veiled female rebels in their cause. French administrators adjust their tactics accordingly: "ID checks are ludicrous. If anyone's papers are in order, it's the terrorist's," explains Colonel Philippe Mathieu as he brags about the effectiveness of camera footage in collecting intelligence.

Colonel Mathieu realizes the significance of the panoptical power exercised by cameras hidden at checkpoints. The Casbah is already an open-air prison where French law is suspended. The dispersed cameras succeed, at least temporarily, in streamlining the administration of this large disciplinary structure. The colonel calls this type of surveillance "the policing aspect" and believes that it is far more effective than immediate military power: "To know them is to eliminate them," he instructs his paratroopers.

Before the introduction of strict surveillance methods, "knowing" the native traditionally involved screening outward signs of the bodily "landscape," such as skin color, physiognomy, and, in the case of Algerian women, the veil. Absent other articles of clothing, such as bags, veiled women are usually guaranteed a search-free passage because the French consider them passive, unconcerned with the Algerian cause, and incapable of action by being held back by traditional values and male domination. Fanon aptly describes the French imperial confidence in their ability to "know" the Algerian woman: "With the veil, things become well-defined and ordered. The Algerian woman, in the eyes of the observer, is unmistakable . . . 'she who hides behind a veil'" ([1959] 2007, 34). Ironically, when a woman is wearing a veil, one of the purposes of which is to privatize her body and make it unintelligible to the external gaze, the French military immediately casts her as perfectly intelligible. This means that for surveillance to support constant and operational epistemic housekeeping, bodily features have to be adorned with permanent physical markers.

However, if the military superiority of the French can function only through homogenizing notions of the Other's body and culture, the ability of the colonized to resist and rebel is contingent upon sustainable unintelligibility, which can be achieved only through self-heterogenization. By constantly metamorphosing their Otherness, especially in their strategic reconfiguration of gender roles, Algerian rebels succeed in transforming the status of women from a cultural disability into a political and cultural leverage. By rendering their "Otherly" markers unreadable, Algerian rebels are always one step ahead of the colonizing state's knowledge apparatus.

When traditional screening methods at checkpoints are repeatedly infiltrated and the colonial regime suffers significant losses, the French realize that there are loopholes in their intelligence-gathering system. Their orientalist regime of knowledge has become dysfunctional because the empire's eyes are overtrained on native normalcy. The new native rebel has an evasive rather than paramount appearance. Accordingly, imperial surveillance has to adapt to what Colonel Mathieu describes as "a faceless enemy, unrecognizable, blending in with hundreds of others." The phrase "faceless enemy" literally refers to the Algerians' clandestine mutinies under the guise of the veil but also alludes to the limits of imperial knowledge.

Surveillance cameras are installed because the imperial gaze needs to furnish the enemy with a knowable face and rewrite it as a stable sign. But as the French intelligence personnel pore over the collected surveillance footage, they are forced for the first time to redirect their gaze from what they define as the familiar markers of race and gender toward uncategorical signs of native agency. All Algerians become suspects. As a result, unindividuated indigenous subjects proverbially salvage from their oppressors the right to misrepresent a type of people. When the colonized subjects cease to represent a type, what they are reclaiming is the right to self-representation and basic ontological variation, originally imperially codified as the exclusive right of free European subjects. But in addition to the surveillance, the French continue to collectively punish the residents of the Algerian Casbah. The revolution, therefore, must self-democratize. The French finally discover that not only men but also unlikely adversaries, such as children and even veiled women, are embroiled in a radical reshuffling of formal Algerian social roles.

The Colonized Female Writes Her Body

Algerian female rebels epitomize Cixous's "female-sexed texts," or text marked by the feminine body (1976, 877). They make political statements with their bodies. The Algerian woman's struggle, interestingly, makes use of a mode of physical westernization that is not politically disinterested. The motives behind the Algerian woman's extrinsic transformation are strategic, and the actualization of the transformation is gradual. In addition to extrinsic transformation, the film emphasizes the distinction between voicelessness and unintelligibility. The fact that the French cannot understand the Muslim female voice does not mean it is not there. After the French authorities discover that some veiled women have been participating in the revolution and smuggling handguns in their baskets, French officers take revenge by blowing up a civilian neighborhood in the Casbah in the middle of the night. Once the Algerians have finished recovering the dead women's and children's bodies from under the rubble, Algerian men and women march spontaneously in the alleys of the Casbah, shouting slogans such as "Huriya!," or freedom, which the French authorities—having strictly enforced French education and showed strong disdain for Arabic—would not comprehend.

Another symbolic hallmark of the extradiscursive transformation of Algerian women occurs when the FLN urges the demonstrators to go back to the Casbah. Jaffar, an FLN leader, placates the demonstrators by promising to avenge their losses. The Algerian women react by ululating. As an exclusively feminine paralanguage and an oxymoronic combination of triumph, mourning, jubilation, and pain, ululation fractures the all-knowing orientalist mindset and foreshadows the radical shift in the role of women in the revolution.[6] What this onomatopoeic expression mimics is a nonessential and shifting native femininity that often gets overlooked or homogenized in colonialist imagination.

Background French commentary, which sounds like a radio broadcast, captures the degree of shock and confusion that this feminine outcry causes the French authorities: "The Muslim quarters still echo with those unintelligible and frightening rhythmic cries." The Algerian woman takes this unintelligibility a step further when she westernizes her appearance. She literally rebrands herself as white. This "conversion" is as textual as it is visual because it endows her body with a new type of signifying power she would have not been able to wield otherwise. She can now pass as French, pose as equal, and incapacitate the racial gaze. In addition to the audiovisual dramatization of the westernization scene discussed earlier, the original script of the film uses language strongly suggestive of a harem shedding its skin: "Djamila . . . removes the veil from her face. Her glance is hard and intense; her face is expressionless. The mirror reflects a large part of the room: it is a bedroom. There are three other girls. . . . Zohra . . . undresses, removing her traditional costume. . . . There is Hassiba who is pouring a bottle of peroxide into a basin. She dips her long black hair into the water to dye it blond. . . . Hassiba . . . seems to be a young European girl who is preparing to go to the beach" (Solinas 1973, 66, ellipses added for omissions).

The Algerian woman's investment in the signifying capacity of her femininity puts her in an extradiscursive, liminal, yet privileged position: just as the French want, she is outside of the "brown man's" harem, despite local traditions. However, she is not outside enough to thank her "new master" for liberating her. Algerian and French androcentric ideologies overlap in their hegemonic directionality. Under both ideologies, the top-down social rules of exchange in a male–female relationship usually

6. It is common for Arab women to defy occupation with jubilant ululation. This happens often in Gaza and the West Bank. In some cases, funeral ceremonies are called "martyrdom celebration" out of defiance. Colonial discourse usually misreads this as love of death.

mandate submission: sexual, economic, political, or otherwise. Both Algerian and French power structures—although each is shaped by unique and complex cultural, economic, and ideological strands—recruit the female as the Other of gender relationships. The woman's body is consequently always positioned at the receiving end of the ideological codifications of morality and social roles of both sociopolitical formations, the colonizing and the colonized.

By juxtaposing the traditional marriage of Mahmud and Fatiha with the prostitution that Algerian nationalists believe the French have introduced to their society, Pontecorvo's film certainly oversimplifies the contrast between what the French want from the body of Algerian women and what male Algerian rebels want. Whereas marriage represents the nostalgic regression to a pure precolonial stage now lamentably lost, the exaggerated emphasis on the dilemma of prostitution probably results from the fear of moral decadence that the rebels believe the French are spreading to disintegrate the traditional Algerian family and defuse the revolution. At the dawn of the revolution, therefore, Ali La Pointe and other guerrilla leaders are adamant on emphasizing traditional values and eliminating prostitution. In spite of this polarization, the film succeeds at least in highlighting the frequent objectification of women's bodies in the Algerian War of Independence. Both the Algerian and French men want "things" from Algerian women's bodies. After the French discover that veiled women are participating in the struggle, Algerian women resort to tactics that are unorthodox by the standards of both French and Algerian essentialist cultural values: the new rebel arrives at the point of no return. Nationalistic liberation discourse, being only vaguely religious, does not call for women to reveil after the revolution.[7]

The notion of repurposing the oppressor's identity markers permeates fiction, but Algerians take it to a new level when they abruptly and willingly abandon a banal fixture, the veil, that France has been trying to systemically remove for decades. Westernization of the Algerian body

7. Postcolonial religious revivalism undertook the task of reveiling in North African in general, blaming unveiling on the West instead of acknowledging the homegrown aspects of Arab secularism.

is strategic in the sense that it is Calibanistic; that is, like Shakespeare's famous character Caliban in *The Tempest*, it exploits the loopholes of the oppressor's ideology and dismantles it from within rather than completely abandoning one's older self in submission to a new master.

By unveiling and becoming "white," Algerian women do not become more European and less Arab. The master–slave motif is not new to Europe, especially regarding North Africa. Algerian women become French only to the degree that Caliban, the North African island native, becomes Italian when he uses the language of his master to curse him:

> You taught me language; and my profit on't
> Is, I know how to curse. The red plague rid you
> For learning me your language!
>   ([1610–11] 1914, 1.2.62–64)

Like the Tunisian Caliban, Algerian female rebels gain leverage and muddy the master–slave dialectic by brandishing the "master's" tools of oppression in his face. Unlike Friday in *Robinson Crusoe* (Defoe [1719] 1994) or Kurtz's slave in *Heart of Darkness* (Conrad [1899] 2011), Algerian women are not using the colonizer's language to say "master." Their Europeanized body is to the French what Caliban's broken Italian is to Prospero: a curse.

Nevertheless, in resistant discourse, to westernize is to sacrifice part of oneself. In *Black Skin, White Masks*, Fanon dubs the desire among some women of color to pass off as white and be desired by white men as pathological "lactification." He attacks Mayotte Capécia's *I Am a Martinican Woman* (Capécia [1948/1950] 1997) as "a third-rate book, advocating unhealthy behavior." According to Fanon, "unable to blacken or negrify [*sic*] the world," the autobiographical heroine of the book "endeavors to whiten it in her body and mind" ([1952] 2008, 29, 25, 28, 9). In contrast with the desperate desire for racial mobility that forced Capécia to abandon her Blackness, the lingual and physical lactification of Algerian women in the film is only skin-deep.

Conclusion: The Fatherless "Birth" of Algerian Feminism

The political rhetoric of postcolonial state formation is usually replete with images of birth, regeneration, emancipation from the colonial past, and restoration of a national grand narrative based on imagined historic, religious, and cultural unity. In Algeria as well as in many other postcolonial North African countries, memories of the colonial past continue to shape a wide spectrum of ideological formations. The effort to erase traces of the colonial history is in itself a confusing love–hate affair with that past. However, Algerian postcolonial feminists, in spite of their usual idealization of the female rebels of the colonial era, have generally rejected extreme dogmatic structures.

Susan Slyomovics, a Near Eastern studies scholar who writes frequently on gender issues in Morocco and Algeria, detects this trend in the postcolonial condition of Algeria in the 1990s. She gives the example of Hassiba, the Algerian rebel who is seen dying her hair blond in Pontecorvo's film. Slyomovics recounts how Algerian feminists, who marched in two cities to protest the Islamists' rise to power in the 1990s, commemorated Hassiba's anticolonial struggle in their slogans: "Hassiba Ben Bouali, If You Could See Our Algeria" and "Hassiba Ben Bouali, We Will Not Betray You" (1995, 8). The commemoration of Hassiba in these prosecular demonstrations almost three decades after the gaining of Algerian independence in 1962 underlines the feminists' vehement disapproval of two masculine discourses: colonial and religious.

Some people might perceive unveiling as an act of defection to the West, but this is a false dichotomy belied by history. Unveiling in North Africa surged under Arab pan-nationalist regimes fiercely opposed to Western interests in the Arab world. Before those regimes took over, Huda Sha'rawi, a strong opponent of British rule in Egypt, turned unveiling into a political statement and became a role model for many feminists in the Arab world. Unveiling can simultaneously be a personal choice and a political statement, but its politics, although influenced by the materiality of history, do not necessarily gratify patriarchal expectations.

Works Cited

Abouzeid, Leila. 2009. *Life of the Prophet: A Biography of Prophet Mohammed.* Rabat, Morocco: Imprimerie El Maarif al Jadida.

———. 2010. *The Last Chapter.* Cairo: American Univ. in Cairo Press.

———. 2014. *America: The Other Face.* Beirut: Arab Scientific.

"Al-Ahzab." N.d. At http://quran.com/33/59.

Alloula, Malek. 1986. *The Colonial Harem*. Translated by Mirna Godzich and Wlad Godzich. Minneapolis: Univ. of Minnesota Press.

"'Awrah of Female Slaves in Sharia." 2008. Nov. 3. At http://fatwa.islamweb.net /fatwa/index.php?page=showfatwa&Option=FatwaId&Id=114264.

Baaqeel, Nuha. 2015. "An Interview with Ahlam Mosteghanemi." *Women: A Cultural Review* 26, nos. 1–2: 143–53. At https://doi.org/10.1080/09574042.2015 .1035055.

Bakr, Abdulaziz. 2015. "Novelist Abouzeid: Are Arab Secularists Undermining Their Own Culture While Their Peers in the West Are Restoring Theirs?" Apr. 20. At http://www.lahaonline.com/articles/view/47878.htm.

Caillé, Patricia. 2007. "The Illegitimate Legitimacy of *The Battle of Algiers* in French Film Culture." *Interventions* 9, no. 3: 371–88. At https://doi.org/10 .1080/13698010701618604.

Capécia, Mayotte. [1948/1950] 1997. I Am a Martinican Woman & The White Negress: *Two Novelettes*. Translated by Beatrice Stith Clark. Pueblo, CO: Passeggiata.

Cixous, Hélène. 1976. "The Laugh of the Medusa." Translated by Keith Cohen and Paula Cohen. *Signs* 1, no. 4: 875–93. At https://www.jstor.org/stable/3173239.

———. 1998. *Stigmata: Escaping Texts*. Translated by Eric Preno. London: Routledge.

Conrad, Joseph. [1899] 2011. *Heart of Darkness*. Edited by Ross C. Murfin. Boston: Bedford–St. Martins.

Defoe, Daniel. [1719] 1994. *Robinson Crusoe*. Edited by Michael Shinagel. New York: W. W. Norton.

Djebar, Assia. 1994. *Far from Medina*. London: Quartet.

Djebar, Assia, and Clarisse Zimra. 2005. Afterword to Assia Djebar, *Children of the New World: A Novel of the Algerian War*, 201–29. New York: Feminist Press at the City Univ. of New York.

El Saadawi, Nawal. 2009. *A Daughter of Isis: The Autobiography of Nawal El Saadawi*. New York: Zed.

Fanon, Frantz. [1959] 2007. *A Dying Colonialism*. Edited by Adolfo Gilly. Translated by Haakon Chevalier. New York: Grove Press.

———. [1952] 2008. *Black Skin, White Masks*. Translated by Richard Philcox. New York: Grove Press.

Ginio, Ruth. 2006. *French Colonialism Unmasked: The Vichy Years in French West Africa*. Lincoln: Univ. of Nebraska Press.

Harlow, Barbara. 1986. Introduction to Malek Alloula, *The Colonial Harem*, translated by Mirna Godzich and Wlad Godzich, ix–xx. Minneapolis: Univ. of Minnesota Press.

Hoodfar, Homa. 1993. "The Veil in Their Minds and on Our Heads: The Persistence of Colonial Images of Muslim Women." *Resources for Feminist Research* 22, nos. 3–4: 5–18. At https://www.proquest.com/scholarly-journals /veil-their-minds-on-our-heads-persistence/docview/194879317/se-2.

Ibn Abbas. N.d. "Dress: Men Who Are in the Similitude of Women, and Women Who Are in the Similitude of Men." At http://sunnah.com/bukhari/77/102.

Ibn Umar, Abdullah. N.d. "Clothing (Kitab al-Libas): A Garment of Fame and Vanity." At http://sunnah.com/abudawud/34/12.

Al-Khudri, Abu Sa'id. N.d. "The Book of Knowledge: Following the Ways of the Jews and Christians." At http://sunnah.com/muslim/47/7.

Lazreg, Marnia. 1994. *The Eloquence of Silence: Algerian Women in Question*. New York: Routledge.

Mernissi, Fatima. [1975] 1987. *Beyond the Veil: Male–Female Dynamics in Modern Muslim Society*. Rev. ed. Bloomington: Indiana Univ. Press.

———. 1994. *Dreams of Trespass: Tales of a Harem Girlhood*. With photographs by Ruth V. Ward. New York: Perseus.

———. 2001. *Scheherazade Goes West: Different Cultures, Different Harems*. New York: Washington Square Press.

Moore, L. C. 2003. "The Veil of Nationalism: Frantz Fanon's 'Algeria Unveiled' and Gillo Pontecorvo's *The Battle of Algiers*." *Kunapipi: Journal of Postcolonial Writing* 25, no. 2: 56–73. At https://eprints.lancs.ac.uk/id/eprint /3849.

Mosteghanemi, Ahlam. [1993] 2003. *Memory in the Flesh*. Cairo: American Univ. in Cairo Press.

———. 2015. *Chaos of the Senses*. Translated by Nancy Roberts. London: Bloomsbury.

Roberts, Katherine A. 2007. "Constrained Militants: Algerian Women 'in-between' in Gillo Pontecorvo's *The Battle of Algiers* and Bourlem Guerdjou's *Living in Paradise*." *Journal of North African Studies* 12, no. 4: 381–93. At https://doi.org/10.1080/13629380701307043.

Said, Edward W. 1978. *Orientalism*. New York: Vintage.

Shakespeare, William. [c. 1610–11] 1914. *The Tempest*. Edited by W. J. Craig. London: Oxford Univ. Press. At https://www.bartleby.com/70/index11.html.

Slyomovics, Susan. 1995. "'Hassiba Ben Bouali, If You Could See Our Algeria': Women and Public Space in Algeria." *Middle East Report*, no. 192: 8–13. At https://doi.org/10.2307/3013348.

Solinas, Franco. 1973. *Gillo Pontecorvo's* The Battle of Algiers. Edited by PierNico Solinas. New York: Scribner.

Spivak, Gayatri Chakravorty. 1988. "Can the Subaltern Speak?" In *Marxism and the Interpretation of Culture*, edited by Nelson Cary and Lawrence Grossberg, 271–313. Urbana: Univ. of Illinois Press.

3

Roots and Routes of the Veil in the Maghreb

Rachida Yassine

Women's bodies are used everywhere to symbolize and project collective ideals. Perhaps nowhere has this been more the case than in the Maghreb, where women's bodies, women's dress, women's presence in particular spaces have always been used as a way of characterizing a host of moral, political, and religious notions. Both Eurocentric and Islamocentric discourses on Maghrebi Muslim women seem to be framed by the dichotomy between Islamic tradition and Western modernity. In the former discourse, the Muslim woman is victimized by Islamic tradition and can be liberated only through the magical act of removing the veil. The latter is characterized by two dissenting views: that of the modernist male elite, which calls for women's emancipation through abolishing the veil, and that of the Salafi (traditional or conservative) trend, which considers the veil an essential component of girls' and women's Islamic identity.

The Maghreb is the area in North Africa that comprises the modern nation-states Morocco, Algeria, and Tunisia. The word *maghreb* in Arabic signifies the direction west. This region occupies an ambiguous geopolitical position that is at once "Western" from the standpoint of the Arabs of the Mashreq (the Middle East) and "Oriental" from the standpoint of Europe. The Maghreb is also an area characterized by a rich cultural and historical mix, a plurality of identity and experience. For many centuries, European-based empires controlled the Maghreb: the Romans, the Byzantine emperors, and finally the French during their imperial heyday

(Algeria, for instance, gained its independence from France only as recently as 1962).

This chapter seeks to explore some of the historical, sociopolitical, cultural, and religious factors that have had an impact on the perception and representation of the veil in the Maghreb. First, I consider the impact of colonial history and Western cultural discourses that disseminated detrimental stereotypes of Arab/Muslim women through literature, photography, film, television, and the media. These stereotypes continue to shape the image of Arab women in the West. For instance, though orientalist pictorial/visual representations have encompassed all facets of North Africa, they have been particularly pernicious to feminine identity. Just as colonial Europeans fostered detrimental clichés of the Maghrebi subjects and culture, they also created narrow, self-serving visions of Maghrebi women. The image of these women in both racial and sexual terms was more than a codified stereotype for the West. Concealed behind their veils, the women were hidden from the prying eyes of the colonizers and the West in general. As a consequence, their identity was easily forged into an erotic feminine collective in orientalist literature, painting, photography, and cinema, which contributed to the stifling of the Maghrebi feminine voice and subjectivity even further. In these genres, the women are often represented as cloistered within harems but unveiled and even denuded for the aesthetic pleasure of the viewer or the reader: a catharsis of pleasure through tragedy. Second, I examine the impact of the nationalist ideologies during the struggle for independence when the veil became no longer just a traditional garb but also the most significant bastion of resistance. Basing my study on Frantz Fanon's nationalist discourse in his book *Studies in a Dying Colonialism* (1965), I demonstrate the way this discourse politicizes the veil, thereby reconstituting colonialism as the project of "unveiling colonized societies" and stressing the extent to which the nation authenticates its distinct cultural identity through its veiled women.

The Veil and Colonial History

Tunisia, Algeria, and Morocco constitute a geocultural entity. They all went through a period of French colonization and became independent roughly in the late 1950s and early 1960s. The common type of veil that a Maghrebi woman wore in the nineteenth and early twentieth century consisted of a *hayek*, a loose-fitting piece of cloth enveloping all the body, and a face cover that allowed only the eyes to be seen. Sometimes women used the *hayek* to cover the body and the face, allowing but one eye to be seen and to guide a woman while she was walking. Some women wore a djeballa when stepping outside, a long, loose-fitting robe that has almost the same function as the *hayek*. During the colonial era, the Maghrebi female body, thus covered up, became the object of material, aesthetic, scientific, and erotic examinations. As a matter of fact, history knows of no other group of women as comprehensively painted, portrayed, and photographed as North African and Middle Eastern women. For instance, painters such as Eugène Delacroix (1798–1863), Auguste Renoir (1814–1919), and Henri Matisse (1869–1954) as well as colonial photographers such as Marcelin Flandrin (1889–1957) and many others showed their fascination with Maghrebi women and mis/represented them in many ways.[1] What those mis/representations have in common is their audacity to unveil and denude women in a society where nakedness violates local customs and religious practices.

The act of unveiling Maghrebi women was an iconic sign of French domination because it attempted to reverse the common facts known about women in Muslim countries, who were barely noticed in society, let alone being exposed naked to the camera of a photographer or the gaze of a painter. Historically, Arabs and Muslims believed that the veil covered the body to discipline, reassure, protect, and comfort women as they participated in society. The veil was a way of ensuring that the moral boundaries between unrelated men and women were respected. For the colonizer, the veil was a tool of oppression and an unequivocal sign of Muslims', especially Muslim women's, backwardness. For this reason, portraying unveiled and naked women in colonial photography was part of the so-called civilizing mission to "liberate" these women and a cunning disclosure of a Muslim secret that had preoccupied Europeans for centuries.

---

1. Some examples of such representation in literature are Gustave Flaubert's Kuchuk-Hanem in *Voyages en Orient* (1850) and *Correspondance* (1853) and Eugène Fromentin's Haouâ in *Une année dans le Sahel* (1858).

Thus, a series of early twentieth-century French postcards and photographs depicting eroticized scenes from Morocco, Algeria, and Tunisia under colonial rule circulated in France between 1900 and 1930.[2] They portrayed Maghrebi women in various guises: nude and odalisque-like, surrounded by "Oriental" props and festoons. These postcards anchored Maghrebi women in the realm of the exotic and represented a European phantasm of the "Oriental" female. According to the Algerian postcolonial critic Malek Alloula, these postcards are "photographed discourse" (1986, 130), an illustrated form of colonialist discourse that reproduced the Oriental stereotypes and participated in the exercise of colonial power to support the larger French colonial project in the Maghreb, especially in Algeria. In this sense, these postcards usurped Maghrebi identity by a process of misrepresentation. They did not represent Maghrebi women; rather, they represented the French phantasm of the Oriental female and her inaccessibility behind the veil in the forbidden harem. They were part of a colonialist strategy of social coercion targeting the institution of the family. As Klaus Karl argues, "Women from the Maghreb did not strip, especially in front of strangers. Those that agreed to do so were mercenary accomplices, bought by the eye behind the lens for the pleasure of voyeurs deceived as to the reality of images" (2011, 122).

It should be noted that colonial photography of nakedness was restricted to the Quartier *réservé* and to places such as the Bousbir, an infamous brothel built in Casablanca in the 1920s, and the studio only. The French photographers could not get those nude images in any place but a brothel or a studio. Most of the mis/representations were studio portraits constructed in such a way to give the sensation of a sly, dishonest glance into the intimacy of the Muslim household's interior, which was increasingly open to imagined public view by the end of the nineteenth century. It was commonly known that most women serving as prostitutes in the Quartier *réservé* were female peasants from the Atlas or clandestine women coming from Europe or Africa to accompany the army, and, hence, they can in no way be representative of Maghrebi women.

2. For further details about these postcards, see Boëtsch and Ferrié 1993, 193–96.

Even as the French cunningly tried to undermine the religious and traditional connotations of the veil, they discovered that women served national resistance effectively through the veil. Women were not seen, but they could see. Women could carry anything under their veil without being noticed. Moreover, wearing the *hayek* was a solution for wanted men resisting French colonialism to circulate freely from one place to another without being detected by the French army. Resistance chronicles in Morocco, Algeria, and Tunisia immortalize stories of women carrying weapons for men hiding in the woods and on mountains, of men wearing the traditional *hayek* and transferring news and information to the leaders of resistance, and of assassinations of colonial administration members or their native supporters carried out with the help of the veil. The veil in this case became an effective instrument of camouflage and gender passing for the sake of resistance.

The Veil and the Discourse of Nationalism

During the Algerian War of Independence (1954–62), the French generals, determined to keep Algeria French, choreographed a public ceremony in Algiers on May 16, 1958, in which they rounded up native Algerian women in the Casbah and forced them to unveil while singing the French national hymn "La marseillaise" and the military "Chant des Africains" (Lazreg 1994, 135). Because the French saw in the act of unveiling the body of the "Algerian woman" a French military victory over the native Muslim Arab population, the Algerian male leaders of the National Liberation Front (Front de libération nationale, FLN) transmogrified the veil as an icon of nationalist resistance and a symbol of Maghrebi Muslim identity.

For example, the anticolonial writer and FLN leader Frantz Fanon can be considered exemplary for recognizing gender as a formative dimension of nationalism. In his book *Studies in a Dying Colonialism* (1959, translated into English in 1965), he presented a problematic analysis of the gendering of the national formation. He revealed the extent to which the nation authenticates its distinct cultural identity through its women. In his analysis of the dialectical relationship between the colonized and the colonizer, the Algerian woman became a central force. She was the axis upon and around which the colonizing mission and anticolonial resistance often spun. In "Algeria Unveiled," one of the essays in *Studies in a Dying Colonialism*, Fanon explained the intricacies and developments of the Algerian War of Independence. He used the image of the "unveiling of Algeria" to draw a connection among the land, the nation, women, and their bodies. His account of the French presence in Algeria is in essence the account of the colonial power's attempt to unveil the Algerian woman. The veil, according to Fanon, functioned for the colonizer as an exotic signifier, invested with all the properties of a sexual fetish. Faced with a veiled Algerian woman, Fanon wrote, the European colonizer was consumed with a desire to see, a desire that in colonialism's highly sexualized economy of looking also operated as an urge for violent possession (1965, 42).

Like Fanon, Alloula identifies "one of the chief objectives of colonization" as "the breakup of the very kernel of the resistance to colonial penetration: the traditional family" (1986, 39) Therefore, for Alloula the veil is a sign of an authentic cultural identity and an emblem of resistance. It is a challenge to the colonial gaze because it discourages what Alloula terms "the scopic" desire—that is to say, the photographer's voyeurism. In Alloula's male-centered discourse, the veil also represents "the closure of private space. It signifies an injunction of no trespassing upon this space" (13).

Fanon's nationalist discourse regarding the status of Algerian women during the War of Independence revealed that the struggle over the veil in colonial Algeria was parallel to the struggle over sati, or widow sacrifice, in India. Fanon's metaphorical relationship between the land and women was shared by both the French and the Algerians: in both colonial and nationalist discourse, Algerian women were depicted as key symbols of Algeria's cultural identity. In the colonialist fantasy, to possess Algeria's women was to possess Algeria. This metaphor illustrates what Ashis Nandy describes as the colonial homology between sexual dominance and political dominance (1983, 4). Algerian women were at once the symbol of Algeria's refusal to surrender to France's "emancipatory seed" and the passageway to penetration of the colonized land. Thus, not only was Algeria imagined as a woman to be possessed, but possessing an Algerian woman was also a step toward possessing Algeria. In nationalist/resistance discourse, in contrast, the land is a female body whose violation by the colonizer requires the male natives to rush to her defense. This metaphor places the male subject as defender of the nation and the female subject as its embodiment. As Fanon's title "Algeria Unveiled" suggests, this equating of land and woman was especially focused on the veiled woman. The veil was thought to be the most significant bastion of resistance.

In *A Dying Colonialism*, Fanon outlined the Algerian resistance to what was seen as the premeditated colonial plot to erase Algeria's cultural originality, to defeat and fragment the Algerian nation by unveiling its women and forcing modernity on the colonized for colonialist purposes. According to Fanon, the French occupiers' "frenzy" to unveil Algerian women aimed at reducing colonial domination to a cultural issue symbolized by women. This project, as Fanon viewed it, was part of a campaign to weaken indigenous culture and destroy anticolonial resistance. Fanon's position on this issue is akin to Abdul JanMohamed's subsequent view of the dialectic between the colonized self and the colonizing other, which is based on the suppression of colonial identity and culture. According to JanMohamed, the colonial power "destroys without any significant qualms the effectiveness of indigenous economic, social, political, legal, and moral systems and imposes its own versions of these structures on the Other" (1986, 85). This colonialist process of negation and appropriation engenders a paradoxical sense of alterity on the part of the colonized subject, which manifests in the colonized's tendency not only to see themselves through the gaze of the other but also to draw on aspects of the colonizer's model in order to elaborate their own sense of subjectivity.

Fanon's discourse exposed the colonial paradigm to reduce the identity of the colonized by inverting traditional forms. This discourse politicized the veil, thereby reconstituting colonialism as the project of "unveiling Algeria." In his book, Algeria is depicted as a veiled woman, threatened with unveiling, which is synonymous with rape. According to Fanon, in the collective psychology this unveiling/rape—colonial domination either of the land or of the nation—led to Algerian/male dishonor:

> This veil, one of the elements of the traditional Algerian garb, was to become the bone of contention in a grandiose battle, on account of which the occupation forces were to mobilize their most powerful and

most varied resources, and in the course of which the colonized were to display a surprising force of inertia. Taken as a whole, colonial society, with its values, its areas of strength, and its philosophy, reacts to the veil in a rather homogeneous way. The decisive battle was launched before 1954, more precisely during the early 1930's. The officials of the French administration in Algeria, committed to destroying the people's originality, and under instructions to bring about the disintegration, at whatever cost, of forms of existence likely to evoke a national reality directly or indirectly, were to concentrate their efforts on the wearing of the veil, which was looked upon at this juncture as a symbol of the status of the Algerian woman. (1965, 36–37)

Fanon thus established the wearing of the veil as symbolic in the anticolonial struggle, which focused on the perceived status of the Algerian woman. He paraphrased the colonial administration's political doctrine as follows: "If we [the French] want to destroy the structure of Algerian society, its capacity for resistance, we must first of all conquer the women; we must go and find them behind the veil where they hide themselves and in the houses where the men keep them out of sight" (1965, 37–38). The contention is that the French wished to gain control of women's attitude toward the veil and thus in a sense gain control of their bodies. This control of their bodies, which was at least in certain aspects seen to be the prerogative of Algerian men—of fathers, husbands, brothers, and sons—was to be lost to the Algerians and, according to Fanon, thus lead to an end of the country's resistance to colonization: "Every rejected veil disclosed to the eyes of the colonialists horizons until then forbidden, and revealed to them, piece by piece, the flesh of Algeria laid bare. . . . Every veil that fell, everybody that became liberated from the traditional embrace of the *haik*, every face that offered itself to the bold and impatient glance of the occupier, was a negative expression of the fact that Algeria was beginning to deny herself and was accepting the rape of the colonizer" (42). Thus, Fanon posited the wearing of the veil as a resistance to French cultural hegemony and to the colonial paradigm that was intended to reduce the colonized people's identity by inverting traditional cultural forms. He concluded that a woman's wearing of the veil was an indication of her patriotism or dedication to the struggle: "The attitude of a given Algerian woman with respect to the veil will be constantly related to her overall attitude with respect to the foreign occupation" (47). He further argued that at one point in the War of Independence the veil was removed, and Algerian women fighters westernized themselves (light-skinned, blond women were favored in this scheme) to fool French soldiers at the blockades and pass unsuspected guns and bombs in handbags and baskets to the French quarter of Algiers. They returned to traditional dress when strategy dictated they carry larger arms. The veil became "a technique of camouflage" (Bhabha 1994, 63). Fanon took care to remind his readers that despite the Algerian woman's co-option in the resistance, she never relinquished her individuality, independence, and integrity, nor did she relinquish her role in Algerian culture. Her individuality, according to Fanon, was fully anchored in the culture of her society.

In describing what he called "the new dialectic of the body and of the world" for the revolutionary woman, Fanon detailed the relationship between the veil, the body, and self-image as follows: "The veil protects, reassures, isolates. . . . Without the veil she [the recently unveiled woman] has an impression of her body being cut up into bits, put adrift; the limbs seem to lengthen indefinitely. She has the impression of being improperly dressed, even of being naked. . . . The absence of the veil distorts the Algerian woman's corporal pattern. . . . The Algerian woman who walks stark naked into the European city relearns her body, re-establishes it in a totally revolutionary fashion" (1965, 59). As these lines imply, however important the psychological effects of colonialism, Fanon posited the body of the colonized as the prime target of control and therefore as a prime location of resistance. In this respect, according to Fanon, the formerly veiled woman experiences the veil as holding her body in a defined space. In addition, she equates the part with the whole, the veil with her clothes. Without the veil, she feels not only naked but also not whole. She senses no lines of demarcation between herself and her environment, the exterior world beyond her body. This sense of intermingling with the outside world is not a positive experience but rather a source of anxiety. Yet because Fanon was writing about revolutionary transformations, his statement that she "re-establishes her body in a totally revolutionary fashion" can be considered a positive valuation of unveiling. Fanon was convinced that through the revolutionary process, the traditional attitude toward the veil would undergo drastic modifications. He affirmed that when Algeria gained "her" independence, the question of the veil would not be raised (47–48) because the unveiled Algerian woman, who assumed an increasingly important place in revolutionary action and developed her personality, would not revert to the past. She would have forged a new place for herself by her heroic participation in the liberation struggle. By contributing to the writing of the heroic pages of Algerian history, she was challenging the patriarchal structure of Algerian society, earning free access to public space, and abolishing the shackles of her past enclosure. She was, in Fanon's words, "at the same time participating in the destruction of colonialism and in the birth of a new woman" (107).

Thus, in the Maghreb, because of the history of struggle around it, the veil as a cultural and religious signifier came to comprehend significations far broader than merely the position of women. It can be considered a borderline between points of contact, East/West, modernity/traditionalism, and male/female. The veil also acts as a meeting point for confrontational perspectives, providing a contentious image to initiate debates on women's emancipation and critiques of patriarchal formations. These critiques vary from considering the veil as an instrument of oppression and a mechanism of control of women's sexuality, as the Algerian feminist writer Marnia Lazreg (1994, 2009) sees it, to approaching the veil more as a matter of social status than of religious injunction, as the Moroccan feminist Fatema Mernissi (1991) maintains.

Works Cited

Alloula, Malek. 1986. *The Colonial Harem*. Translated by Mirna Godzich and Wlad Godzich. Minneapolis: Univ. of Minnesota Press.

Bhabha, Homi. 1994. *The Location of Culture*. London: Routledge.

Boëtsch, Gilles, and Jean-Noël Ferrié. 1993. "La Mauresque aux seins nus: L'imaginaire erotique colonial dans la carte postale." In *Images et colonies*, edited by Pascal Blanchard and Armelle Chatelier, 192–217. Paris: Syros.

Fanon, Frantz. 1965. *Studies in a Dying Colonialism*. Translated by Hakoon Chevalier. New York: Grove Weidenfeld.

JanMohamed, Abdul R. 1986. "The Economy of Manichean Allegory: The Function of Racial Difference in Colonialist Literature." In *Race, Writing and Difference*, edited by Henry Louis Gates Jr., 78–106. Chicago: Univ. of Chicago Press.

Karl, Klaus. 2011. *Erotic Photography*. London: Parkstone International.

Lazreg, Marnia. 1994. *The Eloquence of Silence: Algerian Women in Question*. New York: Routledge.

———. 2009. *Questioning the Veil: Open Letters to Muslim Women*. Princeton, NJ: Princeton Univ. Press.

Mernissi, Fatema. 1991. *The Veil and the Male Elite: A Feminist Interpretation of Women's Rights in Islam*. Translated by Mary Jo Lakeland. New York: Basic.

Nandy, Ashis. 1983. *The Intimate Enemy: Loss and Recovery of Self under Colonialism*. Delhi: Oxford Univ. Press.

Part 2 Immigrant Women and the Veil in Fiction

Patriarchy, Negotiations, and Agency

4

Fictionizing the Veil

Patriarchy, Matriarchy, and Jihad
in Fadia Faqir's *Willow Trees Don't Weep*

Dallel Sarnou

The terrorist attacks on the Twin Towers and the Pentagon on September 11, 2001, were a turning point in the history of the United States of America. The event was also a major climacteric for Arabs and hyphenated people of Arabic origins, who have witnessed a terrifying rise in phobia since this event, often the outcome of a biased misrepresentation of Arabs and Muslims. Muslim and Arab women in particular can be considered a main target of anti-Arab and anti-Muslim expression. The latest bans on wearing the burka (face veil), the headscarf, and the burkini (Islamic swimsuit for women) have increased the tension between Muslim and Arab people living in Western countries and non-Muslim natives of these nations. The headscarf or veil of the Muslim woman has now become a representation either of oppression for non-Muslims or of personal liberty for Muslims. However, many intellectuals—Muslims and non-Muslims—who may hold a neutral position believe that radical attitudes toward the veil, both pro-veil and antiveil, are against the freedom of women. Arab women authors who write in English are among the most courageous

An earlier version of this chapter was published as "Re-thinking the Veil, Jihad and Home in Fadia Faqir's Willow Trees Don't Weep (2014)," *Open Cultural Studies* 1, no. 1 (2017): 155–60, at https://doi.org/10.1515/culture-2017-0014. Available under a CC-BY-NC-ND license.

voices that have often called for the freedom of Arab and Muslim women both in their home countries and in the Diaspora. In fact, a commitment to voicing liminal and misrepresented individuals is a priority for most Anglophone Arab writers, and the British Jordanian novelist Fadia Faqir is one of the most acclaimed Arab writers in the West who has kept writing for and about Arabs and Arab/Muslim women in the Diaspora. In her novel *Willow Trees Don't Weep* (2014), she negotiates the meanings of women's freedom, love, jihad, fathering, and wars.

In fact, Faqir has become a leading figure in Arab British literature. Since the publication of her fifth novel, the reception of her books in the West has reached an important increase owing to the rise of interest in understanding the "Other" who is considered a threat to the West. In *Willow Trees Don't Weep*, Faqir defeated censorship and phobia in writing about the life of a terrorist and his deserted family. The novel exposes the predicament of thinking of oneself as a jihadi even while one is transforming into a terrorist. This is the case of the protagonist's father, who began his journey to save the Islamic world but wound up a terrorist. Najwa, his daughter, sets out to save herself, but she eventually ends up a dislocated immigrant in Durham, England. A story of hatred and love, freedom and oppression, matriarchy and patriarchy, forgiveness and accusation, broken promises and dreams, a father and daughter, *Willow Trees Don't Weep* takes the reader on an epic journey with the protagonist to discover the mysterious country of Afghanistan and to learn untold truths about jihad and Islamism. The novel also exposes how religious fundamentalism and secular extremism can be two sides of the same coin.

Initially titled *The Terrorist's Daughter*, Faqir's most recent novel, *Willow Trees Don't Weep* (2014), has made a difference in Anglophone Arab literature and world literature by fictionizing a journey that is considered a threat to the Western world. The decision to write about a man who left home to join al-Qaeda when his daughter was a child may be considered an outspoken act of bravery by this Arab woman author writing in English—and mostly for a Western readership. About the novel, the writer said in an interview in 2014: "It was different because *Willow Trees Don't Weep* is partly set in Afghanistan, a country I could not visit no matter how hard I tried. . . . What made the task of writing *Willow Trees Don't Weep* harder is constructing a country out of research material and photographs. The difficulty in relying on books is that you need to read a hundred to get a few useful facts that you could use in fiction. It is an arduous journey, but I hope I did justice to Afghanistan and its brave people" (Faqir 2014a, ellipses in original, qtd. in Sarnou 2017, 156). In another interview where the author introduced her book for the first time, she explained that she wanted the innocent—that is, the young daughter—to go on a journey that is difficult and is going to change her into someone who is possibly aware of what is happening in the world (Hebron Books 2014).

Najwa's journey represents a multiplicity of discoveries: discovering the meaning of jihad and fathering, discovering oneself, discovering universal womanhood, and discovering love and beauty in a dreary place in the world (Afghanistan). Here, therefore, I seek to inspect how and why a young girl who has been raised by a secular mother traces her jihadi father. Moreover, I set out to question how the veil, in particular the burka, is represented in this novel.

The curious case of Najwa, whose mother is an extreme secularist and father a radical Islamist, may for the reader embody where moderate Islam should be located and must be viewed. In the novel, the protagonist realizes that standing at the crossroads of her father's extremism and her mother's radicalism may save her dreams. In fact, Najwa's self-discovery is the end result of her journey to different countries but, more importantly, to Afghanistan. In this strange place, she recognizes how the face veil may symbolize freedom for some Afghani women, including her father's Afghani wife, Gulnar, and her own stepsister, Amani.

The headscarf and the face veil have become central issues debated in the West. Joan Wallach Scott proclaims that the West has long encouraged the secularization of the East (2007, ix). For Scott, one of these attempts to secularize the East, which is mostly Muslim majority, is to condemn the veil—the headscarf or what is known in Islam as the hijab—as being the most terrible garment to impose on women. In fact, the colonization of the Orient (from North Africa to South Asia) and the subsequent Europeanization of the postindependence elite in the former colonies of France, Britain, Spain, and other colonial powers resulted in a wave of early Arab feminists who saw the veil as belittling and demeaning of women's right to uncover their own bodies. Among the early pioneers of this movement is the Moroccan sociologist Fatima Mernissi, whose works have indeed reinforced the European view of the hijab. In her most prominent book, *Beyond the Veil: Male–Female Dynamics in Muslim Society* ([1975] 2011), the author strongly denounces how the scarf or the veil is a symbol of unjust male authority over women (136).

However, the late 1980s, the 1990s, and the early 2000s were marked by the rise of a more moderate Arab feminism and less westernized Arab women writers; many younger female intellectuals who had the opportunity to be educated abroad are often positioned as liminal for their in-between-ness regarding their Arabness/Muslimness and their modernizing convictions. Ahdaf Soueif, Leila Aboulela, Mohja Kahf, Leila Alalami, Ahlem Mostaghanemi, Safinez Kazem, Fadia Faqir, and many other contemporary Arab women authors writing in Arabic, English, and French hold less extremist antisharia views.

Fadia Faqir articulated her standpoint vis-à-vis her Arabness in an interview from March 2010 published in the *Journal of Postcolonial Writing* in 2012: "If the discourse in the metropolis aims to de-humanise Arabs and make them disappear in order to justify 'collateral damage,' my fiction and writing aims [*sic*] to humanise not only the Arabs, but the English, the Americans, the Indians etc. It is harder, perhaps, to shoot someone you know very well" (Bower 2012). Starting from the last sentence of Faqir's statement, one can notice that many Anglophone Arab women writers—including those listed earlier—who have lived between their Arab countries and the Diaspora, know both cultures and thus, because of their open-mindedness and tolerance, both understand and represent well people from different backgrounds.

Willow Trees Don't Weep is an epitome of Faqir's previous statement because it is a story that unveils unexpected truths about jihad, jihadis, women's rights in Muslim countries, secularism, and parenting. Following a short summary of the story, in an attempt to highlight scenes where major truths about Najwa's homeland, Jordan, are being narrated, I offer both a thematic and a literary analysis of the novel.

Raised by her mother and grandmother, Najwa knows her father only through her ill mother's stories of how he betrayed her. Najwa and her mother were abandoned by her father when she was three years old. However, after the death of her ill mother, the grown-up Najwa decides to trace her father, who has long represented for her the figurehead of patriarchy. In this journey, Najwa keeps traveling from one extreme to another: from Pakistan to the center of Taliban training, to Afghanistan, and eventually to a Europe where she metamorphoses into a freer woman but is still a strange person.

Faqir's novel explores eccentric journeys of discovering oneself, whether the father's or his daughter's. It leads the reader to some conclusions about those jihadis who have prioritized religion over their loved ones, for whatever reasons. In the case of Omar Rahmane, Najwa's father, the main reason for his metamorphosis into a jihadi is his first wife's (Najwa's mother's) cruelty. We read that the latter could not fill his heart with love the way his Afghani wife does. He also willingly takes on this transformation out of love for a friend.

Through the novel, the reader travels along with Najwa, who while searching for her father unveils bitter truths about women's status in Jordan and the other countries she visits during her journey. For instance, in chapter 1, "Behind the Poppy Field," Najwa's grandmother unveils a first truth about single women living on their own in Jordan: "You know how it is in Amman and particularly in this neighbourhood. Chaste women don't live on their own" (Faqir 2014b, 6).[1]

Najwa was aware of her alienness as a woman and as the daughter of a jihadi father and a secular mother. She confesses: "I knew I was different. I was not allowed to cover my head, wear a long school uniform or trousers, recite the Qur'an, participate in the Ramadan procession or wear prayer clothes and go to the mosque in the evening with the other children, who carried lanterns" (9). For Najwa, both her father and her mother are to blame for this feeling of alienness and dislocation: "You're as bad as each other. You (for the father) abandoned me and she (for the mother)" (7, parenthetical insertions in the original). However, Najwa is neither an extremist secular nor a religious fundamentalist. For instance, she admits

---

1. Subsequent citations to *Willow Trees Don't Weep* give page numbers only.

that the Quran can heal people: "If only she [her mother] had read this verse [chapter 94] from the Qur'an, she would have realised that each trial carried the seeds of healing within it" (79).

The novel also reveals many aspects of women's life in different places and countries. In Jordan, the life of Najwa, her mother, and her grandmother represents the life of Arab women who are caught within patriarchal practices, misinterpreted religious texts, and failed attempts to get liberated. In Afghanistan, Najwa's stepmother, Gulnar, and half-sister, Amani, are archetypes of Afghani women who were accidently trapped in a war zone under Taliban rule but still have love and affection because their men are romantic and caring. Even in London, we hear and meet other female characters who were deserted for one reason or another. The lonely, kind Isabel is one example. Therefore, this novel may also be considered a women's book in essence, besides being the story of a father and daughter.

The novel is unique in many ways, and one of these ways is how Faqir depicts women wearing the face veil and burka in Afghanistan. Najwa comes across many veiled and headscarfed women in different places—Amman, Pakistan, Afghanistan, and London. Yet, in fact, her first encounter with the headscarf was in her childhood when she was among the girls of her neighborhood, from whom she was detached by her mother. If we apply Carla Brewington's notion of emotional exile as a separation caused by trauma, heartbreak, relationship breakdown, or withdrawal (2013, 30), then we can see Najwa's emotionally exiled subjectivity. Najwa feels separated not only from her mother and father—a mother who died and a father who gave up on her when she was a child—but also from the entire Ammani community: "Children in the nearby kindergarten sang rhythmically, 'I am a bird, I could fly, I could also say goodbye.' I was not a bird and I could neither fly nor say goodbye. Although I was free to breathe, walk, work, I felt like a prisoner, condemned to my life" (5). We can infer, therefore, that even when growing up as a secular female, Najwa was not free. It is the same case for Najwa's mother, Raneen, who "when he [Najwa's father] left, twenty-four years ago, changed. She took off her veil, cut her hair, packed my father's clothes, Qur'ans, books, prayers beads, aftershave comb and tweezers in suitcase, hurled it in the loft" (7) but was never happy or free even when she became secular, took off the veil, and was trying to be herself.

Najwa makes an interesting comparison between her secular, unveiled mother and the Afghani women veiled head to toe: "The women flocked in burqas in all the colours of the rainbow. They flung them off as soon as they stepped in. Happy to have them in her house, Gulnar embraced and welcomed them. . . . Life was a journey for her, not a source of anguish, like it had been for my late mother" (136–37, ellipses in original).

Najwa's journey in tracing her father also represents a journey of finding a home for her unprotected femininity. In fact, what disturbs Najwa is the missing part in her past where the father should have been present. We read: "No, you must go and look for your father. The past might make you whole" (28). Interestingly, Faqir's novel portrays *home* in different ways. Home is at first a gynecocracy, a social system ruled by a woman and inhabited only by women. It must be a different home where matriarchy reigns. However, after the death of Najwa's mother, Raneen, this matriarchy collapses, and the daughter decides to restore the patriarchy that was excluded or forced to leave the house. Najwa says: "A few weeks after the death of my mother, the imposer of rules and regulations, I had been free to search the house for clues, photos, documents—anything that would help me construct a father" (34).

The many letters that she finds hidden in a box represent a revelation, an unveiling of many truths related to decisive queries that could make her whole again. The letters that her father had sent to her through the years of his absence help her reconstruct the father she barely remembers. A first truth she unearths is that her father was a secular student of nursing and that in four years, he changed from a normal loving father and husband into a vagabond (36). It is this first truth and the many letters she comes across that will drive her journey to find a fatherly home after being deserted and exiled from her father's society for more than twenty years.

Omar Rahmane's letters contain detailed stories of Taliban camps, battles, training, and social life. The Taliban is described as a home that Najwa's father was forced to inhabit but had to get used to. We read: "When

Hani[2] and I arrived here [Aybak, Afghanistan], we knew what we were doing: we were fighting the communist Soviets and trying to get them out. I was not and didn't wish to be a combatant like him, no matter how hard the warlords tried" (114–15). In fact, we could argue that the home Omar was looking for was, rather, the love his wife could not offer after a few years of marriage. His journey to Afghanistan was at heart a journey of love for his best friend, Hani. In Peshawar, Omar meets Gulnar and falls in love with her, but during the long years he stayed in Afghanistan to fight, he was not himself. About the love he found in and with Gulnar, who becomes his Afghani wife, Omar says: "Was I Qays Ibn al-Mulawwah, the poet who roamed the deserts reciting love poetry for Leila? . . . I looked for the sea in her, migrating birds, fields of wheat swaying in the wind. I searched for a centre, a walled garden with grape vines and jasmine, my country" (143, ellipses in original). Indeed, Gulnar, the veiled Afghani woman, was Omar's new home and new country after he was displaced while away from his cruel, westernized wife and little daughter.

Similarly, Najwa's home is not Amman, not Peshawar, and not even Durham, where she ends up residing. Najwa is looking for an emotional home where she can be reterritorialized after being exiled in all the places she goes to. One may conclude that her father represents this home, yet many other clues lead us to reconfigure this home according to the state of being the protagonist experiences in every place she visits and with the different people she meets. In this respect, Faqir's *Willow Trees Don't Weep* redefines, renarrates, and re-represents masculinity versus femininity and patriarchy versus matriarchy. The father in this case—though he deserted his family and gave up on his young daughter—is not an oppressor patriarch. In the novel, guilt must be shared between Najwa's father and mother, both of whom Najwa keeps blaming for her disturbed and fragmented identity. She cannot, as a grown-up woman, decide whether she wants to be religious or secular: "After we finished they did their ablutions, then stood in a line to pray. I felt awkward sitting there and kept fiddling

2. Hani was Omar's best friend, whom he wanted to help and sustain in his journey to Afghanistan.

with my pendant. Was I a Muslim? Why did I find bowing to Allah so dif-ficult, even humiliating?" (111).

During her journey to different countries, Najwa is looking for a home where she can settle peacefully, the only place where she can reter-ritorialize—to use Deleuze and Guattari's concept[3]—the identity she lost between her mother's extreme secularism and her father's extreme funda-mentalism. All she is looking for is herself: "Yes. Lucky indeed. Unlike me, my grandmother knew who she was, where she came from and what she believed in" (138).

While trying to trace her father from one place to another—from Pak-istan to Afghanistan and then to the United Kingdom—Najwa also expe-riences odd moments that will help her reconstruct her lost identity. In Afghanistan, for instance, while traveling in a car to Peshawar, she wears a chador, her head wrapped in a hijab, and sits next to a woman wearing a burka: "My mother, who went out of her way to secularise me, would vomit blood, if she saw me wearing the blue shroud" (101–2). Also, when Najwa meets her stepmother, Gulnar, and half-sister, Amani, she discovers the cruel, dark side of her own personality, which she owes to the absence of affection in her life: "Amani sat next to me playing with a cloth doll. . . . Perhaps you [Najwa and Amani's father] had spoilt her so much that she could hang on to her childhood? You must have showered her with your love. . . . Her tears spurt out at the least provocation. I, the abandoned daughter, on the other hand, weathered and dried-up like a prune, would always remain dry-eyed" (151, ellipses in original). Even when her sister is murdered, Najwa "couldn't shed a tear" (162). In this passage, Najwa understands that the abandonment by her father is behind her cruelty. After the death of her half-sister, Najwa leaves "the land of the wronged, of victims and hard-done-bys, and entered the country of the guilty" (161),

---

3. The French scholars Gilles Deleuze and Félix Guattari (1986) coined the terms *deterritorialization* and *reterritorialization* to characterize a constant process of trans-formation: whereas deterritorialization is the process in which to undo what has already been done, reterritorialization usually follows as the process of redoing what has been undone back to what has already been done.

Britain, comprehending that Afghanistan is never the home she can belong to, just like her father, Omar.

Arriving in Britain, Najwa meets her father in Durham, where he went after being sentenced to death in Afghanistan; she also meets other British people there. Some are orientalists, such as Andy, with whom she has her first sexual experience. After hosting her with unexpected generosity in their "pigeon loft," Andy and his mother give up on her, knowing she comes from the Middle East and is the daughter of a terrorist: "I got up and walked towards him. He stepped back. . . . Why was he so cold with me? My grandmother had said that men were predators. . . . He might not have wanted to get involved with a foreigner" (208–10, ellipses in original).

However, Najwa also meets good, tolerant British people in Durham, in particular Elizabeth; Najwa can find inner peace and tranquility in Elizabeth's house. While there, she is interested in knowing all the trees in the neighborhood: "As the days got longer and the nights shorter, I began to wake up early and go for a walk by the river just after sunrise. I took Herbert Edlin's book *Trees*, which I borrowed from Elizabeth's library, with me and tried to recognize some of them" (251). At the end of her journey, she finally feels liberated after realizing that her father's love for Hani, his friend, was the only reason why he left his family: "You loved him dad? He took off his glasses and wiped them. Too much, perhaps" (274). She feels released after having seen and talked to her father. She becomes what her name indicates in Arabic: "Najwa: a whisper or a secret conversation" (269). Her father explains to her: "At dawn and after morning prayers, I imagined you. . . . I whispered my answers and blew them, hoping that the breeze would carry them to you. Also, life is secret conversation" (269, ellipses in original). Najwa's final home is liberation, daring and knowing: "Liberated by the spaciousness, I stretched my arms out and said to the chariot-shaped cloud, 'Peace be upon you, wherever you are!' After months of studying British trees, and much quizzing by Elizabeth over many dinners, I had begun to recognize them. . . . I must go back to sweep my mother's grave" (276, ellipses in original). By this last sentence of the novel, one can guess that Najwa has decided to go back to Jordan to work against some repressive traditions her society has long been practicing. I also contend that Najwa is finally able to distance herself from her father's fundamentalism and her mother's secularism. The novel represents different forms of extremism, but it also represents how those who are ethnically, religiously, and ideologically different should be tolerated.

Works Cited

Bower, Rachel. 2012. "Interview with Fadia Faqir, 23 March 2010." *Journal of Postcolonial Writing* 48, no. 1 (Feb. 1). At https://doi.org/10.1080/17449855.2011.569380.

Brewington, Carla. 2013. *The Sacred Place of Exile: Pioneering Women and the Need for a New Women's Missionary*. Eugene, OR: Wipf & Stock.

Deleuze, Gilles, and Félix Guattari. 1986. *Kafka: Toward a Minor Literature*. Translated by Dana Polan. Minneapolis: Univ. of Minnesota Press.

Faqir, Fadia. 2014a. "The Shambolic State of World Affairs with Fadia Faqir." Interview. *Inkapture Magazine*, June. Formerly at inkapturemagazine.co.uk/2014/06/the-shambolic-state-of-world-affairs-with-fadia-faqir/. No longer available.

———. 2014b. *Willow Trees Don't Weep*. London: Hebron.

Hebron Books. 2014. "Fadia Faqir Introduces Willow Trees Don't Weep." YouTube. At https://www.youtube.com/watch?v=tK4K1V8SreA.

Mernissi, Fatima. [1975] 2011. *Beyond the Veil: Male–Female Dynamics in Muslim Society*. Rev. ed. with a new introduction. London: Saqi.

Sarnou, Dallel. 2017. "Re-thinking the Veil, Jihad and Home in Fadia Faqir's *Willow Trees Don't Weep* (2014)." *Open Cultural Studies* 1, no. 1: 155–60. At https://doi.org/10.1515/culture-2017-0014.

Scott, Joan Wallach. 2007. *The Politics of the Veil*. Princeton, NJ: Princeton Univ. Press.

Part 3 Television and the Veil

Reinforcement of the Veil

5

Veiling and Ideology

The Islamic State's Use of Iranian TV Series to Propagate Its Gender Ideals through Veiling

Cherie Taraghi

Compulsory veiling has been enforced in Iran since 1980. Within the borders of the country, no female, regardless of nationality, creed, or religion, is permitted to enter a public space without covering her head and body. As an issue, compulsory veiling has been controversial since the very first days of the revolution. It is a staunch and extremely symbolic aspect of state ideology, a signature cultural issue that is an essential part of the regime's identity. As such, veiling itself cannot be easily questioned, but the significance of the various types of veiling that have emerged over the years since the revolution can be. Through an analysis of three Iranian TV series, *Miveye mamnoo'e* (Forbidden Fruit), *Tanhai'ye Leyla* (Leyla's Loneliness) and *Madine*, which have been vetted and permitted to be broadcast on television in Iran, this chapter explores the regime's ideology regarding women and veiling, ranging from what the regime considers to be superior veiling and hence the ideal type of lifestyle and woman to inferior veiling or the type of woman and lifestyle the regime would be happy to extract from society to achieve its claim to be the ultimate puritanical Islamic republic.

In 1979, Ayatollah Ruhollah Khomeini announced that women should observe the Islamic dress code (Hoodfar 1993). Hijab became mandatory by law for all women in 1983. Compulsory hijab was rapidly linked to morality and Islamic virtue, and wearing the hijab was defined as "moral cleansing."

Over the years since then, the regime's ideal and ideologically correct compulsory cover has been the traditional veil or chador (Shahidian 2002; Zahedi 2007), which has historically been used by pious women in Iran. The chador is a long, wide, semicircular piece of fabric that is draped over the head like a shawl. It covers the whole body from head to toe. The chador has no fasteners; it is held in place under the neck by hand. As a result, it is usually worn over another cover such as a headscarf or *maghna'e*, a piece of cloth that fits around the head using an elastic string. In public, the preferred color for a chador is black, but colorful or floral-patterned chadors are used inside the house or at the mosque. The chador is known as *hejab'e bartar* (the superior form of the hijab) and is ideologically preferred because of its history as a symbol of religiosity and because it cannot be embellished, altered, or turned into a fashion accessory. However, from the time the hijab law was passed, the regime has been unable to impose the chador as the only hijab option available to women. The reason for this is that long before the revolution, female proponents of the movement for culturally authentic Muslim women had already popularized modest Islamic clothing. They had been wearing the headscarf or *roosari* along with the dark-colored manteau or *rupush*, an oversize long coat meant to cover women's curves. The *rupush-roosari* immediately became the uniform of women who did not believe in the importance of maintaining hijab but were left with no choice but to cover.

Islamic Republic of Iran Broadcasting

Islamic Republic of Iran Broadcasting (IRIB) is run by the state and has the monopoly on domestic media services in Iran. It offers both domestic and foreign radio and television services. For its national audience, IRIB TV currently broadcasts twelve domestic channels. By law, it is independent of the Iranian government and under direct control of the Office of the Supreme Leader (Semati 2009). Under Ayatollah Ali Hosseini Khamenei, IRIB has been kept close to the conservative and hardline factions (Azizi 2014). Because it is a state-run network and the biggest disseminator of culture and the government's political message, its programming is manipulated to educate its audience with religious or ideological content at all times. This is clearly defined in its charter, "General Policies and

Principles of the Programs of the Organization." In fact, article 5 of the charter states, "IRIB must work as a public university to promote the public awareness in various ideological, political, social, cultural and military issues," and, distinctly relevant to this chapter's main subject, article 45 states that IRIB needs to "define and explain the high status of women in Islam," to "introduce the real values of women aimed at giving them their actual Islamic nature," and to "eliminate the false values" by "restoring moral values in families and helping the consolidation of family ties" (IRIB n.d.).

To achieve the aims established for IRIB, the "red line" of censorship and control is an inseparable aspect of its programming. However, it is extremely difficult to identify the red line. There are no strict and clearly defined themes or rules regarding what is allowed or forbidden. The Islamic Republic's ideology is based on tenets of politicized religion, and religion plays a role in all aspects of life, so the red line of censorship does not delineate only political issues that may be a threat to the well-being of the state. Rather, all aspects of life are under scrutiny. All programs, including sports, entertainment, and children's shows, are under control. For example, IRIB was criticized for trying to hide the presence of the Iranian Diaspora, particularly the exuberant, loud, and hijabless female fans, at the matches played by the Iranian national football team at the Asian Cup Football tournament in 2015 (Younesipoor 2015). Musicians often criticize IRIB because it does not broadcast concerts of legal pop bands. In fact, IRIB is not allowed to show orchestras and musicians and singers at a concert at the same time, which means individuals interested in watching Iranian musical concerts on TV have to turn to broadcasts on satellite (*FreeMuse* 2016). A scene depicting a brief dance sequence featuring one man in the locally produced Iranian film *Rooz fereshteh* (Day of the Angel) was censored, and the dance sequence was frozen so as not to show movement when the film was broadcast on television. TV channels have also had trouble rebroadcasting Iranian TV series produced after the revolution. Many series have been revetted and censored once more before a permit is issued for them to be shown again. Content in IRIB programming is a reflection of state ideology rather than of the reality of society that IRIB's audience experience on a day-to-day basis.

Iranian TV Series

The various IRIB channels air about thirty to forty locally produced television series per year. Although IRIB has produced some genuinely wonderful, interesting, and audience-gripping series, most of its programming in recent years has been of low quality. The need to conform, financial problems, and the decision to spend most of the budget on programs for specific occasions, such as the fourteen days of Nowrooz (Iranian New Year celebrations) and the month of Ramadan, have resulted in a situation where programming during much of the rest of the year is weak and low in quality. Specifically with regard to serials, storylines have been simplistic, artificial, didactic, and often quite predictable or boring.[1]

In a speech delivered to IRIB staff on July 3, 2010, Supreme Leader Ali Khamenei stated, "There are certain red lines that have to be observed. By red lines I do not mean political red lines, as I am mainly concerned about ethics, religion and other such things. . . . It is not appropriate to show some of the romantic relationships which are reflected in our films. Reflecting such relationships can create moral corruption[;] . . . it is harmful to reflect an inappropriate romantic relationship—such as love triangles and squares. There is nothing one can do in such cases. We should just avoid reflecting such things in our film" (Khamenei 2010). Based on the supreme leader's speech, Iranian serials can portray evil so long as an emphasis is placed on the hero's selfless efforts to counter this evil; poverty can be shown, but the hero's main motivation needs to be to fight poverty or prove that poverty is the will of God, so that an unrealistically bleak picture of Iranian society is not painted. IRIB is required to make series that uphold the foundations of the family, modesty, and hijab (Khamenei 2010). Correct content is far more important than ratings, and teaching the audience correct behavior is a worthier task than entertaining or even keeping the audience interested in the content being broadcast.

---

1. For more detail and information, see a review of all thirty-one Iranian TV series shown on various IRIB channels during 1393 (2014) at 93 های سریال بدترین و بهترین, Tebyan News website, Mar. 8, 2015.

The scenario for a series is completed, vetted, and censored before production and most definitely before it is permitted to be broadcast. There is lack of transparency on issues or themes that cannot be shown on TV. Material is censored and controlled on all levels: the writer self-censors, the producer censors, the channel overseer censors, the director and actors censor, and so on and so forth. The product finally aired on TV is ideologically cleansed and purified.

The need for censorship and control of the content and scenes depicted in a TV series in Iran means that there can be no rambling, never-ending storylines. A writer predetermines the number of episodes in the series—typically between fifteen and thirty, although there is a distinct effort in recent years to produce longer series or to produce sequels with another thirty episodes continuing the saga of the same group of people introduced in the original. The series *Payetakht* (Capital City) has had five sequels to date. Another important aspect to keep in mind is the trend to produce series that can be broadcast during a special occasion in the year, such as two-week-long series during the fourteen days of Nowrooz holidays or a one-month long series to coincide with Ramadan or Moharram. These special occasions are times of the year when families get together and spend time watching television. Nowrooz is a holiday, so whole families are home and have extra time for relaxing and enjoying the TV specials. Ramadan is the month of fasting, and the breaking of the fast is often a combination of families getting together to feast and watch television. TV stations allocate larger chunks of funding for series that are produced for these special occasions. Writers and producers make an extra effort to ensure that the quality of their product is good enough to be broadcast at these lucrative times of the year, and audiences look forward to these occasions when they can enjoy the cream of Iranian television.

Iranian television series are, like their counterparts in other parts of the world, melodramas. Some have historical and religious storylines, depicting the life of an imam, such as the highly popular series *Imam Ali*, or a historical Shi'a religious hero, as in the series *Mokhtar*. A few series have focused on more recent history, such as *Madare sefr darajeh* (Zero Degree Latitude), which is set during the Second World War, and *Kolahe*

Pahlavi (Pahlavi Hat), which takes place in the 1930s. In the early 2000s, a trend toward the supernatural emerged, with series typically depicting the effects of the presence of a disguised angel or devil among ordinary citizens—for example, the series *Oo yek fereshte bood* (She Was an Angel). But most series are about the trials and tribulations of ordinary people living in current-day Iran.

Iranian TV series include all clichéd aspects of a good melodrama and are quite realistic in accepting the fact that Iranian society has people from all walks of life and that Iran has its fair share of social issues, such as poverty, corruption, and drug problems. There is no attempt to obfuscate reality as a form of background setting for a scenario. The series do not portray perfect societies. Quite the contrary, to expound the ideological pedagogy, they need to show that situations other than the ideological ideal exist.

A few signature cultural issues for the Islamic Republic regularly feature in series. They are issues that the Islamic Republic relies upon for the self-sustenance of its identity. Veiling is obviously one such issue. As Farideh Farhi has most eloquently stated, "On the streets of Iran, without enforced veiling, very little physical manifestation of what the Islamic Republic looks like remains" (2004). The threat of and the need to combat Western cultural influences form another tell-tale signature issue. Yet another is the regime's deference to the bazaris and the lower economic classes, segments of Iranian society that formed the revolution's primary social base and support (Farhi 2004). The regime has always been sensitive to the needs and demands of the poorer classes and has always maintained a clear suspicion of Iran's traditional landed gentry and wealthier upper classes. The latter classes historically benefited from the former Pahlavi monarchy's regime, and from the early days of the revolution they were identified as the propagators of the Pahlavi regime's Western values and ideals. Yet another signature issue is self-identification as a regime that places God-centered morality and submission to the power and will of God before all else. These signature issues form a core sense of identity that repeatedly manifests itself in series after series.

Veiling is an extremely potent feature of Iranian society, defining a woman's identity, character, and fate. By law, all women must be covered regardless of their lifestyle, creed, or background, but the degree and gradations of veiling carry strong nuances. As one of the main purveyors of the regime's ideology, IRIB series openly emphasize the depth of faith in the chador as a symbol of the selfless, virtuous, caring, kind, house-bound wife who is rewarded and venerated. The *rupush-roosari*-clad woman, by contrast, is a second-class citizen, even though she represents the vast majority of women in the country. She is tolerated. She is rather innocuous and colorless in a patriarchal world where most decisions are made and led by men. But the more colorful and striking her *rupush-roosari*, the greater threat she poses to the morals and virtues of society. The bright, colorful, chic, or elegant fitted jacket and loose head cover are symbolic of components of a secular and Western lifestyle, with values that tempt, harm, and derail the virtues of the true adherent of Islam. Within an ideological context, this woman is to be shunned from society. More often than not, in television series she and her harmful effects are forcibly removed—for example, by conveniently putting her in a road accident and then in a coma.

The three TV series selected for analysis in this chapter are examples of the popular "ordinary people" melodrama genre. All three were produced and broadcast as special-occasion series shown during the month of Ramadan, although in different years: *Miveye mamnoo'e* (Forbidden Fruit, 2008), *Tanhai'ye Leyla* (Leyla's Loneliness, 2015), and *Madine* (titled after the lead female character, 2015). The series have been selected specifically because they revolve around the experiences of a strong, independent-minded, stubborn female lead character.

Among the three, *Miveye mamnoo'e* is the most interesting, with a complex and challenging storyline. An important aspect of it is its leading female character, a young, attractive female engineer, Hasti Shayegan. Hasti is intelligent, street-smart, and gutsy. She is forced to take over control and operation of a large car-part factory, and she must singlehandedly deal with a loud-mouthed, powerful, threatening, patronizing, corrupt businessman and his henchmen. She is self-confident and self-aware enough to haggle with men of all classes and backgrounds and to succeed in a male environment.

It is important to point out that Hasti is a wealthy, traditionally upper-class, secular character. She dons a *rupush-roosari* (overcoat and headscarf) throughout the series. The audience never sees her in a chador. In some of the scenes, her *rupush-roosari*s are beautiful examples of a fashion statement. They are also thus prime examples of "bad hijabi" (loose morality and disrespect). In many scenes, her *roosari* is made of bright-colored silk or a bright-colored shawl that is wrapped around her face, and her *rupush* is an open (buttonless) autumn jacket. In some scenes, this jacket is extremely elegant, made in red cotton with black-and-white stripes at the wide arms.

Halfway through the series, Hasti's father is murdered. The murderer is none other than the corrupt businessman, Hasti's archnemesis who is making her life miserable. Through plot twists, Hasti flirts her way into becoming engaged to her nemesis's father, Haj Agha Fotuhi, an older gentleman of faith who has spent his life living according to godly principles: working hard, doing good, never cheating or lying or harming anyone in business. He pays alms, and, as his name indicates, he has been to Mecca and has really become a haji.[2] A great deal is made of the fact that Haj Agha Fotuhi is a respectable, honest man. He has never needed to worry about his "face"—that is, his reputation. He has been a successful cloth merchant, a religious man, a husband, and the father of four grown children. His success has allowed him to acquire a big, beautiful house and a new Mercedes-Benz.

An alert Iranian viewer would be aware of the signs that there is something wrong here, though. A good Muslim haji should not place so much emphasis on material goods. Material goods are the signs of the fallen idol, items that one falsely worship. Haj Agha Fotuhi is a good man, but he has started to place too much value on material wealth and respectable, financially beneficial marriages for his daughters: an outward respectability rather than an inner, spiritual one. The fact that he falls in love with Hasti and intends to divorce his wife and marry Hasti instead cements

2. In Iran, it is customary to call respectable men "haji" as a sign of respect. But in *Miveye mamnoo'e* the audience is told that Haj Agha Fotuhi really has been on a pilgrimage and that his title is genuine. In the series *Tanhai'ye Leyla*, the character Haj Agha Seyfedin is an example of a man who is called "Haj Agha" out of respect because he is the village elder and a man who is wise and worthy, like a haji.

the suspicion that his faith has waned, and so, according to the tenets of a superior Islamic melodrama, he must enter a period of suffering and spiritual self-doubt. It is important to understand that his love for Hasti is not to be seen as a midlife crisis, the need to sow wild oats, or any other "Western" notion. In an Iranian series, such a sequence of events can be interpreted only as inner religious conflict and the need to regain faith.

In the context of *Miveye mamnoo'e*, Haj Agha Fotuhi can rekindle his faith only if the ultimate fallen idol standing in his way is removed: Hasti, the young, "secular" temptress, the woman who embodies a life-style contrary to the principal dictates of Iran's Islamic regime, needs to be extracted from Haj Agha's life. She is involved in a car accident and falls into a coma. When Haj Agha finds out, he is devastated. He goes to the mosque and has an emotional breakdown as he acknowledges his loss of faith. He questions God's motives: Why is Hasti in a coma? Why is his son Jalal a murderer? Why did his favorite daughter, Ghazaleh, disobey him and marry a poor musician? He determines to resolve the question of his faith by devoting his time purely to praying the namaz and reciting the Quran. Through his prayer, he awakens Hasti's faith or at least urges her to live, for she hears him despite her comatose state and the fact that he is not in her hospital room while praying. She hears him and steps off the path she has taken toward death so that he may extinguish his doubt. When Hasti awakens from her coma, he tells her that he is grateful to her because she reawakened his faith. Thanks to her misfortune, he has come to realize that he had become too fond of material goods. He gives much of his fortune away in alms. He recognizes that he was angry with his daughter because he valued her material comfort more than her happiness with a worthy, extremely devout man. He forgives his corrupt, murderer son and determines to help him rediscover his faith and inner goodness. He also informs Hasti that her presence in his life was "God's test" so he could rediscover his faith, and he ends his engagement with her. Hasti's traditional landed-gentry wealth and secular lifestyle are defined as the fallen idol that tempted and led Haj Agha astray. They must be rejected. The series ends with Haj Agha happy in the company of his family, while Hasti is shown all alone, lighting a candle as a sign that she must pray for forgiveness and find a path to the light of God.

It is interesting to note that the screenwriter offered Hasti the perfect alter ego: Ghazaleh, Haj Agha Fotuhi's favorite daughter. Ghazaleh is another strong, determined, and stubborn female character. In the beginning of the series, despite her deep love and respect for her father, she disobeys his wishes by marrying the man she loves. Her beloved is a charming, caring man who has lost his whole family, fortune, even his house in an earthquake. Yet even with his incredible misfortune, he has not become bitter or lost his faith. He has carried on, and God has smiled upon him by introducing Ghazaleh into his life. Her disobedience to her father is selfless: she has chosen her husband because of his purity and goodness rather than his wealth or status. She embodies the character that rejects status, pride, material goods. and material comfort, all the signs of temptation against the will of God and Islamic morality.

Like Hasti, Ghazaleh is young, energetic, and well educated: she is a lawyer. Unlike Hasti, she is the perfect housekeeper, a wonderful cook, and a loving, nurturing wife, sister, and daughter. Hasti has no housekeeping skills. She is never shown cooking or taking care of her dwelling. In scenes where she is shown at home, she is usually busy completing a puzzle depicting Edvard Munch's *The Scream*, something very "Western" and a reflection of her life. Hasti is shown to love her father, but he turns out to be a conniving, ruthless, materialistic man with a penchant for revenge, so her general ability to love and nurture are misguided. Hasti is ambitious and is determined to work and save the factory. She is also against marriage. When Haj Agha confesses love and proposes to her, she abuses this confession by exacting humiliating and extremely difficult conditions supposedly for him to prove his devotion to her but really to deter him and to enact the revenge her father desires to take upon Haj Agha's family. When a young, male accountant who becomes her sidekick in trying to solve the mystery of her father's disappearance and murder proposes to her, she ridicules him for assuming that his attempts to help her in her time of distress would result in her needing him as a life partner. Ghazaleh, by contrast, gets a home-based part-time job to make sure she is always home and able to take care of the house and her husband's needs. Most important of all for the main subject of this chapter, Ghazaleh is a chador-wearing woman—even in the privacy of her own home, and in the company of her family, she dons a thick, tight scarf and chador. She is unquestionably the Islamic Republic's ideal woman: she is selfless, virtuous, and modest. She limits her life to the private sphere, and her priorities are her house and husband, followed by the integrity and well-being of her family. In one scene, Ghazaleh, clad in a black *maghna'e* and white chador, visits her mother and siblings in her childhood home. The family congregates to discuss the future of Mr. and Mrs. Fotouhi's marriage. Even in times of crisis, ideal women maintain their modesty and virtue.

The series *Tanhai'ye Leyla* is very different from *Miveye mamnoo'e*. Whereas *Miveye mamnoo'e* is urban, modern, and filled with a variety of characters with varying shades of black, white, and gray qualities, *Tanhai'ye Leyla* is set in a little, conservative town where black and white are distinct. *Tanhai'ye Leyla* is of particular interest to the main subject of this book because it explores the (mis)fortunes of a young woman, Leyla, who returns to Iran from the United States, where she has lived most of her life. Like Hasti, she is well-to-do, educated, and from a secular background. *Tanhai'ye Leyla* is the story of Leyla's journey from shallow Western secularism to the depths of Muslim faith. Along the way, the series has elements of traditional melodrama, for Leyla's journey inward is initiated when she inexplicably falls in love with a poor, extremely devout, orphan man. Naturally, her wealthy, secular family is against her choice, and she is disowned. A former beau by the name of Shayan emerges to tempt her back home, but her notion of home has already shifted. She no longer welcomes the comforts of urban life and material wealth. Her happiness is fulfilled by being the modest, respectful, nurturing, caring wife and home keeper.

This is a story of "God's test," and Leyla's faith needs to be pushed to the limits. She is tormented by her former beau. Her husband dies on the day she gives birth to their son. She is a lone woman in a patriarchal, conservative town, and the townspeople question her every action and seek ulterior, sinful motives. But Leyla perseveres. She becomes a selfless angel, helping and forgiving everyone, regardless of previous harm incurred by them. She lives an honorable and respectable life of modesty, existing with a loyal and devout memory of her love for her deceased husband and with her love for God.

The series commences with Leyla's return to Tehran and a party given by her family to help her reunite with old friends. The party scenes are important as a contrast, introducing the viewer to the world of wealth and pleasure: pretty clothes, ladies in golden shawls and sparkly *rupush*, endless skewers of kebab cooked on a BBQ in the vast garden by the pool, talk of party drugs and the possibility of having a boyfriend before marriage. This is the world of sin and temptation, the worship of idol materialism and Western values. Leyla watches the party unfold with discomfort. She is jetlagged and has a headache, and she keeps seeing a ghostlike figure of an elderly lady who tells her to leave the party and go to bed. At this stage in the story, Leyla is a secular woman. She wears a plain *rupush-roosari*, and she does not know how to pray the namaz. After one of her initial trips to the little town that she eventually settles down in, she puts on a chador for the first time, picks up a hand-scribbled script of the surahs recited during namaz, and prays.

The town is presented as a traditional, conservative one. All the women wear the chador in public. The most honorable women wear the chador indoors, too. Leyla becomes self-conscious and in a charming scene asks her husband if he is ashamed of having a wife who does not wear a chador. He tells her he loves the chador. It is his favorite form of veil and the one he prefers, but the chador is a path that she must arrive at. It is her veil, not his. Leyla has a strong sense of halal and haram. She is modest and has self-respect. He is not ashamed of her.

The subject comes up once more a few scenes later. Husband and wife return home from a little gathering arranged in honor of their marriage. Leyla's husband walks into the room to see her standing in front of a mirror adjusting a chador. He smiles flirtatiously and asks what she is wearing. She responds that it is a gift. He says she better put it away until she is ready to use it. She looks at herself in the mirror and says, "I like it on me. I am ready." From that scene on, the chador is an integral part of Leyla's life. There is not a single scene in which she is not wearing a chador. Acknowledging the depth of her faith is a turning point in the story. Once she recognizes how deep her faith is, she is ready for God to test her. From here on, she is challenged in every way possible. She faces the death of her husband, rejection by the community, the kidnapping of her son, harassment by her previous beau, poverty, and extreme loneliness. She comes close to giving up and returning to her own family, which would mean a rejection of faith and a return to secularism and wealth, but she perseveres and is eventually rewarded with acceptance and a genuine place in the community.

The storyline of the third series, *Madine*, revolves around a lady by the name of Madine and her attempts to act as a moral beacon to her stepson, Bahman. The series commences with Madine cooking in a large industrial kitchen. The scene immediately informs the viewer that her husband owns this successful packaged-food company. In the first episode, the audience also learns that she has been married, divorced, and remarried and is now a widow. She is infertile, which explains why her first husband divorced her. Her partnership with her now deceased second husband revolved around the desire to make the company they own grow and become a country-wide famous brand. In short, Madine bears all the tell-tale signs of the fallen idol: not a good homemaker, unable to fulfill her duty as a woman by bearing children, too involved in business and working outside the house. But there is a catch: Madine is from a lower-middle-class, religious background, and she wears the chador. In every single scene where she appears, she wears the Islamic Republic's most venerated black chador on top of a dark-gray or black headscarf. Although several different characters in the series don the chador on different occasions, Madine is the only consistent chadori woman.

The series *Madine* is in effect a reversal of expectations, for the storyline proceeds to unravel a different truth. Yes, Madine is infertile, but she has been the perfect, caring, loving, nurturing mother to her second husband's son, Bahman. Bahman prefers her to his biological mother, Roohi, to the point where he has married Madine's brother's daughter Haniye rather than Roohi's brother's daughter, even though Roohi's brother is extremely wealthy, and his daughter is heiress to factories. Bahman has learned from Madine's principles. He has preferred the middle-class values of a housewife who will love and nurture over the trappings of wealth, comfort, and a spoilt wife. Madine spent much of her second marriage helping her husband develop his business, but she did this selflessly. Her husband, his partner, and his son own the company, the house Madine lives in, and other property. Nothing is in her name. She has simply of-fered her time, her good business instincts, and her skills to help cultivate her husband's career. She is also the honorary CEO of a children's charity that takes care of girls in need. Most importantly, she is extremely prin-cipled and lives by clear moral example.

As the scenario unfolds, Bahman repeatedly makes morally dubious choices to save his father's company from going under, at one stage re-sorting to usury to buy out an unethical business partner and at another stage agreeing to leave his wife and get engaged to the sister of the compa-ny's new owner. Madine is devastated but consistently tries to be a moral beacon, offering calm, sound advice. She unswervingly asks Bahman to face his mistakes rather than take further steps down a path that leads to shame and loss of honor and reputation. Madine is the only person in Bahman's life who steadfastly offers long-term, difficult, but sound advice. All the others, in particular all the other women in the series (it is valu-able to note that only Madine wears a chador in the series, all the other women wearing varying forms of colorful to plain black *rupush-roosari*), offer short-term, often lie-riddled solutions to his problems.

The serial's storyline revolves primarily around the consequences of Bahman's inexperienced youth. He has the erroneous belief that his worth and honor are bound to making money and maintaining the company his father worked hard to build—external, material value as opposed to internal, spiritual worthiness. His choices lead to acts of haram: lowered quality of the food products produced by the company, usury, and so on. In the end, he is even sought by the police for allegedly intending to harm the sister of the company's new owner. As in *Miveye mamnoo'e*, haram actions can be cleared only through faith and submission to the will of God. Faith is rekindled and achieved through the forced extraction of the ultimate idolatrous tempter: a secular, bright-color-shawl-bearing, chic, open-jacket-*rupush*-wearing, ambitious, selfish, uncaring, homewrecking woman. Bita, the sister of the company's new owner, symbolizes all the negative qualities that the audience is taught to avoid. Her fate is an un-fortunate (although probably suspected) one: she has an accident and falls into a coma.

Unlike in *Miveye mamnoo'e*, where Haj Agha's rekindled faith is sufficient, in *Madine* neither Bahman's nor Madine's faith is enough. It is his young, hurt, betrayed wife (Bahman has let her believe that he is planning to divorce her and get married to the sister of the company's new owner) who recognizes that she has been selfish; she has nagged and complained to her husband and blamed him for the consequences of his mistakes, pushing him away. Selflessly, she forgives and promises to stand by her man if only he will return to her. She spends the whole night in her chador, praying the namaz in supplication that Bita may rise from her comatose state and inform the police that she slipped down an electrical escalator; Bahman did not push or harm her. Of course, it is noteworthy to mention that praying the namaz requires donning the chador. It is the first time in the series that the audience sees this youthful, spoiled young lady who normally wears an ordinary *rupush-roosari* submit to genuine faith. The shift to the chador is the symbolic bind letting the audience know that her prayers will be answered. Her selflessness and virtue result in Bita awakening from coma.

The character Bita is necessary as a trope that can be used to push temptation to its limits, so that when the temptation is removed, balance and harmony can be reestablished. She is in many ways like Hasti or Leyla. She is young, vivacious, highly educated, self-confident, and intelligent. She is from a modern, middle-class, religious family, but she has no faith in God. She is the only character in the series who wears well-fitted, chic, colorful jackets and bright, loose shawls (over a *maghna'e*).[3] In the final scene before her accident, Bita is at her most alluring, dressed in a shiny, gold jacket with brown patches that match the color of the loose, brown shawl covering her head. In this scene, she rejects her brother's supplication that she stay in Iran. She rejects family, modesty, and virtue for love and money. She is just steps away from being taught the error of her ways and beliefs.

---

3. The series, being a product of the Islamic Republic, can imply "bad hijabi" but cannot actually show it. The audience is permitted to imagine that Bita in reality would, like many of the wealthy North Tehrani women she represents, don only the loose shawl.

Deeply devoted to her father, Bita is hurt and vengeful because her father loved her brother more. When the characters Bita and Salar Mosh-fegh are first introduced about halfway through the series, their father is already deceased. Before his death, off-screen, Bita has spent several years squandering money, flirting, and continuing a relationship with a swin-dler, who is deeply in debt. All this occurs off-screen because a secular, Western lifestyle of partying and out-of-marriage relationships that will be punished can be implied but not portrayed on an IRIB TV series. Her father has set the firm, humiliating condition in his will that she can re-ceive her share of inheritance money only if she is married to a man her perfect brother approves of. But Bita is in love with the swindler and un-willing to change her mind.

When her brother buys the packaged-food company, Bita suggests Bahman leave his wife and pretend to want to marry her. Because he is a man from a solid family background, marriage with him will entitle her to her inheritance. In return, she will transfer one-sixth of the company to Bahman. As the scenes leading to her accident proceed, she is shown as in-creasingly losing control of her morality. She even records a confession on her phone informing the audience that she is becoming immoral and bad. Although Bahman accepts her offer, she does not honor their agreement. She cheats him and tries to escape to Turkey with the money. Bahman follows her to the airport, where she slips down an electrical escalator, is knocked unconscious, and falls into a coma. Afraid, Bahman flees, leav-ing the impression that he pushed her. It is only with the removal of all that Bita represents—the Western ideals and lifestyle, the arrogance, the blind desire for money and self-satisfaction at the cost of self-respect and sexual integrity—that Bahman's wife can forgive and Bahman's eyes can be opened to his errors. Eventually, with his face turned toward a mosque, listening to the evening *azan* (call to prayers), he realizes that he should swallow his pride, work hard, and earn a halal living to be worthy of his now constantly chador-wearing wife, his baby, and Madine's love and acceptance.

Through IRIB, its main ideological voice, the Islamic regime of Iran informs the Iranian audience of the distinct interlink it perceives between the choice of veil and a woman's identity, character, and fate. There are in essence three types of veiling in Iran. The regime's optimal choice is the chador. It is the symbol of traditional, conservative, deep faith, virtue, and modesty in a woman. It epitomizes the image of the woman the regime has tried to promote as ideal since the early days of the revolution. The chadori woman is like Ghazaleh or Madine. The focus of her life is on being a good housemaker, wife, and mother. The chadori woman is self-less and kind. She does not care for material wealth. In fact, she shuns and denies wealth and all its worldly, idolatrous trappings. The second type of woman prefers to wear a *rupush* and *roosari* (overcoat and headscarf). This woman represents the majority of women in Iranian society. She has faith but is not deeply religious. She is benign and tries her best to blend in by choosing dark colors and loose-fitting overcoats that hide her. In a patrimonial society, she is the second-class citizen who is accepted but has little say until or unless she dons the chador. Examples of this woman are Leyla and Bahman's wife, Haniye (until they become chadori women). The third type of veil is the high-fashion *rupush-roosari*: the woman chooses to make her presence noticed by wearing bright colors; tighter, fitted over-coats with an elegant cut or stitched detail; and a loose, colorful shawl that is draped over the head rather than tightly knotted at the throat or a headscarf that is colorful, attractive, and visible. This woman symbolizes self-awareness (as opposed to selflessness), personal ambition, and desire, characteristics that are unbecoming to the female sex. She usually belongs to higher classes of society and covets wealth and material goods to advance her own pleasure and enjoyment. She is morally dubious and harmful to society. She also tends to represent the secular and Western values and lifestyle that the Islamic Republic abhors and seeks to eliminate. Be it Hasti or Bita, this woman in her bright veil must go into a coma.

Works Cited

Azizi, Arash. 2014. "Can Iran's New TV Chief Bring IRIB, Rouhani Closer?" *Al-Monitor*, Nov. At https://www.al-monitor.com/pulse/originals/2014/11/iran-irib-sarafraz-press-tv.html#ixzz3mitdJZ9t.

Farhi, Farideh. 2004. "Cultural Policies in Islamic Republic of Iran." Woodrow Wilson International Center for Scholars, Nov. At https://www.wilsoncenter.org/sites/default/files/FaridehFarhiFinal.pdf.

FreeMuse. 2016. "Iran: Musical Instruments Still Not Allowed on Iranian TV." Mar. 15. Formerly at https://en.unesco.org/creativity/sites/creativity/files/free muse-annual-statistics-art-under-threat-2016.pdf. No longer available.

Hoodfar, Homa. 1993. "The Veil in Their Minds and on Our Heads: The Persistence of Colonial Images of Muslim Women." *Resources for Feminist Research (RFR) / Documentation sur la recherche féministe (DRF)* 22, nos. 3–4 (Fall): 5–18.

Islamic Republic of Iran Broadcasting (IRIB). N.d. "General Policies and Principles of the Programs of the Organization." Iran Human Rights Documentation Center. At https://iranhrdc.org/general-policies-and-principles-of-the -programs-of-the-organization-irib-islamic-republic-of-iran-broadcasting -irib/

Khamenei, Ali. 2010. "Supreme Leader's Address to IRIB Artists and Staff." July 3. At https://english.khamenei.ir/index.php?option=com_content&task=view &id=1333&Itemid=4.

Semati, Mehdi. 2009. "Communication, Media and Popular Culture in Post-revolutionary Iran." Middle East Institute, Jan. 29. At https://www.mei.edu /publications/communication-media-and-popular-culture-post-revolutionary -iran.

Shahidian, Hammed. 2002. *Women in Iran: Emerging Voices in the Women's Movement.* Westport, CT: Greenwood.

Younesipoor, Payam. 2015. "IRIB Censorship of Iranian Women in Australia." Iran-Varzeshi, Jan. At https://www.persianfootball.com/forums/showthread .php?113729-IRIB-censorship-of-Iranian-women-in-Australia.

Zahedi, Ashraf. 2007. "Contested Meaning of the Veil and Political Ideologies of Iranian Regimes." *Journal of Middle East Women's Studies* 3, no. 3 (Fall). At https://people.ucsc.edu/~rlipsch/migrated/AFRICOM/Zahedi.pdf.

Part 4 Cinema and the Veil

Dismantling the Master Narrative

6

Representations of Veiling in Bollywood Cinema

Nishat Haider

Foregrounding the frames of veiled women in Bollywood cinema, this chapter examines the ways in which these frames dominate and seduce by investing power in the signifier, trope, and description of veiling/unveiling/reveiling in films. The trope of the veiled woman is so powerful a motif that, as Meyda Yegenoglu argues, "There is always more to the veil than the veil" (qtd. in Lewis and Mills 2003, 14). Though often dialogized on the screen as a signifier that silences Muslim women's sexuality, the veil also represents a liberating force, a recovery of the female space, a reclamation of the female gaze, and ownership of both the scopic and haptic zones of the body.

As the noted Urdu poet Israr-ul-Haq Majaz said, "Tere maathe pe ye aanchal bahut hi khoob hai lekin / Tu is aanchal se ek parcham bana leti to achcha tha [This veil that covers your head is beautiful indeed / It would be better if you transformed it into a banner of revolt]" (qtd. in Mir and Mir 2006, 146). In line with the complexities of the veil and its diverse conceptions that are reflected in the multiple words used to denote the different types of veils (*purdah, burka, chador, dupatta*, and *niqab*, among others), veiling can be defined as a complex system that establishes itself through multiple veils: social practices, architectural features or patterns (such as latticed windows), and segregated spaces (zenanas). Veiling as a social practice embraces not only clothing/bodily covering but also values and behavior "reflecting different conceptions of female modesty" that often stem from a regionally specific history of sartorial practice and sociocultural traditions (Amer 2014, 65). Although Hindu and Sikh women also observe veiling practices of some kind (*ghoonghat*, chador, and purdah), this chapter offers a situated and embodied understanding of Muslim veiling and zenanas with examples from four major shifts in Bollywood cinema representing Islamicate cultures:[1] the Muslim historical, the Muslim courtesan, the Muslim social, and the post-9/11 (i.e., after September 11, 2001) Muslim narratives. It is true that the forms and idioms of Islamicate cultural imaginary pervade all genres of Hindustani cinema (the language of Bollywood is a blend of Hindi and Urdu), but they are most intensely realized in the distinctive Muslim inflections of the historical, courtesan, social, and post-9/11 films. This chapter does not intend to construct clear lines of distinction and chronology among these shifts, but it aims to explore how these generic shifts under the impetus of a changing national scene represent a certain line of transformation in the way Muslim women have been looked at within the discourses of cinema. To map out the contours of such a pattern, however, is not to assert the total substitution of traditional ways of figuring genre, gender, and identity, which are conceivably more fluid, porous, and spread out in their formulation.

India has the second-largest population of Muslims in the world after Indonesia. Mapping the richness of the cultural territory of the Indian subcontinent and the way in which cinema has intersected with Islamicate popular performance culture, including the tradition of the *tawa'if*, or courtesan, Kaushik Bhaumik argues that by the mid-1930s Bombay had taken over the personnel, narratives, and performance culture of Lahore in Pakistan, thus subverting Lahore's position as a distinct

---

1. According to Ira Bhaskar and Richard Allen, the term *Islamicate* "does not refer to the Islamic religion per se, but to the social and cultural complex historically associated with Islam and the Muslims, both among Muslims themselves and even when found among non-Muslims" (2009, 3). In *Hermeneutics and Honor: Negotiating Female "Public" Space in Islamic/ate Societies* (1999), Asma Afsaruddin distinguishes between Muslim or Islamic societies and Islamicate societies. For her, *Islamicate* is the term to designate "such countries where allegiance to Islam is cast in emotive, broadly cultural, and experiential terms rather than in legal and theological terms" (4).

film-production center. Although the Bombay (now Mumbai) film industry maintained something of the earlier hybrid cinema culture, albeit in a
more complex cultural and political context, Ravi Vasudevan says, "This
was the period when a substantial critical discourse started developing,
what Bhaumik calls the formation of a Hindu ethnoscape, in which many
of the marks of hybridity of the earlier period, whether in terms of language, dress, setting, or music, came under attack, and critics demanded
the institutionalization of authentic representations of Hindu culture"
(2015, 30–31). In Bollywood cinema, the implied "Indian" viewer is always
a Hindu male (Gehlawat 2010, vi). In fact, such "a religious paradigm"
for "the viewers of Hindi films is based on the 'Hindi/Hindu' equivoca-
tion, in which Indians are characterized as 'Hindu'" (Gehlawat 2010, xvi).
Hence, in contradistinction to Laura Mulvey's contention that the male
audience derives scopophilic pleasure from looking at on-screen women,
this chapter suggests that in Bollywood films the direction of the gaze is
formed not just by gender identity but by national/religious/ethnic identity as well, and, hence, the male audience (predominantly Hindu) often
differentiates between the women they define as legitimate objects of the
gaze and those whom they consider should be protected from it. Foregrounding concrete analysis of Hindi films, this chapter explores haptic
images and their connections to representations of gender/cultural difference framed by means of both "the skin of the film" (Marks 2000, 1) and
the thin, evocative veil. Though the Muslims in India do not constitute a
monolithic group, the Muslim ocular regime and the mainstream Indian
visual semiosis convey a notion of shared values and common membership within this perceived group.

Mapping the Field: The Veil, the Gaze, and Haptic Visuality

This section reexamines the aesthetic, affective, and haptic import of Bollywood filmic images by opening up the field of investigation through a
mapping out of the wider historical and theoretical view of the cinematic
medium in order to explicate the representations of the embodied socio-
cultural/religious practice of veiling (purdah, hijab) on-screen. The most
interesting aspect of cinema representing veiled women is the fact that
women previously concealed by the hijab in the public domain now found

themselves visible on the other side of the hijab, or "screen." One of the Urdu words for the screen of cinema is *purdah*, which literally means "something that veils or conceals." This connotation underscores that the screen as a two-faced metaphor has become the ontological problem of the Indian cinema. The association of the screen with purdah (the invisible) rather than with the visible highlights the significance of the issues of visuality, the politics of vision, screen, and gaze. As the visuality is made up of "the entire sum of discourses inserted between the subject and the world," when we look through the screen, "what we see is caught up in a network that comes to us from the outside: mobile tesserae of signification, a mosaic that moves" (Bryson 1988, 92). As in Norman Bryson's (1988) example of the twentieth-century Japanese philosopher Kitaro Nishida and his student and translator Keiji Nishitani, it can be said that the subject–object relationship is mediated through a screen, a network of signs and signifiers that is based on socially constructed cultural knowledge. As opposed to Cartesian perspectivalism, which privileges an ahistorical, disembodied subject completely outside of the world it proclaims to understand only from a distance, with the screen-mediated subject–object relationship one must recognize and emphasize the significance of "the idea of the body as sensory envelope, as perceptual membrane and material–mental interface, in relation to the cinematic image and to audio-visual perception" (Elsaesser and Hagener 2015, 11). Complementing "the paradigm of cinema as skin" is the notion of the "gender-determined" nature of skin in culture, which "negotiates and re-distributes the relation between inside and outside[,] between Self and Other" (Elsaesser and Hagener 2015, 136–37). While the importance of the skin as a sensory organ and the envelope of the body is indisputable, it must be admitted that the body enters the field of vision for the most part clothed—wearing what Edmund Bergler calls its "improved skin" (1953, xxiii). In psychoanalytical feminist theory, mass culture substitutes for the Freudian individual ego, for the former serves as "a massive screen on which collective fantasy, anxiety, fear, and their effects can be projected. In this sense, it speaks to the blind spots of a culture and finds forms that make manifest socially traumatic material through distortion, defense, and disguise" (Mulvey 1993, 6). The screen that used to conceal from the gaze now imagines the spectator in an ambivalent position that involves a new viewing pleasure at recognizing the private sphere, in which women previously supposed to be veiled now find themselves visible on the other side of the purdah, or "screen."

The purdah or the veil in the cinematic screen is "a metaphysics of principled concealment[,] and it [is], over-all, a mechanized interplay of surfaces" in which "the image move[s] across spaces, and in doing so, acquire[s] a haptic quality and gravitate[s] away from an unflinching iconic stance" (Basu 2013, 142). Fabrics, human skin, clothing, the tactile possession of living things construct the world just as much as communication does, which also depends on touch because of the discordance between linguistic and cultural systems. The theories of cinema as a tactile experience, in addition to an experience that grants the eye "haptic" faculties aside from the more common "optic" dimension, make cinema a "contact space with Otherness, to account for the fact that cinema brings faraway places closer and renders absent people present" (Elsaesser and Hagener 2015, 10). In fact, the title of Laura U. Marks's book *The Skin of the Film* (2000) suggests the image of a viewer touching a film with their eyes in what she calls "haptic visuality." Thus, the screen is no longer a two-dimensional plane surface but rather a transvergent interface with a woman's world that has otherwise been consigned behind purdah.

Indian popular films have a distinct visuality and synaesthetic discourse that are exemplified by the ideology and practice of darshan, *nazar,* and *nigah.* "Darshan" refers to the auspicious sight of a god or a special person, when the camera invites the viewer "to gaze through the deity's (or star's) eyes," which "heightens the experience of the reciprocity of *darshan,* closing an experiential loop to evoke (in a characteristically Hindu move) an underlying unity" (Lutgendorf 2014, 47). In Indo-Islamic religious discourse, the words *nazar* and *nigah,* borrowed from Arabic and Persian, respectively, have similar implications of tangible exchange. However, unlike darshan, the notions of *nazar* and *nigah* apply not only to "the benign gaze of Ṣufi masters, which watches over and protects their disciples," but also to "the eye contact of lovers, especially the first sight that arouses passion" (Lutgendorf 2014, 46). Compared to *nazar,* the term *nigah* connotes "a more potent contact," an essentially voyeuristic peek in the context of "a culture that idealized (and sometimes practiced) the veiling of respectable women, an illicit glimpse that . . . is disruptive of social and familial hierarchy" (Lutgendorf 2014, 46). Therefore, the "act of gazing" conveyed by the terms *nazar* and *nigah* takes "the place of touching" and "is itself transformed into the aim of sexual activity," leading to "a twisted form of penetrating the other" (Bronfen 1996, 60). While the veil is a significant "visible" signifier of South Asian traditions and modesty pertaining to Muslim women in real life as well in popular culture, the *nazar/nigah* in cinema unveils the invisibility of Muslim women behind the purdah. Hence, the intersubjective, haptic potential of *nazar/nigah* is essential for understanding the women covered by the hijab in the public sphere, now exposed on the other "side" of the hijab or purdah (screen).

Because film perspective, apparatus, genre, and authorship are swayed by the vectors of gender, power, religion, ideology, and politics, to understand the meaningful relation between cinema and gendered sensate bodies we must engage with a synaesthetic discourse to foreground the major shifts in the different genres of Bollywood cinema in which veil as a trope, veiling practices, and gendered spaces make significant interventions in the representation and interpretation of Muslim identity.

The Veil and Muslim Identity: Major Shifts in Bollywood Cinema

The Muslim Historical

Through evaluation of specific Muslim historical films, this section discusses haptic images and their connections to the representations of embodiment and veiling practices. Although the historical film established itself as a significant genre of nation-building by the early 1920s and gained momentum with the rise of the nationalist movement, the genre dwindled with the end of the Nehru era in the 1960s, but then had a resurgence in the twenty-first century when the Hindu Right (especially the Bhartiya Janata Party and Shiv Sena) in the western state of Maharashtra (where Bombay/Mumbai is situated) influenced Bollywood filmmaking to domesticate India's Muslim population in post-Hindutva India (Merivirta 2016, 458). In Hindi cinema, popular Muslim historicals include *Nurjehan* (Jamahedji Jehangirji Madan, 1923), *Razia Begum* (Nanubhai B. Desai and

Bhagwati Prasad Mishra, 1924), *Shahjahan* (Naval Gandhi and Ardeshir Irani, 1924), *Mumtaz Mahal* (Homi Master, 1926), *Shiraj-ud-Daula* (Dhanjibhai K. Desai, 1927), *Shiraz* (Franz Osten, 1928), *Chandbibi* (Narayanrao D. Sarpotder, 1931), *Sikander* (Sohrab Modi, 1941), *Humayun* (Mehboob Khan, 1945), *Anarkali* (Nandlal Jaswantlal, 1953), *Adl-e-Jahangir* (Gopaldas Parmanand Sippy, 1955), *Mughal-e-Azam* (Karimuddin Asif, 1960), *Shahjahan* (Abdul Rashid Kardar, 1946), *Taj Mahal* (M. Sadiq, 1963), *Mirza Ghalib* (Sohrab Modi, 1954), *Jodhaa Akbar* (Ashutosh Gowarikar, 2006), *Mangal Pandey/The Rising* (Ketan Mehta, 2005), and *Taj Mahal: An Eternal Love Story* (Akbar Khan, 2005). Though many historical films have celebrated the glories of the ancient past or the action-ridden tales from militant Maratha and Rajput histories, the Hindi historical as a genre owes its enormous popularity to the Mughal themes. Karimuddin Asif's film *Mughal-e-Azam* was one of the most successful of films of all times, but the more recent film *Jodhaa Akbar*, directed by Ashutosh Gowarikar, was banned in several states, including Madhya Pradesh, Uttar Pradesh, Haryana, and Rajasthan, because the Rajputs saw the representation of the Rajput Hindu princess Jodhaa Bai as the Mughal emperor Akbar's wife as an insult to their community. While *Mughal-e-Azam* masks the complexity of a Mughal emperor's relationship with a Rajput princess, *Jodhaa Akbar* enunciates that "acceptance and inter-communal harmony are the desired goals—but on Hindu terms, regardless of the fact that the Emperor of the historical period depicted is a Muslim" (Merivirta 2016, 468). This comparison illustrates that Hindi historical cinema is increasingly becoming the site of ideological and identitarian struggles. In these films, the haptic female body is either reified as the uncontaminated representation of the nation or reduced to the corrupting influence that prevents the state from becoming a nation.

Mughal-e-Azam tells the story of the Great Mughal, Akbar (r. 1556–1605), and his conflict with his son, Prince Salim (Dilip Kumar), because his son falls in love with Anarkali (Madhubala), a dancing girl in the Mughal court. Emperor Akbar (Prithviraj Kapoor) prohibits Salim from continuing this relationship, but the prince rebels against his father and spearheads a battle against him. Though the veracity of Anarkali as a historical figure is disputable, the deliberate usage of myth and metaphor invites us "to read Mughal social conventions as the social institutions and class structure of modern-day India" (Sardar 1998, 25). In her *mujra* (song-and-dance performance), Anarkali defiantly sings, "Pyar kiya to darna kya [Why be afraid when you have loved]?"[2]

The love story of Salim and Anarkali in the film lifts the veil from the false sense of propriety. In this song, Anarkali challenges social conventions and their meanings: "Purdah naheen jab koyee Khudha sé, / bandon sé purdah karnaa kyaa [When I don't wear a purdah before God / why should I veil myself before men]?" In the next shot, the emperor averts his gaze, looking down. The intimate and proximate close-ups collapse not only the distance between the viewer and the image but also the partition of the sensible established by the frame and invest the spectator with a haptic mode of perception in which "the looker is also implicated. . . . This being-for-the-Other is the basis of the ethical relation for Levinas" (Marks 1998, 345). The frames of visual and haptic erotics enable the Indian audiences to identify the undercurrents of Otherness that undergird the filmic narrative through the perceived Otherness of Anarkali, a dancing girl. The performance and the alluring "spectacle of cinema, the dance of the slave, and the male gaze reinforce the diffused power of historical imaginaries," which underpin "social conventions such as sexism, objectified gender performance, and female exploitation, in this case circulated through film imaginaries" (Singh 2016). The film "speaks to the political and cultural project of nation-building in multiple and conflicting ways" (Singh 2016). Since cinema is an audiovisual form, the privileged evidence of the historical "truth" in a specific era is conveyed through images, songs, dances, and soundtracks.

Like *Mughal-e-Azam*, Ashutosh Gowarikar's *Jodhaa Akbar* was also a very popular, albeit controversial, film. The historical personae Akbar and Jodhaa have supporting roles in *Mughal-e-Azam* but are the central characters in *Jodhaa Akbar*. The film is a lavish historical epic that revived the Muslim historical in the aftermath of the Gujarat communal riots in 2001, which created acrimonious fault lines between the Hindus

---

2. I give my own translations of quotes from films unless otherwise noted.

and Muslims throughout the country. The film narrates the coming to the throne of Jalaluddin Muhammad Akbar (Hrithik Roshan), the third Mughal emperor of India (born October 15, 1542), whose ancestors included the warriors and rulers Timur and Genghis Khan from Central Asia. Akbar is considerably esteemed as the harbinger of peace between his Hindu and Muslim subjects in India, a place that he has endeavored to make his home, and he marries a Hindu princess, commonly known as Jodhaa Bai (Aishwarya Rai Bachchan). However, the protagonists are estranged by the manipulations of Maham Anga, a woman who had served as a nurse to Akbar and is now the chief adviser at his court. The film frames Jodhaa with veils, saris, and floating drapes, which repetitively underscore her position between the private and the national realms. In the Indian national imaginary, the Hindu woman embodies the nation, so her body is forbidden to the Muslim Other. However, *Jodhaa Akbar's* narrative articulates a new language of desire that not only allows interreligious coupling but also situates a desiring female gaze at the center of the historical process.

Though the film *Jodhaa Akbar* returns us to the earlier setting of the Bollywood classic *Mughal-e-Azam*, it gives a more expansive peep inside private female spaces, from Jodhaa's childhood zenana in a Rajput palace to her personal quarters in the Mughal palace, making the past accessible as a present reality for the contemporary viewer (as filmgoer, tourist, or property buyer). Describing the narration of the nation in the form of narrating the woman, Anustup Basu says, "A whole discourse on Indian modernity has focused on the casting of the figure of woman, or a 'recasting of it' in an interiorized ethical diagram of the home or the Bharat Mata or Mother India as an iconic imagination of the nation" (2013, 139). In the film, we see "a Muslim masculinity threatened by an aggressive Hindu femininity. . . . Jodhaa's agency, however, does not serve her own desire. Instead it focuses on serving her community—only in the space sanctioned by familial duty does she come to love Akbar" (Khan 2011, 134). As a revisionist history, the film implies that as long as Jodhaa, who symbolizes the nation, domesticates the extreme sexuality and violent risk that the Muslim masculinity poses and indigenizes the Muslim male, she may share her life and live with the Muslim Other.

One of the most erotic and amatory sequences in *Jodhaa Akbar* consists of a sword fight between Akbar and Jodhaa in which Akbar hopes to overcome Jodhaa and bring her back to his palace bedroom. Close-ups of Jodhaa and Akbar dot the long shots of the wide-ranging sword fight. The visual track of the fight charts Akbar's unveiling and veiling of Jodhaa, alternately filmed in long and medium shots. In line with Renata Salecl and Slavoj Žižek's notion that "love is never 'just love' but always the screen, the field, on which the battles for power and domination are fought," the gaze as the "partial object"—leftovers of a jouissance not yet sublated—becomes "the medium of control" as well as of "the fascination that entices the other into submission" (1996, 2–3). During the fight, when Akbar pulls off Jodhaa's turban, revealing her long black hair, she becomes unveiled. Then at a critical point in the swordfight, he cuts the support ropes of a drape, which falls around Jodhaa, veiling her again. The frames of veiling and unveiling are effective metaphorical and psychical enunciations of surrender, autonomy, and agency, which allow us as implicated spectators to reflect on the meanings of "feminine sexuality" and the regulation of jouissance (Barnard and Fink 2002) through masculine and feminine structures of being. The veiling and reveiling of Jodhaa not only highlight the erogeneity that they embody but also construct a tangible image of Akbar's dominance over Jodhaa's body. This revealing and concealing are reminiscent of Luce Irigaray's figurative "curtain-wall-wall-ette" and the divisions made by it (described in both "Belief Itself" and "Plato's Hysteria" [Irigaray 1985, 1993]), which underscore the significance of preserving gender segregation in a libidinal economy that is contingent upon controlling and exploiting female sexuality at the same time as it represses that sexuality. It is precisely such an understanding of corporeal and sartorial practices of veiling/unveiling in Bollywood cinema that the next section brings to bear on *tawa'ifbaazi*, or the courtesan culture.

The Muslim Tawa'if (Courtesan) Films

The construction of Muslim ethnic identity through popular Hindi cinema by means of the trope of the veil and veiling is central not only to "the process of movement and translation from social macrocosm to filmic microcosm" (Chakravarty 1998, 311) but also to the symbolic "return" of the marginalized and the rejects of society, such as *tawa'ifs*, into the body politic. *Tawa'if* is an Urdu-Persian term whose closest equivalent in English is *courtesan* (Qureshi 2006, 317). Although the *tawa'if*, in contradistinction to the Hindu *devdasi*,[3] is usually thought of as a secular institution, in Hindi films the *tawa'ifs* are always popularly imagined in reference to Islamic culture, an imagination that is reinforced through Bollywood's associations of *tawa'ifs* with Urdu *shayari* (poetry), ghazals in particular (Ansari 2008, 300). The most prominent courtesan-based Bollywood films include *Devdas* (Bimal Roy, 1955; Sanjay Leela Bhansali, 2002), *Pakeezah* (Kamal Amrohi, 1971), *Muqaddar ka Sikandar* (Prakash Mehra, 1978), *Umrao Jaan* (Muzaffar Ali, 1981; Jyoti Prakash Dutta, 2006), *Tawa'if* (Baldev Raj Chopra, 1985), *Salma* (Ramanand Sagar, 1985), *Sardari Begum* (Shyam Benegal, 1996), and *Jaanisaar* (Muzaffar Ali, 2015). The elegant *tawa'if* with her inventory of veil gestures, the covering and uncovering with a large *dupatta* (veil/covering) across the body or over the head, is an intrinsic part of the Bollywood courtesan genre. The details of these *gats* (dance movements and forms) are described in the nineteenth-century texts *Sarmaya-i Ishrat* (1884) by Sadat Ali, delineating *nritt* (a Sanskrit term for nonrepresentational dance), *Madun-ul Musiqi* (1869) by Mohammad Karam Imam, and *Bani* (1877) by Wajid Ali Shah. The courtesans in Bollywood cinema are usually Muslim.

The most famous Hindi courtesan film, *Pakeezah* (1971) by Kamal Amrohi, is set at the turn of the twentieth century. At this time, the city of Lucknow was the seat of courtly Muslim culture because the decline of the Mughal Empire in the last quarter of the eighteenth century had led to the mass exodus of female performers, *tawa'ifs*, nautch girls, poets, and artists from Delhi to Lucknow. *Pakeezah* tells the story of Sahebjaan (Meena Kumari), the daughter of a courtesan, Nargis, who was rejected by Sahebjaan's father's aristocratic family. Abandoned and neglected, Nargis dies during childbirth, and her sister, Nawabjaan (Veena), brings up Sahebjaan as a courtesan. One of *Pakeezah*'s most memorable moments

---

3. *Devdasi* means "slave of God." The term is employed for a girl who is ritually married to a Hindu deity or a temple, which David Szanton (2012) calls a ritual prostitution under the terms of the dominant religion in the name of Hindu gods.

is when the hero, Saleem (Raaj Kumar), unknowingly walks into the ladies' compartment in the train and is struck by Sahebjaan's shapely and pretty feet. Unaware that she is a *tawa'if*, he writes her a note: "Your feet are very lovely. Do not place them on the ground. They will get soiled." Talking about the erotogenic powers of feet and foot fetishism, Patricia Uberoi describes "a distinctively South Asian corporeal aesthetic" that is manifested in the film through a "podoerotics" (1997, 148). Rachel Dwyer points out how the courtesan film "fetishizes the woman's body, usually the feet," which are one of the few visible and uncovered parts of her body besides "her hands, hennaed, manicured and bejewelled; and her masklike face, again elaborated, painted and jewelled, her hair tied back, and covered with a veil and more jewels" (2006, 119). In her essay "The Newly Veiled Woman" (1998), Anne-Emmanuelle Berger points to how Luce Irigaray recognizes the feminine habit of using makeup and ornaments as a form of "envelope" (116), as a form of veil, and, hence, according to Amber Fatima Riaz, "as women's internalization of male fetishization of the female body" (Riaz 2008, 147). According to Berger, the Muslim practice of veiling fetishizes the female body in an analogous way, with the variance lying in the in/visibility of women.

The courtesan films employ clothing, song, dance, and music to offer a form of cinematic hapticity and tactility that not only "occurs . . . at the skin or the screen, but traverses all the organs of the spectator's body and the film's body" (Barker 2009, 2). In contradiction to received notions of how gender has been constituted in theory, Stella Bruzzi (1997) has argued, clothing is an essential element of eroticism. This connection is foregrounded in *Pakeezah* as the veil is used as a display of both eroticism and modesty. The film's haptic visuality tears the purdah/screen of the film's surface ideology to unveil the suppressed desires and feelings (Vasudevan 2000, 117). In the first song in *Pakeezah*, "Inhin logon ne" (Those People), Sahebjaan, the courtesan, sings how men have taken her veil, or her modesty: "Inhin logon ne, inhin logon ne, /Inhin logon ne le leena dupatta mera [These are the very people, these are the very people / These are the very people who have taken away my veil from me]." In this song, the red *dupatta* is a "veiled" allusion to virginity or more generally to sexual honor. The *dupatta* in the lyric (loosely translatable as "veil") symbolizes not only Sahebjaan's erotic mystique, refinement, sophistication, and style but also her dignity. The *ghoonghat gats* (dance gestures with the *dupatta*, covering the head and veiling the face) in *mujra* as corporeal play connote the fetishistic absence/presence associated with the subtleties of concealing and revealing.

In Hindi mainstream cinema, the *tawa'if* is imagined through tropes that situate her within particular Muslim historiographies. The courtesan films unravel the numerous ways in which clothing interacts with the body in the development of identity, which can almost always be "linked to certain tropes of Muslim cultural identity and historiography" (Ansari 2008, 291). The courtesan's female skin on the purdah (screen) is more of "a surface" that can be employed as "a movable aperture," which is the site of "display for jewellery and necklaces" and "the canvas on which endless dramas of hiding and revealing, of self-exposure and modesty, of presentation and shame, or veiled allure and absolute vulnerability are played out and staged" (Elsaesser and Hagener 2015, 137). The song "Inhin logon ne" in *Pakeezah*, which was screened after the partition of the Indian subcontinent (1947), alludes to the "gendered violence and the post-facto debate around the recovery of dishonored women and their reinsertion into their legitimate communities" (Das 2010, 18). However, as the "reinsertion" of the recovered women into their own communities violated the patriarchal ideas of female "purity, legitimacy, and honor" (Das 2010, 18), it was very difficult for these women to be readily accepted by their own families. In the film, although Sahebjaan elopes with Salim, she quickly realizes that she cannot escape her fate. When the priest asks her name at the wedding ceremony, performed on an open plateau, she does not answer. The groom answers for her and names her "Pakeezah" (the Virtuous or Pure One). Salim's desire to marry her and his renaming of her as Pakeezah fuel her confusion and self-hatred. The distressed *tawa'if* cries out, "Nahin [No]!," and runs away, her black veil flying out like the wings of an ominous bird. Abandoning Salim at the mosque, she runs away hysterically, her veil catching on a tree. At the end of the film, however, Sahebjaan is ultimately given "the integrity her mother had yearned for, the recognition that, Indian politicians argued post-Partition, was due to women who had been 'recovered,' the respectful reclaiming by society of a 'dishonored' woman as 'pure'" (Das 2010, 21). The film is a relentless haptic experience; throughout it, we see not only close-ups of tightly framed characters but also the filmmaker's use of eyeline matches, which stitch (or "suture") characters' gazes to the world and each other in a coherent unity. Thus, the embodied gaze is the "doubled and crossed situating of the visible in the tangible and of the tangible in the visible" (Sobchack 2004, 134–35). In this interpretation, the gaze is *reversibly mimetic in its shifting address, constant mobility, and fluid identifications. It is, above all, inclusive of alterity*" (Sobchack 2004, 100, emphasis in original). In the courtesan films, this alterity of vision is framed through the mimetic vision of a *tawa'if*.

Set in the post-Hindu-nationalist mobilization years of the 1990s, Shyam Benegal's film *Sardari Begum* (1996) both reworks the main elements of the courtesan film and employs the styles of the classic Muslim social as it gestures to confront a new set of sociopolitical issues that claim Sardari's life in a communal outbreak of violence. The film, framed from the diverse vantage points of select family members and acquaintances, explores not only the trajectory of Sardari Begum's life but also the metamorphosis of the music of the *kotha*s from the nineteenth-century *thumri* idiom performed traditionally by *tawa'if*s in the seclusion of their salons and in the *mehfils* (soirées, often with musical entertainment) at the *havelis* (mansions) of nawabs into the public sphere of the twentieth century through gramophone records and performances in concert halls. Though Sardari (Kirron Kher) is trained in the erotic genres of the *thumri* music of courtesans, she creates her public image as an artist, a classical singer, and a classical musician and severs her connections to the conventions or associations of *tawa'ifbaazi*. She wants her daughter, Sakina (Rajeshwari Sachdev), to become a respected classical musician untainted by the disrepute still attached to the mother. Although at first resisting the career of a performing artist, Sakina finally accepts her destiny. In the last scene of the film, Sakina, dressed in the sari that her mother had worn for her first independent performance at the rich connoisseur Hemraj's *haveli*, picks up her mother's *tanpura* (stringed musical instrument), which marks her advent as an artist.

Through the lives of the two Muslim women, Sardari and Sakina, the film frames the breakdown of a cohesive world of the feudal *haveli* that distributed female energies and virtues into wholly separate parts of the *ghar* (home): the purdah (screen/segregated space) and the *kotha* (abode of the *tawa'ifs*). Space, whether sacred (*ghar* or zenana) or profane (*kotha*), is not produced in a vacuum but rather through "a web of crosscutting power relations" that are themselves situated as embodied practice (Secor 2002, 7–8). The *tawa'if* films frame the *kotha* as "the space of agon" in which "both the conceptual diagrams of modernity and those of tradition were attacked, contaminated, abstracted, revised, and purified" (Basu 2013, 141). The veil is pervasive in Islamicate films as some form of body/head/face covering over either the dress or female-segregated space, and the veiling obliquely embodies, as coded through the courtesan, not only dignity and cultured eroticism apparent on the screen in the maneuverings of the veil but also dishonor revealed in the frames of unveiling. Thus, the courtesan films simultaneously subvert and replicate the gender hierarchy inscribed in the purdah system.

Films such as *Pakeezah* and *Sardari Begum* not only recount nostalgia for the aesthetic and cultural traditions of the past but also frame a thinly veiled representation of the falling fortunes of the postcolonial princely states, the patrons of culture and art, with the curtailment of their power and position after the accession of their kingdoms into the new Indian nation following its independence (1947) from British rule. The imposition of Nehruvian socialism further eroded their influence. When Prime Minister Indira Gandhi abolished traditional forms of capital in the Privy Purse by the Twenty-Sixth Amendment to the Constitution of India in 1971, the courtly patterns of life came to a halt, and aesthetic traditions such as Hindustani music and classical Indian dance as well as the maintenance of royal architectural spaces associated with them, including zenana palaces and *kotha havelis*, appeared to be on the brink of extinction. By exposing the collusion among masculinity, national politics, and religion, the courtesan films not only challenge the traditional concerns associated with women but also foreground the need to reclaim women's bodies from becoming a site and symbol for patriarchal, religious, and institutional control. Within the context of conflicting postcolonial narratives of the Indian subcontinent and its ever-increasing Hindu middle class, this association with a Muslim memory in courtesan films clearly cannot be explained and understood neutrally in terms of religion and culture.

The Muslim Social

Foregrounding the trope of the veil, this section explores the Bollywood films of the Muslim social genre to unpack the gendered geometries of power and privilege in the Islamicate cultures that are enacted in the private and public spaces through categories such as "religion" and the "everyday." Space is a complex concept subject to sociopolitical and religious influences. Although the home is a sacrosanct site for the preservation of religion and culture, where women remain unspoiled by desires, in everyday life it is in these private spaces that sufficient opportunities lie for ordinary women to subvert the traditions that socioreligious institutions impose upon them. Among the Islamicate genres, the Muslim social, which blossomed in the 1940s and 1950s alongside other popular contemporary films that portray an intricate world of Muslim relationships and an Urdu-based domestic and public culture, includes *Najma* (Mehboob Khan, 1943), *Elaan* (Mehboob Khan, 1947), *Mirza Ghalib* (Sohrab Modi, 1954), *Chaudhavin ka chand* (Mohammed Sadiq, 1960), *Barsaat ki raat* (Pyare Lal Santoshi, 1960), *Mere mehboob* (Harnam Singh Rawail, 1963), *Bahu Begum* (Mohammed Sadiq, 1967), *Mehboob ki Mehndi* (Harnam Singh Rawail, 1971), *Garam Hawa* (Mysore Shrinivas Sathyu, 1973), *Nikaah* (Baldev Raj Chopra, 1982), *Salim langade pe mat ro* (Saeed Akhtar Mirza, 1989), and *Maqbool* (Vishal Bhardwaj, 2004), among others.

   Chaudhavin ka chand (1960) is a drama of misrecognition and erroneous identity that occurs because of the confusion caused by veiling. The film is cast within the generic framework of the Muslim social, which explores the mores of Muslim family life, courtship, and culture. It begins with a stolen, forbidden exchange of gazes between the sexes when the Muslim female protagonist, Jameela (Waheeda Rehman), is caught with her veil up in a public space. This deep visual exchange, with detailed shots of both protagonists' eyes, shows an instantaneous attraction that creates a desire for further passionate gazing. In *Chaudhavin ka chand*, the desire set up from the first stolen glance drives the male protagonist, Nawab

Pyare Miyan (Rehman Khan), to find out who this person is and scheme to catch his second sighting of her in the mirrored image that he hopes to see at their own wedding ceremony. Here, not only the gaze but also its movements and operations follow norms of a South Asian visuality that combines darshan, *nazar*, and *nigah*. In the movie, the director, Mohammed Sadiq, deployed the idea of the eroticized *nazar* to generate his love story: the Muslim marriage custom whereby the bride and bridegroom first swap gazes in a mirror during their marriage ceremony. In the film's climax scene, Nawab Pyare does in fact see Jameela again and as a reflection in a mirror, not during their wedding but in the household of a friend, Aslam (Guru Dutt), who has recently married her.

Chaudhavin ka chand engenders *nazar/nigah* as haptic vision, which is "a visual erotics that offers its object to the viewer" (Marks 2002, 16). The filmmaking of *Chaudhavin ka chand* reroutes the vision and gaze toward the tenderly veiled haptic body/image through which the viewer "feels" or tentatively "touches" the loved one's body. Engaging haptic, or tactile, visuality, the film frames the intense gaze mutually exchanged between the lovers that visually expresses the erotic desire. The close-up of Jameela's eyes, otherwise concealed behind her veil, is often adeptly used on the screen to hide and then, as she lifts her burka, to unveil her direct frontal gaze, so the film viewers are given the virtual visual experience of intensely gazing into Waheeda Rehman's eyes, which suggests both hapticity, or the intimacy of touch that customarily remains private and concealed, and a voyeuristic gaze that glares at and around the veil of the female character. The spectator is immersed in the felt environment through "intimate detailed images that invite a small, caressing gaze" (Marks 2000, 169). This haptic visuality rests upon the mimetic faculties, that "sensuous connection between the very body of the perceiver and the perceived" (Taussig 1993, 21). In that state of both viewing and being a viewer, the purdah (both the film screen and the veil) that separates the female beloved and the lover/audience becomes the touched skin. While the cinematic lens provides audiences a visual and haptic participation in the intense exchange of gazes, the veil, as an emblematic cultural marker in the film, not only screens but also identifies the female object that is withheld from the gaze. These practices render the identity of the female wearer visually unmarked and therefore essentially unknown or hidden to those outside the immediate family group.

Chaudhavin ka chand dramatizes the heightened significance these practices bestow upon the revelation of the veil bearer's face and upon the returned gaze that inscribes the emotional impact of the onset of desire as a moment of recognition, which cinema, with its resources of focalization and framing, is uniquely suited to realize. The revelation of the veiled face is dramatized in the film as an inevitable, in the sense of everyday, consequence of modern life and the chance encounters it yields. While the misrecognition that occurs after the face is covered again is initially comic in its consequences—Pyare Mian pursues the wrong woman—it turns tragic when his friend Aslam marries Jameela, the woman whom Pyare Mian loves. In fact, Aslam and Jameela are married at the instigation of Pyare Mian, who, because Jameela is in purdah, remains oblivious of the fact that she is the girl with whom he fell in love at first sight. The film is less a critique of the institution of purdah than a sympathetic portrayal of the conditions of existence under purdah for both genders. The whole film proceeds as a play of gazes, with Aslam not only desiring to see Jameela again but also realizing his desire by seeing her next as a reflection in a marriage mirror. *Chaudhavin ka chand* remains deeply patriarchal in its depiction of the purdah system. Women, as the character Jameela attests, are the property of men, and it is virtuous for them to conceive of themselves in that way. Women are the objects not simply of contestation or rivalry but also of exchange between men. Male friendships are celebrated even to the extent that the woman must be sacrificed, if so required, in the interest of those friendships.

Mere mehboob (1963) reworks the misrecognition plot of *Chaudhavin ka chand*, but the drama is a contemporary one that shows the challenge posed to traditional class hierarchies and gender boundaries by modern institutions and spaces where chance encounters are more likely or where purdah restrictions are relaxed; it also subtly criticizes patriarchal codes of honor that shame the woman who steps outside prescribed roles, traditionally embodied in the figure of the courtesan. *Mere mehboob*, one of the most popular Muslim social films to date, is a romantic narrative set in Lucknow supposedly at the beginning of the twentieth century. In the film, Anwar (Rajendra Kumar), a young student and poet, bumps into a veiled Husna (Sadhana) on campus and goes crazy with love after catching a single glimpse of her. In the film, Husna "lets [herself] be seen without presenting [herself] to be seen" (Metz 1982, 63). At the Aligarh Muslim University poetry competition, Anwar unravels his emotions in the following words:

> Chandnee raat mein nazron se tujhe pyaar karoon
> apnee mehkee huyee zulfon ka sahaara de de.
> . . . .
> samne aake zaraa parda uthhaa de rukh se.
> [On a moonlit night, I will embrace you with my eyes
> Soothe me with the sweet fragrance of your tresses.
> . . . .
> Come forth and lift up the veil from your face.]

As he sings the love poem "Mere mehboob," the film shows the conditions under which the lovers met—an accidental collision, a spilling of books, a touch of the hand, a lifting of the veil, and an exchange of glances. Hence, the hijab of the veiled woman can be seen as the point of both contact and split because the embodiment of the gazing paradox necessitates distance of the object from the eye for the eye to apprehend (or be in contact with) that visual object. The hijab exposes the silhouette of the hidden, which attracts the attention of the unfulfilled, desiring gaze. As the notable Algerian intellectual, philosopher, and anthropologist of religions Malek Chebel points out, "Garments, far from assuming their social function of 'modesty,' exacerbate the tensions between what they mask, the body, and the voyeur. What is or pretends to be 'modest' in a garment thus creates its own 'viewer,' while the garment draws from its own dialectics: eroticism" (qtd. and trans. in Martin 2011, 33). In addition to framing Anwar as the desiring subject in *Mere mehboob*, the dynamics of desire inscribed in the veil produce the same logical paradox for the viewer: Husna, who is hidden from view, essentially invigorates desire and kindles fantasy in both the male protagonist and the audience. The viewer's eyes touch the purdah (screen), what Marks calls "the skin of the film," with his eyes, and this tactile dimension of the film is essentially connected to its affective aspect, beyond its audio-visual factor.

Mere mehboob as haptic cinema shows how the cinematic screen becomes not only a surface of the union achieved by the *nazar* but also the plane on which what generally goes on beyond the veiling of women is projected from the other side of purdah (the screen and the veil)—that is, the ontological awareness of the veiled woman and her world that the film seems to imply rather than show, in a revelation-and-concealment dialectical movement on the purdah (cinematic screen), letting the viewer imagine and feel the indistinct side of the hijab. Using the purdah/screen transvergently, the film invites the *nazar* of the spectator to peep inside the veiled world of the female character. One popular hit song from the film underscores the function of *nazar/nigah* in evoking love and longing:

> Bhool sakti nahin ankhen woh suhana manzar
> Jab tera husn mere ishq se takraya tha
> aur phir raah me bikhre the hazaro naghme
> Mai wo naghme teri aawaaz ko de aaya tha
> Saaz-e-dil ko unhi geeto ka sahara de de
> Mera khoya hua rangin nazara de de
> Mere mehboob tujhe mere mohabbat kee kasam.
> [My eyes cannot forget that delightful sight
> When your beauty encountered my love
> And then a thousand songs lay strewn on the way.
> I dedicated them all to your voice.
> Give my heart the support of the very same mellifluous melodies
> Restore the joys of that lovely sight
> My beloved, in the name of my love.]

The language of popular Bombay film, Urdu, essentially stimulates the concept of vision based on *nazar*, which authorizes an almost corporeal union between lovers in a context when an act of bodily proximity or touching would be prohibited. While singing this song, Anwar is shown recalling the exchange of gazes with his ladylove, an exchange depicted on the screen by alternating close-ups of each actor's eyes, by which the camera simulates both lovers' subject positions. In other words, the audio-visual creation evokes "haptic visuality"—that is, senses other than merely hearing and sight.

The haptic dimensions of both *Mere mehboob* and *Chaudhavin ka chand* are expressed not only through the skin of the film but also through the thin, evocative purdah (veil) of the film. The intense visual exchange, with close-ups of both protagonists' eyes, when the Muslim woman protagonist is caught with her veil up in a public space, is precisely how the director Mohammed Sadiq begins his film *Chaudhavin ka chand*. Though Husna and Anwar in *Mere mehboob* love each other, their hopes of marriage are upset by unfortunate coincidences. Husna's brother Nawab Saheb (Ashok Kumar), who is like a father to her, turns out to be the patron of Anwar's sister, Najma (Nimmi), who is like a mother to Anwar. Though Najma is pure at heart, and her character is unblemished, Nawab Saheb cannot marry her because she eked out a living by singing and dancing for men so that she could raise her brother and educate him to become a doctor like their father. The love between Nawab Saheb and Najma and between Anwar and Husna is threatened not only by the institution of purdah or the code of family honor but also by the social distinctions and hierarchies it is designed to preserve.

In *Mere mehboob* and *Chaudhavin ka chand*, the private spaces occupied by women in zenanas are shown on the screen. The purdah that used to veil/cover from the male gaze now uncovers and draws the spectator's gaze. It positions the spectator in an equivocal position that is not just voyeuristic—as imaging a woman's interior quarters may imply—but also involves a unique viewing pleasure: pleasure at identifying the features of home, or the intimate/private sphere, as opposed to the spectacular. Haptic images thrive in *Mere mehboob* and *Chaudhavin ka chand*, and they have both narrative and aesthetic functions that correspond to Gilles Deleuze and Félix Guattari's concept of the haptic: "A haptic space can be visual, aural, as well as tactile. . . . 'Haptic' is a better word than 'tactile,' since it . . . invites the assumption that the eye itself may fulfill this non-optical function" (1987, 492). The haptic actually gives the viewer a novel way of "interacting" with the film as it offers a back-and-forth between the close intimacy, or the sensation of the object of love/desire, and distance because the film screen is the purdah and separates the viewer from the object. Thus, paradoxically, the cinematic screen, from a haptic perspective, gives viewers the illusion that they have accessed the interior world of the filmic narrative. In *Mere mehboob* and *Chaudhavin ka chand*, the purdah (film screen) is the interface that allows the spectator to take a peek into and interact with the world of the veiled female characters, which has hitherto been imperceptible, inaccessible, or underrepresented in mainstream Hindi cinema. The Muslim social films, very much a political product of their time, placed Muslims, their everyday habitus and practices, in this discourse of cultural difference and sought to negotiate a space on the screen for the Muslim as part of a national imagination.

Post-9/11 Films

In the later twentieth century, while veiling practices became synonymous with Islam and piety for many Muslim women in the West, "'the veil' froze as a signifier of Islamic patriarchy and its despotic exercise of violence" (Kane 2022, 14–15). In Hollywood cinema and global media, the veiled Muslim woman has usually been a fetishized object of a Western gaze that sees concealment (of the female body) as a hazard to democracy, religiosity as a hurdle to assimilation, and exposure as a symbol of (sexual) freedom. Although the long history of orientalism and fetishization of Muslim women and their veils dates back to the early modern travel literature, after the bombings in the United States on September 11, 2001, the popular stereotypes of Muslim women increasingly underscored "Islam's misogyny" (Toor 2011, 167) and labeled the veil as a symbol of Islamist fundamentalism, "a 'mobile prison,' . . . a provocation and, in some instances, a sign of support of terrorism" (Fadil 2018). After 9/11, "hijab," "Islam," and "Muslim woman" became categories that highlight the impact of Islamophobia, which predominantly manifests itself as dislike of or prejudice against veiled women (Zempi and Chakraborti 2014, 2). Though Muslim women and hijab debates have attracted considerable attention in Western media since the 9/11 attacks, few academic publications focus on the cinematic productions that depict Muslim women's reactions to the stereotypes that frame them "as passive, uneducated victims covered by Hijabs, as beautiful and seductive terrorists, as suicide bombers" (Dastgeer and Gade 2016, 1). Some of the prominent post-9/11 Hindi mainstream movies representing Muslim experiences include *Fanaa* (Kunal Kohli, 2006), *Kurbaan* (Rensil D'Silva, 2009), *New York* (Kabir Khan, 2009), *Veer-Zaara* (Yash Chopra, 2004), *My Name Is Khan* (Karan Johar, 2010), and *Haider* (Vishal Bhardwaj, 2015).

My Name Is Khan (2010) is an important post-9/11 film that explores the extent to which visual frames of Muslim women in Bollywood cinema respond to Islamophobia and its effects on their lives. The film is about an Indian Muslim man with Asperger's syndrome, Rizwan Khan (Shah-rukh Khan), living in the San Francisco area and married to an Indian Hindu woman, Mandira Rathore (Kajol). After 9/11, Rizwan sets off on a journey across the United States to meet the president to tell him, "My name is Khan, and I'm not a terrorist." Rizwan's brother, Zakir (Jimmy Sheirgill), is married to Haseena (Sonya Jehan), who is a teacher of psychology at an American university. After the death of Rizwan's mother, Haseena is the strongest influence on him. After 9/11, Zakir convinces Haseena to do away with her hijab when she is assaulted by an unidentified white American attacker who removes it coercively. This "objectification" of bodies and "the fetishization of the 'un-veiling'" inflicts upon Muslim women an epistemic as well as psychological violence (Baldi 2021, 190). In the end, Haseena reclaims the hijab while resuming her job at the university. Examining the correlation between dress and subjectivity, Daniel Miller asserts that clothing not simply serves as "a form of representation, a semiotic sign or symbol of the person[,] [but also] plays a considerable and active part in constituting the particular experience of the self" (2010, 40). Such an approach then underscores the construction of subjectivity. My focus here is not only on the ways in which the act of looking is fraught with gender and power dynamics in the representations of post-9/11 cinema but also on how we might reconfigure debates about gender and agency vis-à-vis religious and cultural practice. *My Name Is Khan* exemplifies how the post-9/11 Islamophobia becomes conflated with racial xenophobia in the normative gaze of an American white male who considers a nonwhite woman, Haseena, an abject Other and who assumes that her Muslim cultural/religious identity and veiling are threats to the American nation.

After 9/11, many loudly vocal conservative Americans identified the veil "as an affront and the flaunting of an identity associated with those who have declared war on the United States" (Haddad 2007, 263). *My Name Is Khan* evocatively portrays Islamophobia and the backlash against veiled Muslim women after 9/11. However, contrary to these developments, Haseena continues to wear the hijab. When Rizwan migrates to the United States after his mother's death, Haseena helps him to adjust and adapt to his new life. Born to South Asian Muslim parents, she performs the role of a negotiator between Rizwan and his brother, Zakir. Besides Rizwan, she is the only other character in the film with a voice-over. Whereas Zakir renounces Rizwan for his wedding to a Hindu, Haseena dismantles the constructed oppositions between "traditional" and "modern," "secular" and "religious," by attending Rizwan's marriage to Mandira. That Haseena wears a hijab is not noticed until after 9/11, when an angry man violently knocks her down in the hallway at her university, saying, "You people [should] go home." The construction of "oppositional categories" in the Western discourse and thought concerning the veil has "the power to naturalise a specific idea of womanhood to which Muslim women in Europe" and America are "blindly asked to conform" (Baldi 2021, 144). That Haseena is an American–born US citizen in a country espousing freedom of religion and freedom of expression is irrelevant to the white American man in his hate-filled diatribe. As a consequence of this attack, though, Haseena's husband, Zakir, directs her to renounce hijab. By denying Haseena an opportunity to make decisions regarding her Muslim identity and veiling, both men (Zakir and the American white male), regardless of their religion and race, infantilize Muslim women, which conveys these men's notions of deep uncertainty regarding women's capability to make decisions and to exercise choices on their own. Visibly shaken, Haseena tearfully accepts Zakir's suggestion that "Allah will understand" if she stops wearing the hijab in public. It is this incident that reunites the two brothers and brings them together as a family. Later, when Rizwan is apprehended as a suspected terrorist and put behind bars without any valid evidence, the media and the common American people embrace Rizwan's cause and clamor for his release. Emotionally validated by the public support, Haseena resumes wearing the hijab. She explains to her university class that the hijab is not just an expression of her religion but a sign of her reality (*wajud*); it is who she is. Such a position has become apparent in the recent phenomenon of "new veiling," as Arlene MacLeod (1991) calls it—that is, women donning the hijab as a political statement. This reveiling demonstrates that "covering can be a form of liberation," too (Bullock 2002, xxxix). Hence, my invocation of the hijab in the discussion of this film is located in the dynamics created when Haseena wears the hijab to screen the panoptic gaze from herself. As Chebel says, "The veil is to be considered as this garment essentially meant to prevent women from being seen and, at the same time, giving them the possibility to gaze at others" (trans. and qtd. in Martin 2011, 34). The veil gives Haseena the privilege of gazing without being gazed at, to perceive others from a nonreciprocal vantage point.

In *My Name Is Khan*, Haseena draws a distinction between an autonomous choice to follow religious authority and dogmas, on the one hand, and an imposed form of authority from an outside force (whether it be a state or a society or a person), on the other. The film positions the veiled Muslim woman subject as an agent of self-empowerment. *My Name Is Khan* provides interesting insights into the rationale for an emerging and complex phenomenon, "new veiling" or the "new hijab." The new meaning of the veil emphasizes that it is not a symbol of "religious revivalism" but rather part of a movement toward "cultural reformation" and returning "to a more authentic and culturally true way of life," which had been diminished by "the loss of traditional values" brought on by the rise of "modernization and development" (MacLeod 1991, 111, 135). In fact, the veil has become a sign of the "reconstruction of identity" (MacLeod 1991, 161). In *My Name Is Khan*, Haseena combines individual freedom of choice with religious piety and veiling practice. For her, hijab serves as a mechanism for affirmation or validation of not only her cultural and gender identity but also her agency. In fact, Haseena's reveiling conveys some measure of audaciousness that pointedly challenges the construction of the voiceless, oppressed Muslim woman stereotype. The film clearly shows Haseena's reveiling as a reaction against the compulsory deveiling. She offers a sobering reminder that the enforced "unveiling" in pursuit of the secularization of society and modernization of Muslim women is as disenfranchising for educated Muslim women as enforced veiling. Hence, agency is linked with performativity and emerges as "the specific ways in which one performs a certain number of operations on one's thoughts, body conduct, and ways of being" in order to "attain a certain kind of state of happiness, purity, wisdom, perfection, or immortality in accord with a particular discursive tradition" (Mahmood 2001, 210). The film shows how the relationship between "visibility" and "agency" is highly fraught as Haseena calls viewers' attention to the issue regarding what is recognized as agential and by whom. She underscores the performativity of veiling practice as an agential politics, for it is an extension of her identity and spiritual disposition.

In contrast to women in films of the past, the Muslim women characters in contemporary Bollywood cinema are as varied, complex, and layered as the women of other communities. The recent films portray a wide array of Muslim women with diverse sartorial preferences, which may or may not include veiling for a variety of reasons other than the religious ones—for example, Saba Taliyar Khan and Alizeh Khan in *Ae dil hai mushkil* (Karan Johar, 2016), Rehana and Shirin in *Lipstick under My Burkha* (Alankrita Shrivastava, 2016), Haseena Parkar as the mafia don's sister in *Haseena Parkar* (Apoorva Lakhia, 2017), Insia Malik in *Secret Superstar* (Advait Chandan, 2017), Sehmat Khan in *Raazi* (Meghna Gulzar, 2018), and Safina in *Gully Boy* (Zoya Akhtar, 2019). In *Secret Superstar*, Insia Malik (Zaira Wasim), a female teenager, wears a burka to camouflage herself from the disapproving gaze of her father while she pursues her dream of becoming a famous pop singer. The film *Lipstick under My Burkha* introduces us to Rehana Abidi (Plabita Borthakur), a freshman in college who sews burkas for her family's store. Although she secretly loves the flamboyant American pop star Miley Cyrus, she is forced to wear a burka, which she rebelliously throws off outside home, flaunting her made-up face and Western jeans and shirt that she wears underneath her burka. Safina (Alia Bhatt), a metropolitan Indian Muslim young woman who is studying medicine in *Gully Boy*, uses the hijab neither as a symbol of oppression nor as a religious prop for the story. In fact, she dons a hijab with the same effortless ease as her headphones and jeans. Where the central focus of the hijab in *Gully Boy* is on culture and identity, not simply on religion, purdah becomes an expression of agency in *Raazi* in the way the heroine, Sehmat (Alia Bhatt), uses the veil to create an interplay of surveillance and subterfuge that allows her to manipulate the Pakistani intelligence officers for her own interests while remaining elusive to their gaze. In this film, the veil can also be seen as "a 'possibility of action,'" a tool through which Sehmat not only achieves her goals but also negotiates a way of life (Baldi 2021, 156). The characterization in these films enunciates the fluidity of contemporary Muslim women's identity, which can be comprehended in terms of the process of "becoming" a Muslim woman who dares to "unveil" her desire, autonomy, and agency. Thus, in the contemporary Hindi films depicting Muslim women, there is a predominant impulse to decenter veiling and religiosity by focusing on the ordinary struggles and pleasures in the everyday lives of gendered Muslims.

Conclusion

If we acknowledge that our customs and mores are constructed in a context where our culture, gender, religion, and politics negotiate with each other in an association that is dialectical, interactive, and iterative, then cinema is the site where that relationship is performed, enunciated, challenged, reconfigured, and preserved. Purdah (screen) is a polysemic surface on which different and inverted images of Muslim women are projected in a unique fashion. The body of the female Muslim woman in veil or segregated spaces in the national imaginary becomes the locus of haptic vision, the palpable medium for recognition to foster not only a more extensive sense of the experience but also a more critical capability for sociopolitical connectedness. This concomitantly interpersonal, transcultural, and phenomenological understanding of haptic visuality in cinema corresponds to an understanding of veiling and the private spaces for women not only as sites of vulnerability and precarity but also as shields or safeguards. Thus, veiling choices are not just sociocultural practices but also decisions defined by women's subjective understandings as they wrestle with notions of femininity, religiosity, and geospatial location. The spectator, too, embedded in particular "power geometries" (Massey 1991) in relation to space, gender, and embodiment, no longer inertly accepts the ocular knowledge but acts as an active person who is wired acoustically, bodily, and affectively in the film. The notion of the body "as sensory envelope, as perceptual membrane and material-mental interface, in relation to the cinematic image" (Elsaesser and Hagener 2015, 11) is the ontological, epistemological, and phenomenological basis for a new way of knowing not only veiled women's experiences of their bodies, affect, and the senses but also the viewer's "corporeal-material being" (Sobchack 2004, 55).

In most of the mainstream Hindi films, the Muslim woman as a subject is either silent or veiled or fragmented or all of these things. The Muslim historical genre depicts the Mughal period as highly oppressive of women in spite of its splendor and courtly refinements. To frame the gendered sociospatial segregation and veiling of the situated and embodied historical referents on the screen, the Muslim historical combined the paradigmatic processes, which are more entrenched in memories, social sensitivities, and perceptions, with the iconic processes that involve archival or architectural sources that signify the time enunciated through appraisal with a modern equivalent. Whereas at the center of the Muslim social films is the figure of the begum (wife), a paragon of virtues, the tawa'if, who symbolizes the fallen singing and dancing women outside purdah and hence under constant public male gaze, is at the center of the courtesan films. Though the tawa'ifs in Muslim courtesan and Muslim social films are good at heart, these genres cannot legitimize them in any other role except as the woman redeemed through marriage and confinement to gender-segregated zenanas, as exemplified by the characters Najma in Chaudhavin ka chand and Sahebjan in Pakeezah. The eponymous heroine of Sardari Begum, however, is a split figure who embodies both the begum and the courtesan. She relinquishes the purdah-bound life and the traditional codes of honor espoused by the figure of the begum to pursue a singing career without any connection to the courtesan culture. The courtesan in Hindi film operates as a fetish that masks women's lack of choice. In fact, the image of the courtesan is a substitute for that choice. However, these enunciations have altered over the years. Though the courtesan defies the diktats of purdah, gender segregation, and confinement of women in public spaces, this rebellion against inequitable gender relations is usually a facade because ultimately it fails to lead its female audience anywhere but back to a wifely, patriarchal femininity fettered within the zenana. However, the veiled women protagonists do not merely serve as symbols of subjugation and disparity. Sometimes the veil acts as spectatorial bait, drawing the audience's notice to the fact that a different regime of looking as well as power is being questioned in these films. The entire veil paradox derives from the principal impossibility of rejecting the erogeneity that it enshrines, which is the essence of seduction in the Muslim historical, the Muslim social, and the courtesan films.

The framing of veiling practices and gendered spaces in Bollywood Islamicate films make significant interventions in the representation and interpretation of Muslim identity. Because the somatic register is the principal register in the Islamic matrix (Mandoki 2007, 223), the Muslim social genre shows how Muslim women's identities are claimed, ascribed, or resisted in everyday situations and everyday use of local spaces and sartorial practices. In the Muslim social, the hero catches a momentary glimpse of the heroine, but her veil often leads to a tragedy arising from misrecognition in films such as *Chaudhavin ka chand* and *Mere mehboob*. No matter how constrained the *nazar*—the gaze or the lens of a camera on a veiled woman—it always finds a way to destabilize the patriarchal disciplinization of female bodies and to enable some measure of freedom from hegemonic institutional control.

However, post-9/11 filmic representations or enunciations of the veil as a trope or practice have altered. In the film *My Name Is Khan*, reveiling is in some measure an assertion of being visibly Muslim; it marks an effective participation within the sphere of public visibility. The very garments that used to signify cruelty, suffering, shame, and death become here subversive symbols of agency. In the context of the reveiling in *My Name Is Khan*, it can be said that veiling does not simply mean blocking the gaze but instead is a matter of mobilizing a particular visual regime that enacts its own aesthetics and ethics. For Haseena, veiled women are not invisible; they are visible in a particular manner, and they are active participants in producing that visibility. After 9/11, Hindi cinema lifted the veil over the suppressed realities of Muslim women and exhorted the desensitized viewer to look at the veiled woman sensitively. The recent Hindi films enunciate in meaningful, transformative, and ethical ways the spectators' relation to the veiled body, which contributes to the shaping of an affective bond between spectators and film characters that can essentially prompt empathy rather than pity and/or fear of the Other. The latest Bollywood films beckon spectators to concern themselves with the vectors of power involved in the films' imaginative construction of the veiled woman and to be conscious of their participation in it.

Works Cited

Afsaruddin, Asma. 1999. "Introduction: The Hermeneutics of Gendered Space and Discourse." In *Hermeneutics and Honor: Negotiating Female "Public" Space in Islamic/ate Societies*, edited by Asma Afsaruddin, 1–28. Cambridge, MA: Center for Middle Eastern Studies, Harvard Univ. Press.

Amer, Sahar. 2014. *What Is Veiling?* Chapel Hill: Univ. of North Carolina Press.

Ansari, Usamah. 2008. "'There Are Thousands Drunk by the Passion of These Eyes.' Bollywood's *Tawai'f*: Narrating the Nation and 'the Muslim.'" *Journal of South Asian Studies* 31, no. 2: 290–316. At https://doi.org/10.1080/0085 6400802192929.

Baldi, Giorgia. 2021. *Un-veiling Dichotomies: European Secularism and Women's Veiling*. Cham, Switzerland: Springer.

Barker, J. M. 2009. *Tactile Eye: Touch and the Cinematic Experience*. Berkeley: Univ. of California Press.

Barnard, Suzanne, and Bruce Fink, eds. 2002. *Reading Seminar XX: Lacan's Major Work on Love, Knowledge, and Feminine Sexuality*. Albany: State Univ. of New York Press.

Basu, Anustup. 2013. "'The Face That Launched a Thousand Ships': Helen and Public Femininity in Hindi Film." In *Figurations in Indian Film*, edited by Meheli Sen and Anustup Basu, 139–57. London: Palgrave Macmillan.

Berger, Anne-Emmanuelle. 1998. "The Newly Veiled Woman: Irigaray, Specularity, and the Islamic Veil." *Diacritics* 28, no. 1 (Spring): 93–119.

Bergler, Edmund. 1953. *Fashion and the Unconscious*. Madison, CT: International Univ. Press.

Bhaskar, Ira, and Richard Allen. 2009. *Islamicate Cultures of Bombay Cinema*. Delhi: Tulika.

Bronfen, Elisabeth. 1996. "Killing Gazes, Killing in the Gaze: On Michael Powell's *Peeping Tom*." In *Gaze and Voice as Love Objects*, edited by Renata Salecl and Slavoj Žižek, 59–89. Chapel Hill, NC: Duke Univ. Press.

Bruzzi, Stella. 1997. *Undressing Cinema: Clothing and Identity in the Movies*. London: Routledge.

Bryson, Norman. 1988. "The Gaze in the Expanded Field." In *Vision and Visuality*, edited by Hal Foster, 87–113. Seattle: Bay Press.

Bullock, Katherine. 2002. *Rethinking Muslim Women and the Veil: Challenging Historical and Modern Stereotypes*. London: International Institute of Islamic Thought.

Chakravarty, Sumita S. 1998. *National Identity in Indian Popular Cinema: 1947–1987*. New Delhi: Oxford Univ. Press.

Das, Srijana Mitra. 2010. "Cinema: Representations in Commercial Films: India." In *Encyclopedia of Women & Islamic Cultures*, edited by Suad Joseph. Leiden, Netherlands: Brill. At https://referenceworks.brillonline.com/entries /encyclopedia-of-women-and-islamic-cultures/cinema-representations-in -commercial-films-india-EWICCOM_0644#d118264404e450.

Dastgeer, Shugofa, and Peter J. Gade. 2016. "Visual Framing of Muslim Women in the Arab Spring: Prominent, Active, and Visible." *International Communication Gazette*, Apr. 19, 1–19.

Deleuze, Gilles, and Félix Guattari. 1987. *A Thousand Plateaus: Capitalism and Schizophrenia*. Translated by Brian Massumi. Minneapolis: Univ. of Minnesota Press.

Dwyer, Rachel. 2006. *Filming the Gods: Religion and Indian Cinema*. London: Routledge.

Elsaesser, Thomas, and Malte Hagener. 2015. *Film Theory: An Introduction through the Senses*. London: Routledge.

Fadil, Nadia. 2018. "Taming the Muslim Woman: The Immanent Frame." *The Immanent Frame: Secularism, Religion, and the Public Sphere*, May 24. At https://tif.ssrc.org/2018/05/24/taming-the-muslim-woman/.

Gehlawat, Ajay. 2010. *Reframing Bollywood: Theories of Popular Hindi Cinema*. New Delhi: Sage.

Haddad, Yvonne Yazbeck. 2007. "The Post-9/11 *Hijab* as Icon." *Sociology of Religion* 68, no. 3: 253–67.

Irigaray, Luce. 1985. "Plato's Hysteria." In *Speculum of the Other Woman*, translated by Gillian C. Gill, 243–365. Ithaca, NY: Cornell Univ. Press.

———. 1993. "Belief Itself." In *Sexes and Genealogies*, translated by Gillian C. Gill, 23–53. New York: Columbia Univ. Press.

Kane, Jean M. 2022. *Muslim Textualities: A Literary Approach to Feminism*. London: Routledge.

Khan, Shahnaz. 2011. "Recovering the Past in Jodhaa Akbar: Masculinities, Femininities and Cultural Politics in Bombay Cinema." *Feminist Review* 91:131–46.

Lewis, Reina, and Sara Mills. 2003. Introduction to *Feminist Postcolonial Theory: A Reader*, edited by Reina Lewis and Sara Mills, 1–22. London: Routledge.

Lutgendorf, Philip. 2014. "Cinema." In *Studying Hinduism: Key Concepts and Methods*, edited by Sushil Mittal and Gene Thursby, 41–58. London: Routledge.

MacLeod, Arlene Elowe. 1991. *Accommodating Protest: Working Women, the New Veiling, and Change in Cairo*. New York: Columbia Univ. Press.

Mahmood, Saba. 2001. "Feminist Theory, Embodiment, and the Docile Agent: Some Reflections on the Egyptian Islamic Revival." *Cultural Anthropology* 16, no. 2: 202–36.

Mandoki, Katya. 2007. *Everyday Aesthetics: Prosaics, the Play of Culture and Social Identities*. London: Routledge.

Marks, Laura U. 1998. "Video Haptics and Erotics." *Screen* 39, no. 4: 331–48.

———. 2000. *The Skin of the Film: Intercultural Cinema, Embodiment and the Senses*. Durham, NC: Duke Univ. Press.

———. 2002. *Touch: Sensuous Theory and Multisensory Media*. Minneapolis: Univ. of Minnesota Press.

Martin, Florence. 2011. *Screens and Veils*. Bloomington: Indiana Univ. Press.

Massey, Doreen. 1991. "A Global Sense of Place." *Marxism Today*, June, 24–28.

Merivirta, Raita. 2016. "Historical Film and Hindu–Muslim Relations in Post-Hindutva India: The Case of *Jodhaa Akbar*." *Quarterly Review of Film and Video* 33, no. 5 (Mar.): 456–77.

Metz, Christian. 1982. *The Imaginary Signifier: Psychoanalysis and the Cinema*. Bloomington: Indiana Univ. Press.

Miller, Daniel. 2010. *Stuff*. Cambridge: Polity.

Mir, Raza, and Husain Mir. 2006. *Anthems of Resistance: A Celebration of Progressive Urdu Poetry*. New Delhi: India Ink Roli.

Mulvey, Laura. 1993. "Some Thoughts on Theories of Fetishism in the Context of Contemporary Culture." *October* 65:3–20.

Qureshi, Regula Burchardt. 2006. "Female Agency and Patrilineal Constraints: Situating Courtesans in Twentieth-Century India." In *The Courtesan's Arts: Cross-Cultural Perspectives*, edited by Martha Feldman and Bonnie Gordon, 312–31. New York: Oxford Univ. Press.

Riaz, Amber Fatima. 2008. "Breaking Down the Walls: Challenging the Concept of Zenana in Blasphemy." In *Women in Dialogue: (M)uses of Culture*, edited by Dilek Direnc, Gunseli Sonmez Isci, and Klara Kolinska, 143–58. Cambridge: Cambridge Scholars.

Salecl, Renata, and Slavoj Žižek. 1996. Introduction to *Gaze and Voice as Love Objects*, edited by Renata Salecl and Slavoj Žižek, 1–4. Durham, NC: Duke Univ. Press.

Sardar, Ziauddin. 1998. "Dilip Kumar Made Me Do It." In *The Secret Politics of Our Desires: Innocence, Culpability and Indian Popular Cinema*, edited by Ashis Nandy, 9–91. New Delhi: Oxford Univ. Press.

Secor, Anna J. 2002. "The Veil and Urban Space in Istanbul: Women's Dress, Mobility and Islamic knowledge." *Gender, Place and Culture* 9, no. 1: 5–22.

Singh, J. P. 2016. "A Subaltern Performance: Circulations of Gender, Islam, and Nation in India's Song of Defiance." *Arts and International Affairs*, Mar. 13. At https://theartsjournal.net/2016/03/13/singh.

Sobchack, Vivian. 2004. *Carnal Thoughts: Embodiment and Moving Image Culture*. Berkeley: Univ. of California Press.

Szanton, David L. 2012. "Mithila Painting: The Dalit Intervention." In *Dalit Art and Visual Imagery*, edited by Gary Michael Tartakov, 219–34. New Delhi: Oxford Univ. Press.

Taussig, Michael. 1993. *Mimesis and Alterity: A Particular History of the Senses*. London: Routledge.

Toor, Saadia. 2011. "How Not to Talk about Muslim Women: Patriarchy, Islam and the Sexual Regulation of Pakistani Women." In *Introducing the New Sexuality Studies*, edited by Steven Seidman, Nancy Fischer, and Chet Meeks, 166–74. London: Routledge.

Uberoi, Patricia. 1997. "Dharma and Desire, Freedom and Destiny: Representing the Man–Woman Relationship in Popular Hindi Cinema." In *Embodiment: Essays on Gender and Identity*, edited by Meenakshi Thapan, 145–71. Delhi: Oxford Univ. Press.

Vasudevan, Ravi S. 2000. "Shifting Codes, Dissolving Identities: The Hindi Social Film of the 1950s as Popular Culture." In *Making Meaning in Indian Cinema*, edited by Ravi S. Vasudevan, 99–121. Delhi: Oxford Univ. Press.

———. 2015. "Film Genres, the Muslim Social, Discourses of Identity c. 1935–1945." *BioScope* 6, no. 1 (Sept. 17): 27–43.

Zempi, Irene, and Neil Chakraborti. 2014. *Islamophobia, Victimisation and the Veil*. London: Palgrave Pivot.

7

Veiled Anxieties in Mani Ratnam's *Bombay*

Afrin Zeenat

The practice of veiling is, in reality, not unique to Islam or to Muslims but has been carried out in various religions and cultures since the very beginning of human civilization. In India, the purdah system, a form of veiling and segregation of women that limits women's movement, was practiced by both Hindu and Muslim elite women since colonial days. The short story "Sultana's Dream" (1905) by Begum Rokeya Sakhawat Hossain subverts the prevalent practice through her portrayal of a fictional Ladyland, where the practice of purdah (veiling) enforced by Muslim patriarchs is questioned. Loaded with revolutionary potential, Hossain's avant-garde representation of Ladyland, a society where women engage in public duties and various intellectual activities, while men remain confined in the *murdana* (male quarters), the inverse of the zenana (female quarters), is considered a visionary feminist utopia. Numerous South Asian Muslim women have successfully pursued education and public service by adorning the burka, which replaced confinement in the zenana. Thus, in relation to the zenana, the burka served a positive role in liberating Muslim women in India. In fact, the burka, or veiling, served as a path to attaining self-sufficiency for them. Yet whereas Hossain's fictional Ladyland spurred Muslim women to play a productive role in society by stepping out of the zenana, a film released approximately one hundred years later, Mani Ratnam's *Bombay* (1995), presents the veiled Shaila Bano as the movie's subject of inquiry in order to condemn the act of veiling as imposed by

Muslim patriarchs. Ratnam's reductionist portrayal of the veiled Shaila Bano in the movie reflects a neoliberal urban Hindu male's concern for the veiled woman's assimilation through voluntary unveiling. The unveiling of Shaila Bano is merely an attempt to shift the patriarchal authority from a Muslim father to a secular Hindu husband. Hossain's vision of Indian Muslim women's defiance in stepping out of the zenana quarters clad in a veil as a symbol of female empowerment becomes for Ratnam a tool for their forced assimilation into the larger identitarian politics that defines the Bollywood entertainment-industrial complex. In this chapter, I undertake an analysis of both Hossain's "Sultana's Dream" and Ratnam's *Bombay* to argue that Ratnam, the Hindu patriarch-savior director, repurposes the Muslim woman's unveiling as expedient for social assimilation simply to further majoritarian beliefs. The act of unveiling, instead of serving as a useful trope for Muslim women's empowerment, is made ineffectual. Thus, by following the dictates of a growing neoliberal Hindu economy and aiming for the social good of India by bringing all "human action under the domain of the market" (Harvey 2005, 3), Ratnam's *Bombay* abounds in the nation's anxieties around Muslims.

As noted earlier, veiling of both women and men has existed from the very beginning of human civilization. In the past, veiling served multifarious functions in different cultures around the world. Although currently the term *veiling* is almost always used in the context of Islam, the practice predates Islam by many centuries (Amer 2014, 7). To disengage the act of veiling from an essentialist understanding of it as a practice limited to Islam, it is important to revisit its history, particularly in relation to Europe. According to D. L. Cairns, the practice can be traced to the Greeks, for whom it often took the form of withdrawal from society or from specific people as a form of protest against a personal affront or even to express anger. He points out numerous instances of veiling in Greek literature and culture to support his claim. One noteworthy example is that of Achilles veiling in the *Iliad*, which Cairns refers to as a form of separation or withdrawal to express anger (2001, 20). Cairns offers a detailed description of the different forms such withdrawal could take, from physical concealment to the refusal of eye contact. Examples of veiling can be further found in early Jewish and Christian tradition. In Christianity, the apostle Paul called for women to cover their head, and Christian women, both Roman Catholics and Protestants, have been known to cover their hair during worship and while attending funerals. Widows formerly wore the nun's veil while mourning the loss of a husband (Patte 2004, 452–54). With changing times, Europe's developments in the philosophical, cultural, and religious realms gradually made veiling practices obsolete and simultaneously influenced the perceptions surrounding the practice of veiling. In recent times, the West has viewed that practice solely through its own narrow historical lens. Such a reductionist approach to veiling creates a dissonance vis-à-vis its immigrants, specifically its Muslim immigrants, who migrate from regions that have different cultural norms. Such an outlook also perpetuates stereotypes of Muslim women (possibly the only group that still veils publicly), which then circulate globally. Other non-Muslim cultures view the practice of veiling in the same vein; thus, stereotypes of women who veil as being backward and in need of intervention are reinforced. Such is the case in India, where Muslims form a sizeable minority (177 million) that practices veiling in large numbers. The majority religious group in India, Hindus, rely on these stereotypes of Muslims to view this Muslim practice as backward, thereby failing to understand both its long tradition and its continued practice even in supposedly modern times.

Even before veiling, commonly referred to as the purdah system, became prevalent among Muslims in India, historically it transcended religious affiliations. Hindu and Muslim women, especially those belonging to the elite classes, practiced some form of purdah. Purdah usually entailed separation from men. Indoors, it implied female seclusion in the zenana (female quarters) and could also imply a physical screen or curtain to deflect the male gaze; outdoors, it implied various forms of veiling—outer covering women put on themselves or a screen on vehicles. Purdah was common in India even before the Muslim invaders arrived in 712 CE. Among lower-class Hindu women even today, the wearing of the *ghoonghat* (face covering) is practiced in the northwestern regions of India. In a chapter titled "Purdah," Virbhadra Singhji elaborates on the practice of purdah among Rajput women. Rejecting the modern popular understanding of veiling as strictly Islamic, he traces the practice of purdah to various forms of seclusion followed in ancient India, the Byzantine Empire, and pre-Islamic Persia. Singhji draws our attention to the Hindu epics *The Ramayana* and *The Mahabharata*, which detail a separate quarter for women (1994, 204). He even mentions the legendary story of Shakuntala and her veiling before she appears in the court (1994, 204). In *Mother-Right in India* (1941), Baron Omar Rolf Ehrenfels corroborates that both purdah and the total veiling of women were foreign to original Islam but were considered a mark of aristocracy in later Islam (200). Another scholar, Arthur Jeffrey, notes that "veiling, seclusion and harem life, none of this originated with Islam" (1959, 56). Despite these scholarly views to the contrary, misguided popular opinion continues to veer on veiling essentially as Islamic even in India, where Hindu women cover their faces with a *ghoonghat* even today.

The advent of British colonialism in India in the early eighteenth century reinforced the purdah system because Indian patriarchs, irrespective of religious affiliations, feared the influence of a Western way of life on their women, even though they themselves embraced many Western practices. Women were given the responsibility of continuing the cultural purdah practices. Shirley A. Fedorak notes that in colonial societies veiling becomes a means of resistance as "a symbol of the . . . rejection of Western morals and political ideology" (2007, 188). According to Eunice de Souza, among upper-class women, both Hindu and Muslim, the practice of purdah enabled social separation from the colonizer's gaze and helped the native upper class to "maintain control over wealth and property" (qtd. in Fedorak 2014, 6). This practice was not very common among the lower classes because of a lack of sufficient physical space to practice it. The British governor General William Bentick and the Hindu social reformer Raja Ram Mohan Roy in Bengal were successful in the abolition of the ancient Hindu custom of sati and later child marriage, which emboldened many Hindu women to gradually come out of their seclusion in the zenana. The lack of similar initiatives from Muslim male leaders (and the British policy of divide and conquer, which was evident in Britain's lack of initiative to reform the Muslim community in equal measure) ensured that the practice of purdah and seclusion in the zenana continued to define Muslim society both in pre-independence and postindependence India. This history shows that Mani Ratnam's conflation of veiling and Muslim women in *Bombay* highlights a lack of historical knowledge about the practice of veiling in India. Begum Rokeya Shakhawat Hossain questioned the practice in "Sultana's Dream," a short story about a dream that its main protagonist, Sultana, has. Although the eponymous Sultana could be the name of a specific person, it also implies any lady belonging to the ruling classes because the title *sultana* implied "wife of the sultan." This dream exemplifies Muslim women's discontent over the practice that relegated them to the zenana and expresses a utopian wish for a world where Muslim women could perform their daily activities without any social restrictions. According to the critic Abul Hussain,

> The extreme measure of secluding men in Ladyland was a reaction to the prevailing oppression and vulnerability of our women. . . . [P]erhaps Mrs. R. S. Hossain wrote this to create a sense of self, confidence among the very vulnerable Bengali women. . . . That women may possess faculties and talents equivalent to or greater than men—that they are capable of developing themselves to a stage where they may attain complete mastery over nature without any help from men and create a new world of perfect beauty, great wealth and goodness—this is what "Sultana's Dream" depicts. . . . I hope the male readers of "Sultana's Dream" would try to motivate the women of their families toward self-realization. (qtd. in Jahan 1993, 2, ellipses as given in Jahan 1993)

Because not much social reform was initiated for Muslim women in pre-independence India, Hossain's short story attempted to motivate male Muslim leaders to take action. Her vision of a Muslim society where women could be free to avail themselves of education is portrayed in the story, which was contrary to Muslim women's reality in India. About the writer of "Sultana's Dream," Susmita Roye informs us that "she could become educated only with the help of a few progressive male relatives (her brother and husband), [for] to even imagine a male-guidance/male-domination-free women's realm is radical to the extreme" (2009, 143). Although many literary scholars in recent times have hailed "Sultana's Dream" to be among the first science-fiction tales to be written by a woman (Roye 2009, 137), it has also been understood to be a work of social protest against Muslim society's failure to offer Muslim women the right to education.

The short story's plot unfolds through a dream, where Sultana is visiting an alternate world, quite appropriately named Ladyland, where gender roles are reversed. She notices the absence of men from public spaces in Ladyland and asks her hostess:

> "Where are the men?" . . .
> "In their proper places, where they ought to be."
> "Pray let me know what you mean by their proper places."
> "O. I see my mistake, you cannot know our customs, as you were never here before. We shut our men indoors."
> "Why? It is not safe for us to come out of the zenana, as we are naturally weak."
> "Yes, it is not safe so long as there are men about the streets, nor is it so when a wild animal enters a marketplace." (Hossain [1905] 2017)

Using tongue-in-cheek humor, Hossain points out that a man freely wandering in the streets is considered a threat in this utopia. Hossain's reversal of the dominant patriarchal view of the woman wandering in the streets as a threat to society becomes even more interesting when we notice that Sultana ventriloquizes patriarchy as she presents the numerous justifications men have offered for imposing purdah or seclusion on women. In contrast, her hostess, the ruler of Ladyland, points out the numerous disadvantages of allowing men freedom of movement in her country as she compares men to wild animals and puts blame on them for all social problems. Just like wild animals who terrorize the other weaker animals roaming in the forest, men, too, have historically imprisoned women indoors and are harmful for society. Hossain's narrative encapsulates the experiences of women of her times, who resisted the forced confinement.

In this connection, Sonia Nishat Amin states that "many Muslim *bhadramahilas* ('gentle-women') of modern Bengal around this time had begun distinguishing between *purdah* and *abarodh*. *Purdah* is seen as 'modesty in dress and behaviour' whereas *abarodh* is a 'patriarchal distortion of purdah which makes women invisible behind the *andarmahal* [inner quarters for women]'" (qtd. in Roye 2009, 140). Roye explains the subtle difference between the terms thus: "Rokeya [Hossain] herself denounced the injustices heaped on a confined woman in *Abarodhbasini* (woman living in *abarodh*)—a series of essays that was written in Bengali and published in 1931. In 'Sultana's Dream,' her subversion of the idea of protecting women's modesty by instead putting men into confinement is a powerfully acerbic critique of the system of *abarodh*" (2009, 140). Both Amin's and Roye's observations of the situation that Hossain and other women faced in pre-independence India explain Hossain's motivation behind writing a story protesting the subjugation of women by Muslim men. The conversation between Sultana and the queen of Ladyland does point out the lower social value of women in Sultana's land based on the notion of women's weakness, as patriarchs wanted society to believe. To comprehend the full import of these notions, we need to remember that when Hossain was writing in 1905, knowledge was disseminated mostly by men, and stereotypes of women as the weaker sex had currency. Amid the preponderance of male views of women and lack of any forceful women's voice rallying for women, Hossain's depiction of Sultana's hostess and the queen of Ladyland, who provide evidence of women's culpability in their inferior status in the society outside Ladyland, is rather groundbreaking for its time. She says, "A lion is stronger than a man, but it does not enable him to dominate the human race. You have neglected the duty you owe to yourselves and you have lost your natural rights by shutting your eyes to your own interests?" (Hossain [1905] 2017). When Sultana inquires about how the men do not complain about the restrictions imposed on them, her hostess informs her:

> "Yes, they wanted to be free. Some of the Police Commissioners and District Magistrates sent word to the Queen to the effect that the Military Officers deserved to be imprisoned for their failure; but they never neglected their duty and therefore they should not be punished and they prayed to be restored to their respective office. Her Royal Highness sent them a circular letter intimating to them that if their services should ever be needed they would be sent for, and that in the meanwhile they should remain where they were.

"Now that they are accustomed to the purdah system and have ceased to grumble at their seclusion, we call the system 'Murdana' instead of 'Zenana.'"

"And since then your country-men never tried to come out of the zenana?" (Hossain [1905] 2017)

Laced with simple logic, the narrative details the various scientific accomplishments of women in that society, thus opening up a range of possibilities for the women readers of Hossain's time, who did not have access to formal education. Our protagonist is amused and surprised to know of the condition of the male citizens of Ladyland. She is also amazed that women control every aspect of that society. Through her utopian vision of a world where women are free to move and participate in public affairs, Hossain offers her colonial women readers a hope that it will be possible for women to step out of the zenana and participate in public affairs. Her utopia does not rely on men for the fulfillment of women's dreams and desires. According to Sally Miller Gearhart,

> Feminist utopian fiction is a sort of fiction political: it contrasts the present world with an idealized society, criticizes contemporary values and conditions, sees men or masculine systems as the major cause of social and political problems (e.g. war), and presents women as equal to or superior to men, having ownership over their reproductive functions. A common solution to gender oppression or social ills in feminist utopian fiction is to remove men, either showing isolated all-female societies as in Charlotte Perkins Gilman's *Herland* or societies where men have died out or been replaced. (1984, qtd. in Siddiqua 2016, 395)

Thus, in "Sultana's Dream" women are shown to be independent and efficient in all the duties they perform. Hossain's story serves as an important text for colonial Muslim women as it attempts to inspire them regarding the immense possibilities for Muslim women to play a bigger public role in society. In addition to her story, her own activism in founding a Muslim girls' school was a step toward the fulfillment of the dream. Hossain rightly identifies the problems that beset Muslim communities in India and, as Roye puts it, inspires Muslim women to imagine a "dream-world . . .

where women run universities and are great scientists. They are one and all highly educated and are also in control of the educational system of their community. Sister Sara mentions that she works in the laboratory and describes to Sultana the various scientific wonders achieved by their women" (2009, 140).

After independence in 1947, Hossain's vision began to be partially fulfilled with new strides in Muslim girls' education. Instead of being restricted indoors, many young girls were allowed to step out of the house to acquire education, but only if they wore a veil. Although veiling or wearing a burka was not practiced by all Muslim families, the veil served an important role in affording Muslim girls some freedom of movement and the right to education. After independence, the burka continued to restrict women but also opened many opportunities and was much better than the seclusion in the zenana practiced during Hossain's time. Hence, interpreting the practice of veiling merely as a marker of social backwardness is obviously reductionist. The burka, when compared to the seclusion of Muslim women that preceded it, was rather emancipatory. In this regard, Daniel Patte attests that although the practice of veiling can be "read as silencing and subordinating of women[,] [it] can become in practice a celebration in gender, ethnicity, and membership in the religious community" (2004, 454). The burka made movement outside the zenana a reality as schools for Muslim girls were opened gradually. Sheikh Abdullah founded a school for girls in Aligarh in 1906 under the patronage of the begum of Bhopal. Hossain's writing and her social activism merged when in 1911 she founded a school for girls in Calcutta, which was quite aptly named the Shakhawat Memorial School. In postindependence India, the dream materialized for a multitude of Muslim women, but they continue to lag behind women from other religious communities in the country. According to India's 2011 census, 51.9 percent of Muslim women were literate, but the percentages for women from other religious communities were higher (Bano 2017, 11). Hossain's writing and activism positively affected Muslim women's lives, and with time the black two–piece burka came to represent Indian Muslim women. In fact, Hossain herself would don the burka, and Barnita Bagchi explains what seems to be a contradiction: "Her reputation for departing from the norm made it all the more difficult for Rokeya to

be accepted as a competent educator by parents who had to garner sufficient faith in her ability as a teacher and in her moral values to entrust her
with the responsibility of educating their daughters" (qtd. in Roye 2009,
139–40). She knew her community too well, and to fulfill her dream of
empowering fellow Muslim women she would have to win the trust of the
community. The practice of veiling, which replaced seclusion, inculcated
a strong sense of identity and alleviated anxieties regarding interreligious
marriages. The burka eventually came to symbolize Muslim women who
would step out of their homes to pursue their dreams.

Although Muslims are a minority in India, the Islamic culture brought
by Muslim invaders has featured prominently in the Bombay film industry
throughout its history (Bhaskar and Allen 2009). While Islamic culture in
Bombay cinema before the 1970s showcased respectable Muslim characters often playing secondary or minor roles, the industry underwent a shift
from the 1970s onward when it started to portray Muslims as antisocial
and antistate (Islam 2007). The burka served many useful cinematic purposes, and the burka trope pervades the products of the industry's century-
long history. Bollywood has successfully deployed the trope of the burka
as the quintessential garment of disguise or camouflage, donned as often
by men as by women. Once it is donned, it offers men free access to the
zenana quarters or exclusive female gatherings, clandestine meetings with
their beloveds, and, most importantly, a disguise to make a getaway from
a difficult situation, as in *Aan: Men at Work* (Madhur Bhandarkar, 2004),
Delhi Belly (Abhinay Deo, 2011), *Jolly LLB* (Subhash Kapoor, 2013), *Jane
bhi do yaaron* (Kundan Shah, 1983), *Ek se bure do* (Tarique Khan, 2009),
and *Bajrangi Bhaijaan* (Kabir Khan, 2015). When seen as a garb adorned
by Muslim women, though, the burka takes on a wholly different meaning. It ceases to be the garment of disguise affording its wearer the ability
to move freely and is instead reduced to a garment that symbolizes backwardness and even takes on negative connotations of evil. Mani Ratnam's
film *Bombay* (1995), a neoliberal attempt at depicting the Hindu–Muslim communal tensions in a post–Babri Masjid India, portrays the Muslim female protagonist who is wearing the burka as the religious Other.
Through this portrayal, Ratnam privileges the Hindu lover, Shekhar, a
Bombay-based journalist. Shaila's veil symbolizes her underdevelopment

and, by extension, the underdevelopment of her community, which imposes this vestment on her and other women, thus justifying her exclusion from the eponymous city when she goes there to be with Shekhar. The initial discomfort Shaila Bano experiences once she is in the city accentuates her "otherness." When she leaves her village for Bombay, she is depicted as donning the burka. On her arrival in Bombay, too, the burka is still on her, but in the next scene, when she accompanies Shekhar to the courthouse to marry, she is seen in a sari. Her transition from a Muslim daughter to a Hindu wife, depicted through her changing sartorial choices, less her own than patriarchal impositions, reduce Shaila to an obedient Hindu wife, with or without the veil. Her "evolution" in the film is merely the result of a change in her overlord from a conservative Muslim father to a neoliberal Hindu husband. Her position does not undergo any change, nor does she offer any hope for other Muslim women. As the veiled Shaila becomes the movie's subject of inquiry, her transition illustrates the neoliberal Hindu male concern for her assimilation through a voluntary eschewing of the practice of veiling. Underlying this concern for the Muslim burka-clad Shaila lies the Hindu patriarchal anxiety pertaining to the Muslim Other, which is easily dismissed through the appropriation of the Muslim female body, the source of future generations of Muslims. As Angie Mallhi points out, "Popular culture, particularly Bollywood films in the Indian context, has the power to disseminate/perpetuate the ideologies and interests of dominant groups by exploiting/misrepresenting those at the margins of that society, in this case, Indian Muslims" (2006, 2). Furthermore, Ratnam's unveiling of Shaila can be understood as Hindu-majority vigilance regarding Muslim practices. The movie comes across as a neoliberal attempt "to maintain . . . [the] pretense of freedom as non-coercion when, in practice, it seems unlikely that most people would freely choose the neoliberal version of the state" (Mirowski 2013, 57). Jamie Peck summarizes such manipulation of the audience as "a self-contradictory form of regulation-in-denial." Ultimately, the goal of neoliberalism is "the remaking and redeployment of the state as the core agency that actively fabricates the subjectivities, social relations suited to making the markets real and consequential" (qtd. in Mirowski 2013, 56, 54). Thus, *Bombay* proves to be a neoliberal attempt at presenting the Muslim, especially the Muslim woman, as the Other to intervene in their assimilation. Under the pretext of portraying Shaila's unveiling as a display of willful agency, the director becomes the representative of the state and the majority-Hindu community trying to police the religious practices of the minority community. In one scene, as Shekhar follows Shaila, Ratnam deploys the burka's ability to conceal and reveal to cause a misunderstanding as Shekhar mistakenly expresses his love to Shaila's friend, who is also clad in a burka. Although initially it is Shaila's concealed beauty in the burka that attracts Shekhar and renders the courtship exciting, to love and marry her neoliberal beau Shaila must surrender her burka.

Bombay managed to offend many people: Hindu groups, Muslim groups, and secular intellectuals. Although Mani Ratnam claims that "my film is about the common man's agony in resolving the question 'why the violence?'" (qtd. in Rai 1995), the controversy surrounding the film's release points to a totally different reality. In a communally charged post–Babri Masjid India, the movie was released after Ratnam secured the blessings of the right-wing Hindu leader of Shiv Sena, Bal Thackeray, which allowed the movie to be shown in Mumbai and the rest of India. Some scenes from the film that presented Hindu mobs' culpability in the riots were deleted, purportedly to please Thackeray and his right-wing Hindu followers (Vasudevan 1996, 55–56). Javed Akhtar, the prominent lyricist, noted in a tongue-in-cheek manner at the time of the film's release, "If you make a film about Germans and Jews, and the Nazi party says it is a good film, then there must be something wrong. The movie is the particular view of a benign, tolerant but communal-minded Hindu" (1995, 30). It comes as no surprise, then, that Muslims in *Bombay* are portrayed as less educated and more aggressive than their Hindu counterparts. Film critics and scholars have agreed that Ratnam's intention was to present a secular view of the riots in order to criticize the communalism in both communities, but he failed in this aim, and his movie finally presents the Muslim community as the more aggressive. Although both fathers in the film are presented as ultraconservative, Shaila Bano's father, Bashir, a brickmaker by profession, is shown brandishing sharp-edged implements—knives, swords, cleavers. Ratnam relies on a stereotypical representation of Muslims as regressive, backward, and violent. Shekhar's father, Narayan, in contrast, seems to have a proclivity only for verbal anger and noticeably backs down in certain exchanges when faced with Bashir's aggressions (Vasudevan 1996, 48). Ravi Vasudevan further adds, "One of the features of the public debate on the film has been the degree to which Muslim aggression has been visibly more evident, especially through the film's tendency to fetishize their image in the white filigreed cap. I believe that this [view regarding a greater emphasis on Muslim aggression] is largely correct, and indicates the premise of a mainstream, and therefore necessarily Hindu secularist narrative dealing with cultural difference as its central theme: in its reconstruction of events, and its bid for inter-communal reconciliation, the narrative cannot neutralise constructions of the Muslim as other" (1996, 49). Shekhar, the neoliberal Hindu Indian—not a practicing Hindu, secular yet symbolizing Hinduism owing to his Hindu ancestry—initiates the love story. Love stories form a necessary ingredient in a Bollywood cinema that has undergone changes since its humble beginnings in Raj Kapoor's films. Regarding the love story genre in Indian cinema in general and Mani Ratnam's revision of the genre in *Bombay* in particular, Lalitha Gopalan notes,

> The love story has always been a successful genre in Indian cinema. In fact, one can look at the different preoccupations of the love story over the last fifty years that press us to consider them as allegories of the nation-state: inter-caste, inter-religious, inter-class stories and so on.
>
> Besides being available for political and social commentary, the genre has allowed its formula-ridden stories to be masterpieces in the hands of a competent director—the most obvious example being Raj Kapoor, whose experiments with the genre have set the standard for future generations of directors. However, the love story too has undergone considerable revision, at times so extreme that we often watch marriage and wedding tales rather than pursue stories of star-crossed lovers. In this cycle of revision, Mani Ratnam emerges as the master of the political love story. . . . [I]n *Bombay*—simultaneously produced in Tamil and Hindi—the durability of a Hindu–Muslim marital union is tested against the backdrop of communal riots in the city. (2003, 372)

In interweaving the love story with a marriage and family plot, Ratnam's film offers audiences an allegory of the nation-state at a significant moment in the nation's history. Thus, *Bombay* through its interreligious marriage aims to foster brotherhood between the two warring communities, but it is a brotherhood that highlights Hindu hegemony and plays by the rules of that hegemony.

Although Shekhar falls in love with the burka-clad Shaila Bano, her burka symbolizes both concealment (or obstacle) and revealment (or opportunity) (Alvi 2013, 177). Ratnam does not waste time in introducing our main couple. The first scene of the movie shows Shekhar returning to his hometown in coastal Malumpur after completing his studies in Bombay. The scene is set near a body of water in the monsoon season. The weather serves as an important force that helps Shekhar get a glimpse of Shaila as her burka's face covering flutters in the wind, making it possible for Shekhar to steal the first glance. Once Shekhar's attraction is communicated to the audience, the following scene creates the occasion for the two to meet for the second time. In the song "Kehna hi kya," Shaila Bano is divested of the veil to complete Shekhar's seduction. The actual burka is replaced by filigreed screens, curtains, and dupatta, concealing and revealing Shaila Bano as a prized trophy to be won. This scene is set in a Muslim wedding being held in a building replete with the arched interiors and long columns redolent of Islamic architecture. Quite surprisingly, the burka-clad Shaila of the previous scene is depicted in this scene without a burka but resplendent in a *sharara*, another type of Muslim attire that is worn on festive occasions. Unlike in the previous scene, in this scene she has jewelry and makeup that add to her beauty, confirming Shekhar's attraction.

Ratnam's direction, at this point, sees it expedient to make Shaila perform a dance to celebrate her friend's wedding. The song-and-dance routine is an integral part of any Bombay movie, so Ratnam finds an occasion early on in *Bombay* to incorporate one for the audience's pleasure. Not only does Ratnam make Shaila dance in the wedding, but he also fails to incorporate even one common reality of orthodox Indian Muslim families in the scene. In addition to requiring that their girls wear the burka when they step outside to further their education, such families do not allow their girls to dance publicly in mixed gatherings. Many such wedding celebrations segregate the genders, and dancing, in fact, is not encouraged in conservative Muslim households in India. Ratnam does borrow some commonly held stereotypes of the Muslims to weave his tale, but this scene displays his willingness to forgo common knowledge of the community in order to appeal to the largely Hindu film audiences, for whom dancing forms an important part of culture. In the song sequence "Kehna hi kya," Shaila's dance shares some semblance with the *mujra*, which Ira Bhaskar and Richard Allen point out was an integral part of the Bombay cinema subgenre known as the "Muslim courtesan film." Although *Bombay* does not fall within the category of the Muslim courtesan film, Ratnam borrows from the genre to present the Muslim female protagonist as a courtesan performing the *mujra* in this scene. A *mujra* was traditionally a performance by a courtesan in the courts of erstwhile Muslim kings of precolonial India. Bhaskar and Allen define the *mujra* as

> a formal musical and dance performance by a courtesan for a gathering, and may be performed in court, at a *mehfil* or at a *kotha*. Both in films with a historical setting and in films located in the contemporary period, the mujra features in non-Courtesan genres as well, where the figure of the courtesan and the way she inhabits the dance underscore both the allure and the threat posed by the public women. It is important to note that neither the Courtesan film nor the performance idiom of the mujra is essentially an Islamicate form. However, because of the valorization of the courtly culture of Muslim elites in Bombay cinema, both in the imagination of nineteenth-century Lucknow, the figure and space of the courtesan came to be dominated by an Islamicate imagination. (2009, 19)

Bhaskar and Allen claim that Bombay cinema has relied heavily on Islamicate culture to render the cinema experience more enjoyable for its Hindu-majority audience through the pomp and glory of the Mughal court. Borrowing the elements from Islamicate culture enables an overall entertaining cinematic experience, hence its significance in Bollywood. The *mujra* is central to this genre, and it often incorporates the rescue narrative in its depiction. The extremely attractive and talented courtesan figure is trapped in her position, and the film focuses on her rescue. The hero is usually the rescuer and fulfills her dream of having a respectable life as wife and mother. Ratnam's movie tends to follow that narrative partially in its depiction of Shaila Bano. Although Shaila Bano is not a courtesan, Ratnam borrows some representational features of the courtesan in his depiction of her, simultaneously presenting her as a woman in purdah and as a woman capable of performing publicly in the song "Kehna hi kya" (and in the consummation song "Humma humma" later in the narrative). Her dance performance at her friend's wedding, then, is replete with most of the elements that define a *mujra* and highlights the contradictions depicted as residing within her. According to Bhaskar and Allen, the *mujra* "becomes the locus for the dramatization of key issues of conflict in the narrative" of courtesan films (2009, 19–20). In *Bombay*, too, the conflict is dramatized in this scene as the unveiled Muslim woman in public poses a threat to unmarried Hindu men. The Muslim household symbolizes a prison as the burka is forced upon her by the Muslim patriarch, and so "in her performance to the appreciative and sometimes lascivious male gaze, we often perceive a defiant resistance on her part to the conditions of her existence" (Bhaskar and Allen 2009, 8). Of course, this representation confirms Bombay cinema's sexist representations of most female actors, but it is especially noteworthy that a Muslim woman, apparently from a conservative family, is depicted in this manner. The depiction tends to perpetuate the notion that the Muslim woman who is under Muslim patriarchal control and who is protected from the male gaze by the burka in reality yearns for male attention and the male gaze.

The burka makes Shaila Bano's female body an object of both Shekhar's desire and his frustration as it is simultaneously glamorized and condemned within a few frames of the movie. Mani Ratnam's representation of the burka, evident in his willful veiling and unveiling of Shaila Bano in the film, aims to inform audiences of the inherent contradictions that reside in Muslim women who wear it. The veil's presence in the movie symbolizes the power of Muslim patriarchy over female Muslim bodies, but its removal by the neoliberal director reinforces the same male power that it seems to implicate, thus rendering the Muslim woman voiceless over what seems to be a struggle between men to control her body. From the outset, the veil is conveniently used to reveal the right amount of Shaila Bano's beauty to make the city dweller fall in love with her. In another scene, Shekhar gets easily frustrated at the veil's ability to erase all distinction between beauty and nonbeauty, an ability that can be potentially liberating for its wearer. The director uses the veil as a mise-en-scène in the first half of the movie. A little later, the burka, like a patriarchal shackle, stops her from meeting Shekhar and needs to be voluntarily surrendered in one of the most controversial scenes of the movie. This scene also foreshadows her later elopement and final abandonment of the patriarchal vestment as it proves inadequate for her new home in Mumbai. Unlike Hossain's story "Sultana's Dream," where the female protagonist wishes to be unveiled to seek knowledge and improve her lot in life, in *Bombay* the unveiling of the female protagonist merely swaps one patriarchal overlord for another.

Similarly, in the song "Humma humma" Ratnam juxtaposes the married couple's lovemaking with a scene in which prostitutes solicit customers in the neighboring brothel. The main dancer in the brothel appears veiled at the beginning, and gradually her veil is removed to disclose a scantily clad prostitute, thus leaving it to the audience's imagination to make the connection between the two women in the song sequence. By creating this montage, Ratnam draws out the negative associations of veiling. The veiling of the prostitute corresponds with Shaila Bano's veiling at the beginning of the movie, and just as the prostitute unveils during the dance performance, Shaila eventually surrenders not just the veil for Shekhar but all her clothes. This song conflates veiling negatively with prostitution and the threat a prostitute poses for society in general. As the practice of selling sexual favors in exchange for money is considered immoral in society, the prostitute who indulges in such acts needs to hide her face out of shame. Her unveiling is presented as an act of immorality. Similarly, Shaila's veiling and unveiling seem to equate her with the public women who veil to hide themselves from society. It only makes sense at this point in the movie that Shaila completely gives up the practice of veiling to assimilate in Bombay.

Marriage to Shekhar affords Shaila Bano the opportunity to be part of the neoliberal city, Bombay, which also serves as the headquarters of the Shiv Sena, the Hindu right-wing party. Ratnam's portrayal of the burka was the cause of much rancor in Muslim communities across India. Muslim religious leaders rallied against the scene where Shaila runs to meet Shekhar at a dilapidated fort, and her burka gets caught, quite symbolically, on an anchor, implying that to secure her future she needs to give up the veil. Ratnam portrays the burka as an impediment to a better future for her. Vasudevan, among many other critics of the film, has contended that Ratnam's film "polices [religious and cultural] practices" of the Muslims living in India by presenting veiling as detrimental to the union of lovers and metaphorically detrimental to Hindu–Muslim amity in the country (2010, 94). Thus, Ratnam's and India's Hindu codes view the Muslim heroine and the veil she wears as a detriment and thus presents Hindu prejudices under the guise of neoliberalism. This neoliberal attempt at depicting interfaith marriage then actually becomes a commercial project of attempting to assimilate Muslim women even while simultaneously equating them with prostitutes who veil themselves in the daytime out of shame. The movie also typecasts Muslim men as more violent and aggressive. Hence, in presenting Shaila's decision to voluntarily give up the practice of veiling as her choice, the movie seems to appeal to audiences as a celebration of Muslim women's freedom from Muslim patriarchal control, which in reality is a subtle form of coercion the neoliberal director wields over the character of the Muslim woman and the Muslim community at large. While Begum Rokeya Shakhawat Hossain's dream of Muslim women's freedom and education in "Sultana's Dream" continues to inspire women, Ratnam's film *Bombay*, on the contrary, merely subjugates them in society.

Works Cited

Akhtar, Javed. 1995. "Lifting the Veil: A Daring Film Explores Hindu–Muslim Relations." *Asiaweek* 21, no. 33: 30–31.

Alvi, Anjum. 2013. "Concealment and Revealment: The Muslim Veil in Context." *Current Anthropology* 54, no. 2: 177–99.

Amer, Sahar. 2014. *What Is Veiling?* Chapel Hill: Univ. of North Carolina Press.

Bano, Ferdous. 2017. "Educational Status of Muslim Women in India: An Overview." *Journal of Humanities and Social Science* 22, no. 6: 10–13.

Bhaskar, Ira, and Richard Allen. 2009. *Islamicate Cultures of Bombay Cinema.* Tamil Nadu, India: Tulika.

Cairns, D. L. 2001. "Anger and the Veil in Ancient Greek Culture." *Greece & Rome* 48, no. 1: 18–32.

Ehrenfels, Baron Omar Rolf. 1941. *Mother-Right in India*. Oxford: Oxford Univ. Press.

Fedorak, Shirley A. 2007. *Anthropology Matters*. 3rd ed. Toronto: Univ. of Toronto Press.

———. 2014. *Global Issues: A Cross-Cultural Perspective*. Toronto: Univ. of Toronto Press.

Gearhart, Sally Miller. 1984. "Future Visions: Today's Politics: Feminist Utopias in Review." In *Women in Search of Utopia: Mavericks and Mythmakers*, edited by Ruby Rohrlich and Elaine Hoffman Baruch, 296–309. New York: Schocken.

Gopalan, Lalitha. 2003. "Indian Cinema." In *An Introduction to Film Studies*, 3rd ed., edited by Jill Nelmes, 359–88. New York: Routledge.

Harvey, David. 2005. *A Brief History of Neoliberalism*. Oxford: Oxford Univ. Press.

Hossain, Begum Rokeya Shakhawat. [1905] 2017. "Sultana's Dream." A Celebration of Women Writers, edited by Mary Mark Ockerbloom, Jan. 6. Univ. of Pennsylvania Digital Library. At htttp://digital.library.upenn.edu/women/sultana/dream/dream.html.

Islam, Maidul. 2007. "Imagining Indian Muslims: Looking through the Lens of Bollywood Cinema." *Indian Journal of Human Development* 1, no. 2: 403–22. At https://www.researchgate.net/publication/318571104_Imagining_Indian_Muslims_Looking_Through_the_Lens_of_Bollywood_Cinema.

Jahan, Roushan. 1993. "'Sultana's Dream': Purdah Reversed." In *"Sultana's Dream: A Feminist Utopia" and Selections from "The Secluded Ones,"* edited and translated by Roushan Jahan, with an afterword by Hanna Papanek, 1–6. New York: Feminist Press at the City Univ. of New York.

Jeffrey, Arthur. 1959. "Family in Islam." In *Family: Its Functions and Destiny*, edited by Ruth Nanda Anshen, 39–72. New York: Harper.

Mallhi, Angie. 2006. "The Illusion of Secularism: Mani Ratnam's *Bombay* and the Consolidation of Hindu Hegemony." At https://www.uvic.ca/research/centres/capi/assets/docs/studentessays/Mallhi_Illusion_of_Secularism.pdf.

Mirowski, Philip. 2013. *Never Let a Serious Crisis Go to Waste: How Neoliberalism Survived the Financial Meltdown*. London: Verso.

Patte, Daniel. 2004. *Global Bible Commentary*. Nashville, TN: Abingdon Press.

Rai, Saritha. 1995. "Mani Ratnam's *Bombay* Views Communalism through Eyes of Common Man." *India Today,* Jan. 15. At https://www.indiatoday.in /magazine/society-the-arts/films/story/19950115-mani-ratnams-bombay -views-communalism-through-eyes-of-common-man-806701-1995-01-15.

Roye, Susmita. 2009. "'Sultana's Dream' vs. Rokeya's Reality: A Study of One of the 'Pioneering' Feminist Science Fictions." *Kunapipi* 31, no. 2: 135–46. At ro.uow.edu.au/kunapipi/vol31/iss2/12.

Siddiqua, Ayesha. 2016. "Explorations into Feminist Utopias: A Critical Study of Kashibai Kanitkar's *The Palanquin Tassel,* Rokeya Sakhawat Hossein's 'Sultana's Dream,' and Charlotte Perkins Gilman's *Herland." Research Journal of English Language and Literature* 4, no. 2 (Apr.–June): 394–402. At http:// www.rjelal.com/4.2.16B/394-402%20AYESHA%20SIDDIQUA.pdf.

Singhji, Virbhadra. 1994. "Purdah." In *The Rajputs of Saurashtra,* 199–207. Bombay: Popular Prakashan.

Vasudevan, Ravi. 1996. "Bombay and Its Public." *Journal of Arts and Ideas,* no. 29 (Jan.): 45–66. At https://dsal.uchicago.edu/books/artsandideas/pager.html ?objectid=HN681.S597_29_058.gif.

———. 2010. "Geographies of the Cinematic Public: Notes on Regional, National, and Global Histories of Indian Cinema." *Journal of the Moving Image,* no. 9 (Dec. 2010): 94–117.

Part 5   Toward a New Discourse

Who Creates the Image?

8

The Enduring Controversy over Veiling in Western Europe Today

Sahar Amer and Martine Antle

> We've been very perturbed about the veil. To see those very young
> girls veiled. . . . Perhaps the veil once said something religious, but
> now it's a sign of oppression. It isn't God; it's men who want it.
> —Anne Hidalgo, deputy mayor of Paris in 2004
> and presidential candidate in 2022

Veiling for Muslims living in western Europe today remains challenging and poses the question of individual freedom to practice one's religion. If you are a Muslim woman living in France, for example, and you wear any sort of face covering or veil, you have no chance of being employed in the public sphere or government sector. If you are a schoolgirl in France, and you decide to adopt the hijab, you must essentially forfeit your education. And if perchance you happen to be a Muslim who wears the niqab, the face-covering veil, you are not allowed to be in public spaces and so must remain at home or in any other private space. The polysemy of the conflicting discourses on veiling explains why an increasing number of veiled and nonveiled Muslim women are refusing to discuss their religious beliefs in public. Even though the veil is a visible sign of their identity and their faith, they continue to assert that veiling is a choice and that this practice should not be limited to the private sphere.

In this chapter, we challenge simplistic understandings of veiling practices, as in France and Europe, and demonstrate that only a multidisciplinary and intersectional approach to veiling can help us better understand Muslim women's veiling practices.

The intensification of the debates on the hijab and the niqab in Europe today reflect both global fears of radical Islamism specifically and Islamophobia more generally. These anxieties are mounting in the aftermath of the Arab Spring and the elections in various Arab Muslim-majority societies that have catapulted conservative Muslim groups into power. The perceived "problem" of Muslim women and of veiling is still alive and well in France and Europe and reveals the extent to which this sartorial practice remains little understood by politicians and the general public alike.

The veiling debates in Europe are also convenient strategies that divert public attention from pressing national socioeconomic challenges. Today, legislating Muslim women's dress has become a convenient platform for many European politicians when they want to show a tough stance in international matters and national-security issues. Not surprisingly, the obsession with veiling coincides regularly with elections and appears on platforms aiming to garner votes by stigmatizing the Muslim population and espousing a hard line toward immigration.

In 2004, the now internationally known French law banned "all ostentatious religious signs" from French public schools. To place the veiling debate in its context, it is important to recall that its onset in France dates to October 3, 1989, when three Muslim middle-school girls (two Moroccans and one Algerian) refused to remove their headscarves in school and were subsequently expelled by the principal, Ernest Chénière, for contravening the principle of secularism (laïcité) and the neutrality of the public school.

As a result, since 2004 Muslim girls have been forced to choose between removing their hijab and continuing to attend public school or holding onto the hijab and leaving school. This is a choice that many Muslim girls still face as early as twelve or thirteen years of age. Moreover, a few years later, in 2010, France became the second European country, after Belgium, to ban the burka (the full-body and face covering that conceals the eyes behind a mesh fabric) and the niqab (the full-body and face covering that leaves a narrow opening for the eyes) from all public spaces, including streets, shops, malls, parks, and sports arenas. And more recently, in response to the terrorist attacks in Paris in November 2015, Switzerland voted against the wearing of the burka in public spaces and instituted a 10,000 euro (approximately US$10,830) fine for those who do not respect the law.

Under the French law, women found wearing a burka or a niqab can be forced by police to uncover their faces, are required to attend citizenship classes, and risk a 175 euro ($190) fine. Men charged with forcing a woman to wear a burka or niqab are more heavily punished: one year in prison as well as a fine of up to 35,000 euros ($38,000). Both penalties are doubled if the "victim" is a minor. In addition, the law makes it possible to revoke the French citizenship of any person accused of wearing the niqab or of forcing a woman to wear it.

The precedent set by both Belgium and France to ban the burka from public spaces has thus created a domino effect and encouraged other European countries—including Spain, the Netherlands, Austria, Italy, and, most recently, Switzerland—to consider whether they too ought to ban the Islamic face veil from government buildings, hospitals, and even public transportation.

Just as there is no European consensus on how to legislate veiling, there is also no consensus within individual European countries on how to deal with the niqab. The divided views of British politicians on the topic offer an illuminating example. In 2006 British prime minister Tony Blair called the Muslim face veil a "mark of separation" and explained that it made the community feel uncomfortable. His views echoed those of Jack Straw, the former leader of the House of Commons, who refused to meet with women in the niqab because their face veils, he said, prevented communication and set their wearers visibly apart. In contrast, Education Secretary Ed Balls issued a statement in 2010 that a law opposing the wearing of the niqab would be contrary to the British tradition of embracing cultural differences.

Driving the debates among European policy makers on how and whether to legislate veiling reveals a general discomfort among the European population toward women who wear headscarves and face veils, especially when confronted with this practice in public spaces. As a matter of fact, the first statistics gathered on Islamophobia in France in 2012 revealed that 84.73 percent of all Islamophobic incidents in France are made against women who wear a veil. This statistic demonstrates how Muslim women's freedom to practice their religion is being used as a shield to hide other political issues. Along the same lines, the Pew Global Project Attitudes poll released in July 2010 showed that majorities in Germany (71 percent), Britain (62 percent), and Spain (59 percent) would support a ban on face veils in their own countries. Most Americans (65 percent), in contrast, indicated they would oppose such a ban (Pew Global Attitude Project 2010).

Reading newspapers and witnessing and following the rapid movement calling for legislation to ban veils throughout Europe, one might easily be misled into thinking that Europe is experiencing an unprecedented increase in the population of veiled Muslim women or that Muslims in Europe are becoming more radicalized and adopting more conservative practices. The perception of threat is, of course, intensified after each terrorist attack.

Yet as official numbers in the press and government agencies illustrate and confirm, of the half-million Muslims living in Belgium, only thirty women wear the niqab. In the Netherlands, which has a Muslim population of one million, it is thought that no more than four hundred women wear niqabs. In France, approximately three hundred women wore the niqab when the debate over face veils began. Today, that number is estimated to be less than one thousand out of a Muslim population considered to be around six million. Given these statistics, it is difficult to believe that legislation banning the burka is motivated solely by the number of cases involved. It is important to open up the debate and situate it in its context, which is the pressing question of the integration of Muslims in France and the constant pressures created by the different waves of immigration.

It is imperative to understand the expanding legislation on Muslim women's dress in Europe and the implications such laws have for Muslims living in European societies today. The constant obsession with veiling matters in Europe is categorically (or indeed) disproportionate if we take into account the number of women wearing the hijab or niqab.

Undoubtedly, the debates and legislation on the Islamic veil in Europe intersect with larger social, economic, and political issues of national and international concern.

France, as the country with the largest and oldest community of Muslim immigrants in western Europe, offers an excellent case study. Today the Muslim population in France is estimated to be in the range of six million people, constituting about 7–8 percent of the population and establishing Islam as the second-largest religion after Christianity.

Debates about veiling in France started more than twenty years ago, well before any other European countries began focusing on their Muslim populations. In this respect, France occupies the role of unofficial European policy setter for issues concerning Islam. Debates and policies on veiling initiated by the French government have direct and indirect implications for other European nations. By understanding what happens in France, the attitudes toward Muslims there, and the various laws adopted toward Muslim veiling, we can better comprehend the various positions espoused by other countries in the European Union as well as the stakes behind mounting European legislation against veiling.[1]

At the international level, the development of the French law also coincided with rising domestic concerns and international crises that centered on Islam. The late 1980s represented the height of a French economic recession with steadily increasing unemployment rates. Such domestic woes fueled the far-right movement and its then-rising leader, Jean-Marie Le Pen. His party gained votes during the legislative elections of 1986 by developing a strong anti-immigration platform and blaming the Arab population for France's high unemployment rate. The headscarf became the symbol of this "threatening" Arab–Muslim community, the scapegoat for France's social and economic problems. More recently, Marine Le Pen, Jean-Marie's daughter, has advocated similar policies.

The previously mentioned incident involving the three girls expelled from their school also coincided with a number of international threats

1. These laws are available on the pedagogical website we have created on veiling: "ReOrienting the Veil," at http://veil.unc.edu, Center for European Studies, University of North Carolina at Chapel Hill.

involving Islam that the media covered excessively. In 1989 Ayatollah Ruhollah Khomeini of Iran issued his fatwa against Salman Rushdie for authoring *The Satanic Verses*; the first Palestinian Intifada against the Israeli occupation was underway (1987–93); and the Islamic Front in Algeria rose to power.

Islamist militancy preoccupied the international community and was heavily covered in the French news. French politicians from all parties, like the population at large, felt anxious about what the rise in Islamist militancy abroad might mean for France's Muslim population at home. It may not be an exaggeration to guess that behind the expulsion of the three middle-school girls in headscarves, France was hiding a perceived fear of an Islamist takeover. In the process, young Muslim girls became scapegoats for both social and political agendas.

Many French politicians and public figures considered Islamic scarves a symbol of oppression, a sign that immigrants at home could not be integrated, that Islamists abroad threatened Muslims everywhere. They assumed a correlation among Iranian chadors, fatwas, book burnings, Palestinians' violence, assassinations in Algeria, and scarf-wearing girls in French middle schools.

Even though the girls themselves attributed their veiling to an effort to distinguish themselves from their parents, who did not veil, and to claim their own identity as young Muslims born or living in France, their views and their act of donning the veil were dismissed as adolescent mischief yet also ironically painted as a threat.

The veil debate evolved and seemed to lose its tenor until it took center stage again in 2003 for its use in photographs affixed to French national identity papers. Minister of Interior Nicolas Sarkozy insisted that veiled Muslim women should be required to pose bareheaded on these documents. For him, women's resistance to be photographed without a scarf represented their failure to embrace the French Republic and to assimilate with its central principles. A refusal to shed the headscarf was a sign that they could not be French citizens.

For many Muslims in France, the debate about photographs on national identification cards was reminiscent of a similar issue in the 1960s, when under French colonization Algerian women had been forced to shed their hijab and be photographed. It invoked the specter of French imperialism all over again. Not surprisingly, the debate on photographs on national identity cards revived the debate on headscarves in French schools.

In July 2003 President Jacques Chirac established the Independent Commission of Reflection on the Application of the Principle of Laicism in the Republic, later known simply as the Stasi Commission, to resolve the question of veiling in addition to broader questions of religious and social diversity in the French Republic. He charged prominent government officials, educators, and scholars with formulating a policy that would both clarify and strengthen the 1905 law on the separation of church and state (better known as the law of secularism). The Stasi Commission was responsible for presenting a revised law of *laïcité* (secularism) just in time for the centennial celebration of the law.

After months of meetings, deliberations, and interviews, the commission offered dozens of recommendations to reaffirm the sacred principle of *laïcité*. From them, Chirac selected the one recommendation related to clothing, which was signed into law on March 15, 2004, and implemented the following academic year in schools.

The sole recommendation that Chirac deemed effective (and presumably sufficient) to strengthen French *laïcité* and to ensure the unity and universality of the French Republic was the outlawing of all conspicuous signs of religious affiliation in public schools. He heralded this new legislation as a means of erasing gender differences and of halting the threat of radical Islam on French soil.

Lest it appear discriminatory and risk being overturned by the European Court of Human Rights, the text of the law was written in language that did not refer to any religion specifically. Its stated goal was to prohibit *all* ostentatious religious signs in public primary and secondary schools that displayed religious affiliation.

Officially, this law prohibited *all* ostentatious signs of religion, including large crosses, Islamic headscarves, Jewish skullcaps, and Sikh turbans, while still permitting smaller adornments, such as a small cross, a Star of David, a hand of Fatima, or a small Quran. Despite the breadth of the law, politicians, the media, and the general public understood the law to be targeting the hijab and Muslims specifically. In fact, in popular discourse and in much of the media, the law quickly came to be known and referred to as the "law against the Muslim headscarf."

Since the passage of this law in 2004, Muslim girls living in France have been prohibited from wearing headscarves in any French public school, whether inside the Hexagon or in its overseas territories. Only those areas with a significant Muslim population (such as the island of Mayotte in the Comoros, northwest of Madagascar) have been allowed to continue to make some accommodations for their veiled Muslim pupils (e.g., replacing the veil with a bandana or a "small" scarf).

Despite opposition from a number of politicians, activists, and feminists from all sides of the political spectrum, the law was voted in 276 to 20 in the French Parliament and supported by roughly 75 percent of the French population surveyed in polls. As in 1989, the decreased tolerance for headscarves can be attributed in part to international events taking place shortly before the law went into effect.

In the early summer of 2004, two French reporters were held hostage in Iraq by a group demanding that France repeal its law against headscarves. This hostage crisis became a watershed event. Not only did it revive French anxieties about the implications of international Islamic terrorism for its citizens, but it also unified those in favor of the law and those who had challenged it. During the hostage crisis, claiming one's right to wear the veil became tantamount to supporting the terrorists.

When the law was implemented in the 2004–5 academic year, some students challenged it by coming to school wearing wigs or with shaved heads. About 550 difficult cases were ultimately successfully resolved though the dialogue period recommended by politicians prior to expulsion. Ultimately, only forty-seven students were expelled for refusing to abide by the law (see Bowen 2008, 65–97).

Although most of the French saw these numbers as a positive step toward the reaffirmation of secularism and the integration of the Muslim population, French Muslims viewed them as just another sign of how unwelcoming France was to its Muslim first-, second-, and even third-generation citizens. These generations continued to claim their right to be both French and Muslim.

The law banning the niqab in France in 2010 unquestionably represents an escalation and a hardening of the French governmental position toward its Muslim population. In fact, while in 2004 the law had been vehemently debated, a surprising consensus existed around the prohibition in 2010. The ban on the niqab proved extremely popular with politicians, passing the Senate with 246 votes to 1 (and 100 abstentions coming mainly from left-leaning politicians); 7 out of every 10 French people also approved it.

These approval rates were particularly astonishing, considering that the number of women actually wearing the burqa or niqab in France remained surprisingly quite small. One central reason why so many people approved the ban may have been that new arguments about national security and women's rights surfaced to justify the proposed law. Members of Parliament in both Belgium and France argued that in the context of heightened global security alerts and the war on terror, it was imperative for police to be able to check people's identities. A person behind a face mask could be anyone posing a potential threat to the public and the nation. Thus, they argued, it was imperative for reasons of national security to ban face masks in all forms. The more convincing arguments, though, concerned women's rights, French notions of gender equality viewed as universally desirable, and what was seen as the oppressive nature of Islam and patriarchy.

At the time, French politicians lumped together veiling, polygamy, genital mutilation, and forced marriages, claiming that Muslim women, veiled ones especially, were subjected to all of these practices. The French secular republic presented itself as the savior of Muslim girls and women from the coercion they presumably suffered at the hands of their fathers, brothers, and husbands. For Muslims in France, this rhetoric uncomfortably recalled nineteenth-century civilizing missions and early Hollywood orientalist films.

The French government borrowed feminist arguments from a newly established and influential Arab and Muslim feminist organization called Ni putes ni soumises (Neither Whores nor Submissive Women). Because the organization was headed by a French-born Algerian woman, Fadela

Amara, many French people assumed that the views it espoused were "authentic" and that the association spoke for a majority of Arab and Muslim women.

Yet the group was by no means an advocacy group speaking on behalf of Arab Muslim women in France. In reality, the French government financed the group's operations, and the French National Assembly and the media recognized the group only because it supported official French doctrine. Members of Ni putes ni soumises did not embrace a feminism that supported women's freedom of choice to practice one's religion and the right to veil. Rather, also in the name of feminism, they claimed that the hijab was an unambiguous symbol of totalitarianism and fundamentalism and urged the French government to support Muslim women's emancipation. From their perspective, any tolerance for headscarves equaled cultural relativism, an unacceptable position concerning women's rights.

Strongly supporting the ban of the burka, President Nicolas Sarkozy advanced the same arguments put forth by Ni putes ni soumises. He, too, invoked a concern for Muslim women and for what he considered their utter subordination symbolized by the burka.

The rhetoric of the 2010 law banning the burka is disturbing for many reasons, not least because it perpetuates the much-cherished myth of a "clash of civilizations." This myth constructs a stark opposition between the ideals of the secular French Republic and a faith-based, misguided Islam, between liberated French women and oppressed veiled Muslim women, between the specter of a violent, radical Islam and a more enlightened, peaceful, and gender-equal Europe. It normalizes through repetition various stereotypes and presents them as accurate portrayals of reality. Ultimately, it lulls people into believing that these myths and stereotypes are true and withdraws them from public scrutiny.

The rhetoric surrounding the ban on veiling and the wearing of the burka in public is also alarming because it has the very real potential of stigmatizing the entire French (and European) Muslim community for the practices of a few. Some politicians have been careful to point out that wearing a veil is different from wearing a niqab because the former is believed to be a religious obligation, while the latter is open to debate. However, most politicians today, including former president François Hollande and members of his team, continue to insist and reaffirm that women who wear the hijab or the burka are manipulated by radical forms of Islam or by their male relatives and are not wearing them of their own volition.

Scholars such as John Bowen (2008) and Joan Wallach Scott (2007), among others, have taken a different stand on the question and have argued that French policies against Muslim headscarves and burkas serve primarily to divert the public's attention from the real social and economic problems that plague French society, problems particularly virulent in the suburbs, where the majority of Muslim immigrants live. In *The Politics of the Veil* (2007), Scott indeed contends that the French government has in fact used the ban on headscarves to reinforce its limitation of immigration and its national identity and to keep Muslims on the margins of French society.

The same scholars have also challenged the work of Ni putes ni soumises as an ideological state apparatus that supports an Islamophobic right-wing political discourse, underlining that this association's and the media's focus on acts of violence in the suburbs obscures the challenges that women everywhere continue to face, regardless of religious background.

Equally important, academic scholarship has produced data indicating that the majority of burka-clad women in France are *not* immigrants, as they have often been referred to by the media and politicians, but are in fact French citizens, many of French descent who converted to Islam.[2] Not only are many of these women French by birth, but they were also educated in France and are fully integrated into the French Republic. These women are *voluntarily* adopting the burka; they are not forced by anyone. They often adopt that practice after their conversion to Islam and marriage to a Muslim.

By perpetuating the long-cherished myth that Islam constitutes a national and global threat, the veil debates in France and elsewhere divert

---

2. See, for instance, Marie-Christine Tabet's editorial published on June 20, 2017, and transmitted on the radio (Europe 1). According to her investigation, there are about 367 women wearing the burka in France and that 75 percent of them are French-born converts. Half of these women are younger than thirty and recently married to converted or migrant men (Tabet 2017).

attention from the real economic and social problems facing countries today. Rather than shed light on the situation of Muslims in Europe, challenge radical Islam, or champion the rights of Muslim women, the growing legislation against Islamic veiling instead exposes European anxieties about issues of "race," integration, unemployment, social violence, and the crisis of a common currency. It highlights a true identity crisis running through Europe concerning the future of the European Union, the Eurozone, and the multiple cultural identities within them. It is also important to note that all official political discourses on veiling in Europe focus solely on Western practices and largely ignore how other non-Western nations approach and deal with this practice. Within Europe, other approaches to veiling do not attract great public attention. Savvy French luxury fashion designers, for instance, have been especially entrepreneurial in ensuring that they maintain and augment the 30 percent of the luxury hijab and niqab business they have in the Persian/Arab Gulf (Al-Qasimi 2010). This is of course ironic because France is also the country that banned both the hijab and the niqab in public schools and public spaces on its own soil. The hijab and niqab may pose challenges to French secularism, as French policymakers like to repeat, but they certainly also represent an economic boon that the French are keen to preserve. A recent Barbie exhibit at the Musée des arts décoratifs in Paris in 2016 also introduced a veiled Barbie that speaks eloquently for the marketing of Barbie on a global scale. In the artistic world, several artists are also working on the polemics surrounding the veil. For example, Boushra Almutawakel from Yemen deconstructs the discourses on veiling in her photography and denounces Western stereotypes—for example, in her series of women covered in burkas made of the tricolor French flag.

Another important aspect of contemporary Islam that challenges Islamophobic discourses on veiling is the rising voice of progressive Muslims in Europe and beyond, a voice yet still too often muffled. Progressive Muslims are male and female Muslim academics, activists, theologians, lawyers, intellectuals, and individuals from diverse backgrounds and occupations (including artists) who challenge perceived notions about Islam and dismantle the assumption that Islam is incompatible with progressive ideals or human rights values. They confront Euro-American stereotypes and escalating Islamophobia and dispute the restrictive interpretations of Islamic texts that conservative Islamic authorities have produced over time.

We can only hope that their voices will be heard because still today at the heart of all the political and public debates about how Muslim women dress in France is the notion that the Muslim veil poses a threat to French *laïcité* (secularism), much more so than the Jewish kippah, for instance, as the recent debates in France make evident. In Europe and the United States, there is a widespread belief that the Muslim veil jeopardizes both Western liberal values and women's fundamental rights. In the minds of many, a veiled Muslim woman is by definition *not* a free woman. She is one whose basic human rights have been violated and whose freedom must be protected. After all, the European Court for Human Rights itself upheld not long ago (July 1, 2014) France's law banning the burka and the niqab and thus annulled the argument presented by the complainants that a burka ban was in fact contrary to six articles of the European Convention of Human Rights.

It is thus imperative to continue challenging contradictory discourses on veiling practices, and, as we have demonstrated here, only a multidisciplinary and intersectional approach to veiling can help us better understand Muslim women's veiling practices and truly uphold their human and civil rights to choose what to wear. Such an approach has allowed us not to engage in misleading binary oppositions: veiling as oppression or veiling as liberation, condemnation or celebration, feminism and gender equality or subordination and coercion, Euro-American women's liberation versus Muslim women's submission, Euro-American democracies against Muslim authoritarian regimes, civilizational advances against religious dogmas, secularism against fanaticism, East versus West.

Works Cited

Bowen, John. 2008. *Why the French Don't Like Headscarves: Islam, the State and Public Space*. Princeton, NJ: Princeton Univ. Press.

Pew Global Attitudes Project. 2010. *Spring Survey Topline Results Survey of 22 Nations*. Washington, DC: Pew Research Center. At https://www.pewresearch .org/wp-content/uploads/sites/2/2010/06/Pew-Global-Attitudes-Spring-2010 -Report-Topline.pdf.

Al-Qasimi, Noor. 2010. "Immodest Modesty: Accommodating Dissent and the 'Abaya-as-Fashion in the Arab Gulf States." *Journal of Middle East Women's Studies* 6, no. 1: 46–74.

Scott, Joan Wallach. 2007. *The Politics of the Veil*. Princeton, NJ: Princeton Univ. Press.

Tabet, Marie-Christine. 2017. "Deux mille femmes portent le voile integrale." *Le journal du dimanche*, June 20. Formerly at https://www.lejdd.fr/Societe /Religion/Deux-mille-femmes-portent-le-voile-integrale-157784-3238187. No longer available.

9

The Veil in Public Space

Critique, Participation, Citizenship

Joseph L. V. Donica

The Muslim feminist poet Mohja Kahf writes in the poem "My Body Is Not Your Battle Ground," "My hair will not bring progress and clean water . . . nor will it save us from our attackers" (qtd. in Layton 2010, 105). In Kahf's poem, the concern over wearing or not wearing the veil is a reductive focus in the discussion of the role of the veil in public life. The veil's role in public life has come under well-documented attacks about what exactly it symbolizes and who should be able to wear it. Broader, public conceptions of the veil have been quite reductive in associating the veil with repression, lack of agency, and, of course, extremism. Elizabeth Bucar addresses these assumptions head on when she calls out "many Westerners'" assumptions that the veil "is the ultimate sign of Muslim women's oppression" (2012, 1). Bucar points out that there is far too much focus on the veil itself rather than on the overall idea of modesty, of which the veil is just one part. Because of the widespread controversies over the veil, that piece of clothing is my focus here. As Bucar rightly notes, in what she calls "pious fashion" (Bucar 2017) the choice of clothing for Muslim women is a nexus of "norms and ideas related to self-identity, moral authority, and consumption" (2012, 2). In my examination of the veil in its various iterations in contemporary Western art, these three functions constantly emerge as evidence that the veil can never be just one thing and, in Bucar's words, is not a 'problem' that needs to be solved" (2012, 2).

As one of the most controversial public symbols, the veil has the ability to offer a critique in public space that other symbols do not. Perhaps this is the reason there has been a rise in its use in public art and renewed controversy and confusion over what the veil means in particular contexts and over the implications of those meanings for the women underneath those veils. In this chapter, I first address the role of the veil in public life in the United States and Europe and how it has conflicted with certain norms yet maintains an ability to critique US domestic and foreign policy, a policy that has defined Muslims as a category of dangerous individuals. I then ask what role the veil might play in offering not only a political critique but also a form of representation for Muslim women that allows space for difference and for leading autonomous lives. To address these points, I turn to the role that the veil has played in public art, specifically street art.

I first look to the #DamnILookGood project, in which two New York artists, Saks Afridi and Qinza Najm, stand on New York City streets in higher-income neighborhoods with hijabs for women to try on and then take a selfie of themselves. Afridi, a Pakistani-born resident of New York, has done most of his work in the corporate sector for brands such as Mercedes-Benz and the fast-food chain White Castle but has exhibited at well-known institutions such as the Tate Modern and Miami Art Basel (Afridi n.d.). Naim is a Pakistani American artist with a PhD in psychology (Qinza Najm n.d.). #DamnILookGood, according to the artists, is an attempt to increase representation of the veil in public spaces because, as they say, "here in New York, it is very brave for someone to wear it out in public" (Warren 2014). Next, I examine the role of the controversial French artist Princess Hijab (PH), who offers an entirely new way of looking at the veil in public life. In major US and European cities, she paints hijabs on public advertisements in subways and in other public places. Her stated goal is countering the "visual capitalist terrorism" of advertisements in public by using the veil to completely change the conversation about the norms that advertisements push on the public (bitch media 2009). I also look to the Italian artist BR1, the well-known street artist Bansky, and the influential former street artist Shepard Fairey, all of whom have deployed representations of the veil as social commentary about its role in public life. Finally, I consider an exhibition held in 2009 at the Austrian Cultural Forum in New York titled *The Seen and the Hidden: (Dis)covering the Veil*. The exhibition featured both Western and Middle Eastern artists and, according to the curators, was "a trans-cultural exploration of the numerous approaches to the ideas that surround both the literal and metaphorical meaning of the veil. It includes works in a variety of media such as video, installation, photography, and painting" (Austrian Cultural Forum 2009). It must be noted that none of these representations of the veil is free of the imposition of Western norms and expectations on the veil. Certainly, the #DamnILookGood project is problematic in encouraging non-Muslim women to "give the hijab a try," as if it is nothing more than a different shade of eye shadow (Warren 2014). However, these artists and performers offer perspectives that address how the veiled Muslim woman represents a controversial and questioning position in the construction of the nation-state. So I begin with the concepts of critique, participation, and citizenship to think through this construction. In looking at the role of the veil in public art, we can begin to see how the veil can simultaneously critique certain norms while also offering Muslim women some form of representation that allows for a discussion of their autonomy (not to mention their safety) and what citizenship has come to mean in the United States and Europe.

Why the Veil Is Such a Powerful Symbol

The veil can and does have the potential to offer a critique of social structures that are confining and often illegal according to US and European law. Some recent contemporary events are most likely at the forefront of your mind as you read through this collection. Refer to this volume's introduction for several examples of the veil's significance. The recent attacks on veiled women as well as the spike in crimes targeting Muslim Americans and those perceived as Muslim since 2016 seem shocking to some and predictable to others who remember similar attacks in the United States after September 11, 2001 (9/11). It is too easy to look just at Donald Trump's rhetoric during his presidential campaign in 2016 as the sole cause of the veil's renewed symbolic power, and his statements are largely to blame for the increased violence against veiled women (Jenkins 2016; *NBC News* 2016a, 2016b; Sakuma 2016). The veil held powerful symbolism long before Trump came on the scene. He simply played to the already-existing meanings that the culture had attached to the veil. The veil's powerful symbolism comes not only from its visibility but also from anxieties over gender, religion, histories of colonialism, geopolitics, and who gets to control the meaning of public symbols.

The history of the veil's symbolism predates 9/11 by centuries. But many assume the veil took on its contemporary symbolism just in the past two decades. Yvonne Haddad breaks down how that symbolic role has played out in Western art for centuries. American media, according to Haddad, could not fathom why in the wake of the liberation women in Kabul "would not cast off their burkas and celebrate" (2007, 255). These attitudes, though, are part of a much longer Western obsession with the veiled Muslim woman's role in public space. Here is a summary of Haddad's analysis of the veiled woman's role in Western art and literature:

Pre-eighteenth century: "The personification of desire"
Eighteenth century: Prisoner of "the harem"
Nineteenth century: "Bizarre and sexually perverse"
Twentieth century: "[A] sad subject[] suffering under illiteracy, polygamy, and seclusion"
After 9/11: "In need of rescue by the West." (2007, 258–62)

The art during the colonial period is replete with images of veiled women and eroticized harems. There was a fascination with the veiled women of the Maghreb, the northwestern corner of Africa, and many artists spent time in Morocco painting actual scenes as well as embellishing scenes of women bathing and reclining nude and in groups. One of the more outrageous uses of the veiled woman during colonization was a series of postcards of Algerian women veiled and often photographed behind bars looking as if they are trapped. These postcards were distributed back in France during the period it occupied Algeria. Sarah Sentilles (2017) argues in the *New Yorker* that the images were used to justify the occupation because these women were clearly in need of rescue. Lalla Essaydi is just one artist among many who plays with the colonial depictions of veiled women. Essaydi claims that the divide between public and private and how these spheres are managed in her home country, Morocco, "helps explain how Arab women became sexualized under a Western gaze" (Errazzouki 2012).

Maysan Haydar points out just how strange it is that veiled Muslim women get singled out for their clothing choices, considering that "the practice of covering hair and body is a choice for many women—and it is not specific to Islam. All the monotheistic religions . . . advocate modesty in dress." "Ironically," she argues, the population that spends millions on beauty products, plastic surgery, and self-help guides is the same one that takes pity on me for being so 'helpless' and 'oppressed'" (2004, 264). This focus on beauty takes a darker edge in Yasmin Jiwani's interpretation of how veiled Afghan women are treated in Canada. The differentiation, Jiwani argues, between "Afghan women living in Canada in contrast to their counterparts in Afghanistan" emphasizes "victimhood, and Canadian benevolence" based on "an imagined community that is reflective of Canada as a white, settler colony" (2009, 728).

Gillian Whitlock emphasizes the import of the depiction of the veil when she argues that people go to war because of the images that they see. She then highlights the different uses of the veil on three mass-market books, all published after 9/11: *My Forbidden Face, Mayada: Daughter of Iraq,* and *Reading* Lolita *in Tehran.* All three of the books share the implied argument that the veil is an instrument of Muslim women's subjugation. Whitlock notices the interesting differences on the covers: *My Forbidden Face* depicts "the totally effaced women in the burka"; *Mayada* uses "the more erotic sexualized gaze over the chador"; and *Reading* depicts in "dark monotone . . . the young veiled women in chador on the sepia cover" (2010, 45). Such is the adaptability of imagery of the veil, but it matters what the veil is being used to communicate. Of great concern to Falguni Sheth ([2009] 2022) is the comparison of the hijab to the sari: the former is vilified, whereas the latter is glorified.

The long history of the representation of the veil certainly came into play after 9/11. Haddad claims that the veil became "a public affirmation of trust in the American system that guarantees freedom of religion and speech." It also symbolized "anti-colonial solidarity and resistance to efforts to eradicate Islam in an American environment that is increasingly seen as anti-Islamic" (2007, 254, 253). The role of the veil in the United States differs from its role in Europe in some essential ways. There are no bans on wearing the veil in public spaces in the United States, and the veil has seen increasing usage in public space there. For example, Muslim women in the military are now allowed to wear the hijab (Myers 2017), and the New York Police Department allows Muslim women officers to gain a religious exemption to the uniform code so that they can wear a hijab. Haddad points out, "The process of re-Islamization has been accelerated in the aftermath of 9/11, as an increasing number of adolescents and young adults (daughters of immigrant Muslims) are assuming a public Islamic identity by wearing the hijab." So the veil has for "American-born Muslim women" become a symbol of solidarity and resistance to efforts to "eradicate the religion of Islam" (2007, 253, 254). An often-cited criticism of the veil, primarily from the left, is that it represents the subjugation of Muslim women as women. But Haddad's work suggests that the veil is anything but simply a symbol of repression—especially since 9/11.

Critique, Participation, Citizenship

The veil's controversial nature is not confined just to those looking from the outside in. Yasmin Alibhai-Brown notes the divisive function of the veil among Muslim women themselves. She says, "For some it is a way of placating their families, so they can follow their dreams, go into higher education and the job market. Others consider the choice a political statement of power. I have met women in full niqab who are spirited and independent, so I am not suggesting this is simple oppression" (2014, xiii). Of course, to see any form of veiling as simply oppression is a reductive view of a very complex practice with deep historical, religious, political, and gendered meanings. The veil has become so controversial that writers such as Alibhai-Brown argue that it should be repudiated:

> For many of us secular Muslims, hijabs concede that parts of a woman's body need to be hidden, that females are a sexual menace or in perpetual danger from males, all of whom are presumed to be predatory. Scarves are so widely worn now that we who object must compromise. At least some women are making them colorful and beautiful. Many of them would not be allowed into post-school education and employment if they showed their hair. . . . It is time to reclaim the right to openly talk about these garments and assert that it is not ungodly, imperialist,

"Islamophobic" or self-loathsome to make the case against various forms of the veil. (2014, 91–92)

She goes on to explain her eighteen reasons for encouraging British Muslim women to refuse the veil. The five that stand out most are (1) resistance to Wahabism; (2) the veil is unfair to men in casting them as animalistic; (3) sisterhood ("Women who make the decision to veil are colluding with gender repression across the Muslim world"); (4) self-segregation damages society; and (5) autonomy and individuality ("This is a society," she says, "that prizes autonomy and gender parity. The burkha offends both of these principles") (2014, 93–104). I take issue with most of the reasons on this list but mostly with the idea that the veil should not offend the sensibilities of Western societies. Muslims in the United States and Europe for the past decade and a half have been resigned to keeping their critiques of US culture under their breath. A sort of uberpatriotism has arisen in Muslim and Arab enclaves in the United States. Dearborn, Michigan, according to many commentators, is the most patriotic city in the country—because it has to be. The veil also takes on an ethical dimension in public space that is both a part of its religious ethic and separate from it. It is a part of that ethic in that the veil is an acknowledgment of one's belief and a signal to others about how one wants to be identified and treated. It is separate from that religious ethic in that it has been so politicized as to be divorced from religious belief in many of its representations.

Elizabeth Bucar examines veiling from the perspective of social ethics, or how, she says, "society should act as a whole." She suggests four functions that the veil is defined to have for society—that is, how many who follow Islam view the veil's functions in public. First, it can "prevent men from being constantly aroused and distracted by women's sexuality in public places." Second, it can encourage "economic productivity by visually segregating women and men so they are not distracted by their sexual desires." Third, some think "the veil allows Muslim women to more fully participate in society by protecting their modesty" and physical safety. Finally, "the veil is seen as a way to prevent social immorality by guarding women from external, especially Western, immoral influences" (2012, 22–23).

These functions are problematic because they reduce the veil to an object that serves only to cover women's sexuality and assumes all men are uncontrollable in their desires—not to mention because of the heteronormative assumptions underlying all of them. The veil has far more productive functions in public spaces. What Bucar does point out, like Haddad, is that the social meaning of the veil is weighed down by the history of colonization and that "Muslim experiences with specific, concrete, and historical events, including non-Muslim critiques of veiling, influenced the contemporary meaning of the veil" (2012, 69). The potential the veil has for offering a critique of gendered, racial, and religious norms in the United States and Europe has only just begun to come into its own. This emerging movement is not attempting to revive the veil as cool, hip, trendy, and cosmopolitan. The latter phenomenon, as in the Mipsterz (Muslim Hipsters) movement, is a different incarnation of the veil's potential. In 2016 Dolce & Gabbana launched a line of hijabs and abayas, and H&M used its first veiled model (Milligan 2016). Such attempts to make the hijab hip can cut both ways. They can remove some of the personal animosity Muslim women might face on an everyday level—always a goal to work toward. Kayla Wheeler, whose work focuses on Black Muslim fashion, takes issue with those who "have the notion that Islam and fashion are incompatible." Further, her focus on Muslim women's wear as fashion emphasizes the "creativity and diverse definitions of Islamic modesty" (Wheeler 2019). Yet attempts to make religious clothing fashionable also have the potential to pull the rug out from under the veil's ability to critique the norms from which the animosity toward it emanates. There are both a political problem and a representative problem in attempts to make the veil cool or hip or just as Western as skinny jeans. These attempts remove not only the veil's religious significance but also its ability to have any critique on US conceptions of what it means to be a citizen and to participate in public life. If the veil is seen as something political or something that critiques white, Western norms, is there something that normalizing the veil does to elide that critique? The answer is not as complex as the question—in theory at least.

A similar discussion occurred among those in queer theory as LGBTQ+ people began to be accepted in the political mainstream. Although normalizing gay marriage certainly helps individuals overcome systemic inequality, many argued that being queer should remain outside the mainstream to offer a critique of the system. The veil has the same dual role in that it still retains the ability to critique the assumptions made in the United States and Europe about Muslim women's bodies and their role in public space. In asking the question about the implications of queer theory for the study of religion, Claudia Schippert states, "In the US American context, over the past ten years, Islam has been portrayed as un-American or even anti-American. This is of course not an entirely new development, as the liberal heritage of toleration always was complicatedly connected to the toleration of religiously defined others by the Christian dominant state. Nonetheless, the vilification of Islam has become especially important to analyze from a queer theoretical perspective in its imbrications with homonormative and homonational strategies" (2011, 66). Schippert's point, which is mine as well, is that the politicization of the veil by non-Muslims is motivated by a very troubling urge toward the homogenization of US culture. However, simply critiquing those norms that are the basis for the discrimination and violence against veiled women does not move us toward greater (or safer) participation of Muslim women in public life. Participation, according to Cindy Patton, is understood "in a broader sense . . . as positive actions by an individual toward their society. . . . As democracies evolved, the idea of a coalition, and thus the idea of participation, also changed to include shared historical and social experience" ([2005] 2013, 252).

Perhaps the best category of analysis we have for talking about the veil in public space at this moment in US history is the shifting concept of citizenship. Citizenship, always an ambiguous category in fields other than the law, seems a more contested category than ever for Muslims. Lauren Berlant's analysis of citizenship in the context of American culture is crucial to examine here. She says, "Citizenship's legal architecture manifests itself and is continually reshaped in the space of transactions between intimates and strangers. . . . But the promise of U.S. citizenship to deliver sovereignty to all of its citizens has always been practiced unevenly, in contradiction with most understandings of democratic ideals" (2007, 41). That distribution of citizenship is always in flux, and the veiled woman is a constant reminder of its unevenness. For better or worse, the veil is the most potent symbol and critique of what citizenship means and what it is coming to mean in the United States. The use of the veil as a primary subject by artists and performers in the spaces of contemporary cities is an indication that its role in defining citizenship and the visual culture of citizenship is growing.

Exploiting the Veil's Symbolism: #DamnILookGood

The New York artists Saks Afridi and Qinza Najm attempt to make the veil less divisive through their project #DamnILookGood, but symbolism happens in the execution, not in the intention, when it comes to certain powerful objects. Afridi describes the project as "a performance art piece . . . where a woman wearing full hijab, takes selfies of herself with others and posts them online using the hashtag #DamnILookGood" (Afridi n.d.). The first woman to wear the hijab is part of the performance, but the women surrounding her often try on the hijab. "The piece," Afridi claims, "is about tolerance, liberation and challenging perceptions of women who wear hijab by choice" (Afridi n.d.). Thomas Gorton, who covered the debut of the project at the Dumbo Arts Festival in Brooklyn, had the following to say about it:

> You can't talk about the hijab in the Western world without somebody butting in to yell about how it's repressive or anti-feminist. But Pakistani-American artists Qinza Najm and Saks Afridi are putting a whole new spin on how people look at the veil—by inviting women to take selfies of themselves in full hijab or niqab and instagramming them under the hashtag #DamnILookGood.
>
> The New York–based pair debuted the project in Brooklyn at the Dumbo Arts Festival in September and were adamant that the hijab is often misrepresented by cultures that don't understand it—chiefly, that many people don't grasp that wearing the veil can be an active expression of choice, personal style and beauty. (2014)

Although #DamnILookGood is certainly a move in the right direction of positioning the veil within a space where it can serve as a symbol of autonomy for Muslim women, it removes the critical power of the veil by normalizing it. And it most certainly raises the problem of the appropriation of a symbol of personal, religious belief. Other artists use the veil in more nuanced ways that achieve—for reasons to be explained in the next section—a balance between emphasizing the autonomy of veiled women in public and allowing the veil to retain its potent critique of Western norms.

The Veil as Capitalist Critique: NiqaBitch and Princess Hijab

Two of the artists who play with the veil's dual role in public space to great impact are NiqaBitch and Princess Hijab (PH). Both are street artists (NiqaBitch is most likely a sort of art collective) who work primarily in France and are anonymous. Anonymity is an obvious, necessary theme among street artists. Their art is produced illegally most of the time. Some street artists, such as Bansky and Shephard Farey, have gained such global renown that they are commissioned to do work. Bansky has retained much of his anonymity, but NiqaBitch and PH take it to the next level. In 2010, just after the French Senate voted to prohibit public face veiling, NiqaBitch released the video *NiqaBitch Shakes Paris* (viewable on YouTube under this title), in which two women walk around the streets of Paris with very short shorts, stiletto heels, and full niqab. Mostly non-Muslim men stop to take pictures, seemingly delighted at the contrast between the veiled woman who is covered from the waist up and sexualized from the waist down. NiqaBitch explains why they used the contrast between the niqab and the short pants: "To wear a simple burqa would have been too easy. Se we asked ourselves, how would the authorities react when faced with women wearing a burqa and mini-shorts? We were not looking to attack or insult the image of fundamentalist Muslims—to each their own—rather, we wanted to challenge the elected officials of the republic who voted for a law that is believed to be largely unconstitutional" (NiqaBitch 2010). Annelis Moors interprets European bans on veiling as an interpretation of Muslim women that assumes they are "simultaneously . . . victims of gender subordination and . . . provocative agents challenging mainstream . . . norms." The power of the NiqaBitch video, according to Moors, is that it creates contending publics. She argues that the video "does not simply invite preexisting publics to air their opinions and feelings but produces virtual publics that contest each other." It is, she continues, "the combination of face veiling with hot pants that engenders the positive, amused reactions among the public; women who combine a face veil with full-length and loose outfits are often the target of far more negative forms of attention." So "NiqaBitch produces contesting publics that are fragmented along multiple lines of differentiation including politics, gender, and aesthetic style" (2011, 129, 132, 133). NiqaBitch certainly uses the symbolism of the veil as a critique of the French state within public space, and they definitely play with the multiple meanings of the veil. But PH goes further with her artistic project of simultaneously allowing the veil to critique while opening up a space for veiled women to have a voice in the public spaces they inhabit—spaces that are often dangerous for them. NiqaBitch causes us to rethink not only how public space can be used to critique how individuals respond to symbols but also the concept of public space generally. Princess Hijab, perhaps the most infamous artist repurposing public space for comments on the veil, reworks an essential public utility for her purposes.

Anyone using the subway in a major city in the United States or Europe daily is familiar with the ubiquitous advertisements lining the walls, hawking fashion brands, films, shows, and other products of those cities. Those ads are in many ways a collective representation of what those cities are about and a finger on the pulse of their culture. In short, they are symbols. The symbolic importance of those ads is not lost on PH. She is best known for her work that transforms those ubiquitous subway advertisements by painting black burkas, hijabs, and niqabs on images of individuals in them. She works very quickly and calls her process "hijabizing" the subjects of her art. She is also the most well-known street artist playing with ideas of the veil in public space. Like NiqaBitch, PH produces contesting publics. She tries to remain as anonymous as possible (which has led to rumors that PH is actually a persona that Bansky takes on), but she has given a couple of interviews with news outlets. In an interview by the *Independent* in 2011, PH stated, "I apprehend advertising in order to transform it. The image of women in publicity is a feature, a fetishist representation of the moment" (Battersby 2011). Moors interprets PH's work as "a form of iconoclasm, an attempt to deface in order to neutralize the power of the image." She says, "The message of Princess Hijab is not sartorial liberalism [as NiqaBitch's is], but a critique of the visual terrorism of market liberalism, or, as she stated in her 2008 manifesto[,] . . . L'Oreal [has] . . . killed her little by little" (2011, 134). The critique of the economic system that relegates veiled women to the realm of the exotic is certainly central to PH's art. However, PH's use of the veil as a critique goes further than just filing a visual complaint about market capitalism.

In another interview on the site Good in 2009, she drove home the point she is trying to make with the representations of the veil she imposes on ads: "Guerilla art is innocent and criminal, ancient and dystopian, intimate and political. I chose the veil because it does what art should do: It challenges, it frightens, and it reimagines" (Wooster Collective 2009). That reimagining is central to how PH disrupts the idea of a strict divide between public and private. In one of her most well-known acts of hijabizing, where she has painted full burqas on underwear-clad male models in a Dolce & Gabbana ad, she causes a reconsideration of what is usually accepted in public. Chiseled men in underwear on a subway is something we in the West take for granted as something appropriate in a public space. But once those men are veiled, the narrative is changed. Many consider the veiled models as inappropriate for public display. When the almost-naked men are made more traditionally modest, they actually become unfit, in some interpretations, for public viewing.

PH uses the veiled woman, she says, "as a challenge." PH is not trying to speak for these women. She states emphatically, "If veiled women want to make a point, they'd do it. If feminists want to do something they're capable of doing it on their own" (Chrisafis 2010). The importance of PH's work is that, as she says, she shows "the veil has many hidden meanings, it can be as profane as it is sacred, consumerist and sanctimonious. From Arabic Gothicism to the condition of man. The interpretations are numerous and of course it carries great symbolism on race, sexuality, and real and imagined geography" (Chrisafis 2010). So PH's primary use of the veil is as a critique of capitalist culture and how that culture enforces unnatural divides between public and private. This idea goes back to my original argument that the veiled woman in liberal democracies represents a truly questioning figure, one of the most radical, perhaps, and PH understands the power that the veil has in public space. Critique is a powerful role that a symbol can take on, and PH is at the forefront of exploring what the veil can accomplish in public space. I turn briefly to three other iterations of the veil before concluding with one of the more contentious, recent uses of the veil in public space by a well-known street artist.

The Everyday Veil: BR1 and Banksy

BR1, short for Bruno, is an Italian artist whose street art is inspired by images from "Arabic magazines that often represent prominent people of the Muslim world" (Morgan 2010). He produces his images in his studio and pastes them onto public walls in US and European cities. His focus is on "veiled women in daily-life situations" (Morgan 2010). He claims his style is social and that all art should convey a social message. His wall art also depicts the diversity of veils and regions in which women veil: the "North African veil, the Afghan burqa, and the Iranian Chador" (Morgan 2010). In an interview in 2013, he explained that he is "particularly interested in the image of the veil and all that it represents, particularly the clash of cultures. I'm intrigued by paradoxes" (Street Art NYC 2013). In emphasizing the everydayness of the veil, he seems to say that the only thing that separates Western women from Middle Eastern and North African women is the veil. Such a distinction is reductive but also challenges any potential critique the veil might have. This "women are the same everywhere" is a major perspective taken by progressives in the United States and a narrative that runs through many cultural forms in the country. A similar interpretation of the veil is put forward in, as ridiculous as it seems to mention, the second *Sex and the City* movie (Michael Patrick King, 2010), in which the main characters discover a group of women in Abu Dhabi who when they unveil are seen to be dressed just like the four American women and who are reading the same Suzanne Sommers book.

Other male artists have tackled the veil as a subject in their art somewhat more successfully. Arguably the most well-known street artist of the past twenty years (Basquiat held claim to that title before then), Banksy, has also used the veil in his art. He is famous for his anonymity but also his extreme success in the art world. In a commissioned show at the Bristol Museum of Art in 2009 titled *Banksy versus Bristol Museum*, the artist "transformed" the museum "into a menagerie of Unnatural History—fishfingers swimming in a gold-fish bowl, hot-dogs and chicken nuggets"

(Bristol Museum and Art Gallery 2009). More than one hundred of his new works were shown at the museum. Among them was one piece titled *How Do You Like Your Eggs?*, which depicts a woman with only her eyes showing through a full burka. She is holding a spatula and a pan with an egg in it. However, over her loose-fitting clothing she is wearing an apron that has the image of a woman's body clothed only in risqué lingerie. The tension in this image is that the woman is clearly modest, but there is a depiction of immodesty on the apron. It is typical of Banksy to play with the viewer's expectations. Like BR1, Banksy also depicts the veiled woman in an everyday activity, but, as Rex Rafanelli argues, he "brings up ideas that this piece is a clash of societies, pitting Muslim standards against western society. Is Banksy, growing up in Britain's Western and more liberal society trying to make a statement regarding the oppression of Muslim women, that they should be able to dress however they please, hence the lingerie apron?" (2011). Rafanelli suggests, though, that the meaning is a bit more obvious in that eggs are a common breakfast food around the world, so a commonality is being signaled here as well as a difference. In this way, Banksy is doing something very similar to BR1 in that he seems to say, "Look, they are just like us." However, there are three things happening in the Bansky piece that make it a more complex representation than BR1's. All three are part of Bansky's always-present irony that frustrates expectation.

First, the assumed oppression of the woman is not her veil but the fact that she is making eggs for the viewers and asking how they want them done. Second, he is making plain the often-prurient desire of viewers to sexualize the veiled woman. Third, he is playing a joke on the viewer, but whether the joke is being delivered by him by objectifying the woman or by the woman herself is unclear. Pointing out the effect of difference in culture has always been a part of Bansky's work, and he understands the power that the veil has to signal difference. In one of his new pieces on a wall in Paris, he takes aim at the Syrian refugee crisis by painting his version of the famous depiction of Napoleon sitting on a gallant horse. In his rendering, Napoleon is fully veiled—thus, the rumors that Bansky and PH are the same person persist. Difference is important to understand if we are ever to have a productively complex understanding of the veil's role in public space. Other exhibits have tackled the very idea of diversity innate in the meanings of the veil. The veil is not just one material item but a set of ideas and practices and assumptions that need to be understood within their own contexts. Many of those assumptions also need to be challenged.

The Veil Is about Us: *(Dis)Covering the Veil*

That complexity was on display in 2009 in an exhibit at the Austrian Cultural Forum in New York titled *The Seen and the Hidden: (Dis)Covering the Veil.* The exhibit featured art by artists from the United States, Europe, and the Middle East. The official statement about the exhibit encapsulates the primary problem I have communicated in this chapter:

> The woman's veil is one of the most symbolically charged pieces of clothing in contemporary dress; it is provocative even when it is not revealing. With roots in the three Abrahamic religions, it has become one of the most visible icons of contemporary Islam. The donning of the veil conveys conflicting ideas of faith, sexuality and public life and thus raises a host of questions and tensions between religion and identity. It represents an important cultural tradition yet remains a very personal practice for women as well as a symbol communicated to others within the public sphere. (Austrian Cultural Forum 2009)

That tension between the private act of veiling and how it is nevertheless such a publicly symbolic act with transcultural implications is on display in such pieces as Negar Ahkami's set of Matryoshka dolls (Russian nesting dolls) with veiled women depicted on them and Ayad Akhadi's mixed-media collages in which the veil on women is replaced with Arabic newspapers.

The director of the forum, Andreas Stadler, said in his statement on the exhibition, "We humans have more potential for hatred when the object of our hatred is part of our own identity." But he also addressed overcoming that hatred by referencing Julia Kristeva's feminist analysis of hatred of the foreign: "Not until we recognize that the foreign is always a part of ourselves can we overcome negative repulsion responses and constructively encounter the foreign as part of the ego." He continued, "On the whole, then, a piece of clothing that has a shared tradition going back thousands of years has become a visual symbol of a cultural conflict between the imagined perceptions of the Islamic and Judeo-Christian worlds, of the 'Orient' and the 'Occident'" (Stadler 2009). As off-putting as Stadler's title to his statement is, "It's Not about the Veil, It's about Us," he is right. The symbolism attached to the veil has been developed by non-Muslim women for the purposes of non-Muslim women. And the implications of that symbolism reach a fever pitch when anxieties about many other things are stoked.

The Veil as Contested Politics of Hope: Shepard Fairey

In the past two years, the veil has become both a symbol of resistance and a symbol of the last line of defense for civil rights. Several times over the past two decades, Muslim communities throughout the United States and Europe have come under increased scrutiny by local officials. The media coverage of this scrutiny and existing Islamophobia in some quarters led to attacks against Muslim women but also gave the veil a more nuanced meaning in public space. Shepard Fairey picked up on this nuance and began using the veil in his work.

Fairey made his name with his brand of clothing OBEY (about which there is now a documentary by Hulu) as well as the now-famous Obama HOPE poster. His status as a street artist is questionable, but his work has become powerfully symbolic for two movements now. Fairey's image of Munira Ahmed in an American flag veil was used extensively at the Women's March the day after the presidential inauguration in 2017. Ahmed was at the time a thirty-two-year-old freelancer from Queens who quickly became the face of the opposition to the Trump administration and its quick attempt to ban Muslims from entering the United States. But she also became a symbol for what it means to be a woman, a feminist, and a progressive in this country. In speaking about her American-flag-veiled image being used as a symbol of resistance, Ahmed said, "It's about saying, 'I am American just as you are'" (qtd. in Helmore 2017). After returning to New York from the march in Washington, she said, "I am American and I am Muslim, and I am very proud of both" (qtd. in Helmore 2017). Fairey's image of Ahmed was part of a series of images commissioned by the Amplifier Foundation to highlight people with the most to lose under the Trump administration. "The intent was to make a strong statement," Adhami, the photographer for the project, said (qtd. in Helmore 2017).

There is a critique, however, of Fairey's use of the American flag for the veil. The Iranian activist Hoda Katebi offers a scathing review of Fairey's image in her article "Please Keep Your American Flags off My Hijab" (2017):

> How are we able to hold up signs of Muslim women wearing the American flag and chant slogans of supposed solidarity while drones carrying the same flag killed our Muslim family in Yemen at the exact same moment and we said nothing? While the women's march was making history, the new administration was already repeating it. Did you even know that Trump has already administered drone strikes? Of course not. You were not supposed to know. You are only supposed to hold our silent faces wrapped in the cloth that has suffocated our voices. Anyway, it's more peaceful that way, isn't it? Next time you are thinking about sharing this image, pasting it on an old wall, saving it as your desktop background, or waving it above your head and pledging your solidarity: Know that if the only time you are comfortable uplifting a Muslim women is when her image has been crafted by a white man and is draped in the American flag, I cannot call you my ally.

What Katebi's critique emphasizes is the often-superficial representation of diversity in public space—a diversity for its own sake. She emphasizes that one cannot rally behind a hijab made with an extremely fraught symbol such as the American flag without having a conversation about the implicit contradiction in the combination of those two symbols. The veil is a complex symbol, and the veiled woman presents a controversial and questioning position in the construction of the nation-state in the West.

Since beginning this essay, I am finding it more useful and, troublingly, more necessary to confront the concept of rights, both civil and human, against that of cosmopolitanism—something the veil once symbolized in US cities. In the summer of 2017, a striking new ad appeared in the New York subway. A veiled woman with a determined look stands in the background with the following text in the foreground: "I should have the right to wear what my faith calls for without being called a threat." A banner at the bottom of the ad states, "You do have the right" (New York City Commission 2017). The banner was a public-service announcement from the

New York City Commission on Human Rights. At one time, the frequent appearance of veiled women on the subway without incident was a signal to the cosmopolitan values of a city long built on its dynamic diversity. Now that diversity is considered a liability—at least according to some corners of the nation. Just months before the commission's ad went up, a picture of a drag queen seated next to a veiled woman on a New York City subway train went viral on Twitter with the comment "this is the future that liberals want" (Crocker 2017). The veil persists as a contentious site of gender, sexual, religious, and state conflict. As French citizens headed to the polls in the spring of 2022 to elect their new president, the far-right candidate Marine Le Pen ran on a platform that included a complete ban of the veil in public—a position that went further than France's current ban on the veil in certain official spaces. From these and multiple other conflicts over the veil in the United States and Europe, we see the veil remains one of the most contentious objects ripe for, at best, projecting one's pet politics onto another and, at worst, attempting to restrain women's bodies through the language of "Islamism." As Irene Zempi and Neil Chakraborti argue, "The wearing of the veil has come under much media, political and public scrutiny in the UK and elsewhere in the West in a post-9/11 climate. Within this framework, the veil is seen as a marker of gender inequality. As such, veiled Muslim women are routinely perceived as oppressed and subjugated, whilst Islam is understood as a misogynist and patriarchal religion" (2014, 2). Clearly, concepts such as critique, participation, and citizenship are always in flux, but the veiled woman, now more than ever perhaps, seems to be at the center of what these concepts are coming to mean currently in our history.

Edward Said's warning disguised as a question in *Orientalism* (1978) regarding the human consequences of dividing human reality into separate cultures and traditions comes to a fine point when questions are raised about the significance of the veil in public space in the United States and Europe. His project in *Orientalism* was to uncover and lay out the history of the European tradition that designated anything from the Middle East and North Africa as foreign, exotic, and completely other. We can easily identify instances of overt othering of the veiled woman. Instances abound in American television series such as *Homeland* and *The Looming*

Tower. As pernicious as the representation of the veiled woman in those shows can be, it is, perhaps, not as dangerous as the more subtle othering that occurs elsewhere. Katebi points out one of those instances. And the tokenizing of the hijab for political purposes by non-Muslims gets to the heart of Mona Eltahawy's argument in *Headscarves and Hymens* (2015). Her argument goes, "They don't hate us because of our freedoms, as the tired post-9/11 American cliché had it. We have no freedoms because they hate us" (4). This feeling of being hated not only for one's identity but for a physical expression of that identity, the veil, makes that expression always-already contested. Princess Hijab's choice of the veil was simple in her telling: "I chose the veil because it does what art should do: It challenges, it frightens, and it reimagines" (qtd. in Ardizzoni 2017, 91). Making a contested symbol more so through engaging its meanings in public space can cut two ways: it can increase the process of othering, or it can give a more complex representation of that symbol and those whose lives depend on that representation. Let us hope that in the case of the veil, more representation means the latter.

Works Cited

Afridi, Saks. N.d. "#DAMNILOOKGOOD." Saks Afridi (website). At https://www.saksafridi.com/damn-i-look-good/.

Alibhai-Brown, Yasmin. 2014. *Refusing the Veil.* London: Biteback.

Ardizzoni, Michela. *Matrix Activism: Global Practices of Resistance.* London: Routledge, 2017.

Austrian Cultural Forum. 2009. "The Seen and the Hidden: (Dis)Covering the Veil." May 22. At https://www.acfny.org/media/press-images-texts/the-seen-and-the-hidden-discovering-the-veil/.

Battersby, Matilda. 2011. "Rare Interview with Urban Artist Princess Hijab." *Independent,* June 16. At https://www.independent.co.uk/arts-entertainment/art/features/rare-interview-with-urban-artist-princess-hijab-2297761.html.

Berlant, Lauren. 2007. "Citizenship." In *Keywords for American Cultural Studies,* edited by Bruce Burgett and Glenn Hendler, 37–42. New York: New York Univ. Press.

bitch media. 2009. "Veiled Threat." Nov. 16. At https://www.bitchmedia.org/article/veiled-threat.

Bristol Museum and Art Gallery. 2009. "*Banksy versus Bristol Museum.*" July 13. At https://www.bristolmuseums.org.uk/bristol-museum-and-art-gallery/whats-on/banksy-versus-bristol-museum/.

Bucar, Elizabeth. 2012. *The Islamic Veil: A Beginner's Guide.* Oxford: Oneworld.

————. 2017. *Pious Fashion: How Muslim Women Dress.* Cambridge, MA: Harvard Univ. Press.

Chrisafis, Angelique. 2010. "Cornered—Princess Hijab, Paris's Elusive Graffiti Artist." *Guardian*, Nov. 10. At https://www.theguardian.com/artanddesign/2010/nov/11/princess-hijab-paris-graffiti-artist.

Crocker, Lizzie. 2017. "How a Drag Queen Launched the 'This Is the Future Liberals Want' Meme." *Daily Beast*, Mar. 3. At https://www.thedailybeast.com/how-a-drag-queen-launched-the-this-is-the-future-liberals-want-meme.

Eltahawy, Mona. 2015. *Headscarves and Hymens: Why the Middle East Needs a Sexual Revolution.* New York: Macmillan.

Errazzouki, Samia. 2012. "Artistic Depictions of Arab Women: An Interview with Artist Lalla Essaydi." *Jadaliyya*, May 16. At https://www.jadaliyya.com/Details/25958/Artistic-Depictions-of-Arab-Women-An-Interview-with-Artist-Lalla-Essaydi.

Gorton, Thomas. 2014. "#DamnILookGood Invites Women to Snap Selfies in Hijab." *Dazed*, Oct. 17. At https://www.dazeddigital.com/artsandculture/article/22213/damnilookgood-invites-women-to-snap-selfies-in-hijab.

Haddad, Yvonne Yazbeck. 2007. "The Post-9/11 'Hijab' as Icon." *Sociology of Religion* 68, no. 3: 253–67.

Haydar, Maysan. 2004. "Veiled Intentions: Don't Judge a Muslim Girl by Her Covering." In *Body Outlaws: Rewriting the Rules of Beauty and Body Image*, edited by Ophira Edut, 258–64. Berkeley, CA: Seal.

Helmore, Edward. 2017. "Munira Ahmed: The Woman Who Became the Face of the Trump Resistance." *Guardian*, Jan. 23. At https://www.theguardian.com/us-news/2017/jan/23/womens-march-poster-munira-ahmed-shepard-fairey-interview.

Jenkins, Jack. 2016. "Just Two Days after Trump's Election, Reports of Anti-Islam Attacks Spike." Think Progress, Nov. 10. At https://thinkprogress.org/islamophobia-two-days-since-election-c4e20bc4c18c/.

Jiwani, Yasmin. 2009. "Helpless Maidens and Chivalrous Knights: Afghan Women in the Canadian Press." *University of Toronto Quarterly* 78, no. 2: 728–44.

Katebi, Hoda. 2017. "Please Keep Your American Flags off My Hijab." *Mondoweiss*, Jan. 25. At https://mondoweiss.net/2017/01/please-american-flags/.

Layton, Rebecca. 2010. *Arab-American and Muslim Writers*. New York: Chelsea House.

Milligan, Lauren. 2016. "Dolce & Gabbana Launches Abaya Collection." *British Vogue*, Jan. 5. At https://www.vogue.co.uk/article/dolce-and-gabbana-hijab-and-abaya-collection.

Moors, Annelis. 2011. "NiqaBitch and Princess Hijab: Niqab Activism, Satire, and Street Art." *Feminist Review*, no. 98: 128–35.

Morgan, Vincent. 2010. "The Veil and Street Art." *Fatcap*, Dec. 6. At https://www.fatcap.com/article/the-veil-and-street-art.html.

Myers, Meghann. 2017. "New Army Policy OKs Soldiers to Wear Hijabs, Turbans and Religious Beards." *Army Times*, Jan. 5. At https://www.armytimes.com/news/your-army/2017/01/05/new-army-policy-oks-soldiers-to-wear-hijabs-turbans-and-religious-beards/.

NBC News. 2016a. "Muslim Woman Harassed on Subway by 3 Men Who Call Her 'Terrorist,' Chant Trump's Name: NYPD." Dec. 2. At https://www.nbcnewyork.com/news/local/Muslim-Woman-Harassed-Subway-Called-Terrorist-Donald-Trump-Chant-404329066.html.

———. 2016b. "NYPD Releases Suspect Sketch after Attack on Muslim MTA Worker." Dec. 7. At https://www.nbcnewyork.com/news/local/police-nypd-release-suspect-sketch-terrorist-grand-central-muslim-assault-attack-mta-employee-405108116.html.

New York City Commission on Human Rights. N.d. "You Do Have the Right." At https://www1.nyc.gov/site/cchr/media/you-have-rights.page.

NiqaBitch. 2010. "Hot Pants and Niqabs: NiqaBitch Stroll through Paris." *MR Online*, Oct. 13. At https://mronline.org/2010/10/13/hot-pants-and-niqabs-niqabitch-stroll-through-paris/.

Patton, Cindy. [2005] 2013. "Participation." In *New Keywords: A Revised Vocabulary of Culture and Society*, edited by Tony Bennett, Lawrence Grossberg, and Meghan Morris, 252–54. Hoboken, NJ: Wiley.

Qinza Najm. N.d. "Bio." At https://www.qinzanajm.com/bio/index.html.

Rafanelli, Rex. 2011. *"How Do You Like Your Eggs?" Seeing Us Seeing Them*, May 15. At https://menandwomencnhs.blogspot.com/2011/05/how-do-you-like-your-eggs.html.

Said, Edward. 1978. *Orientalism*. New York: Vintage.

Sakuma, Amanda. 2016. "Muslim Women Wearing Hijabs Assaulted Just Hours after Trump Win." *NBC News*, Nov. 10. At https://www.nbcnews.com/politics

/2016-election/muslim-women-wearing-hijabs-assaulted-just-hours-after
-trump-win-n681936.

Schippert, Claudia. 2011. "Implications of Queer Theory for the Study of Religion and Gender: Entering the Third Decade." *Religion and Gender* 1, no. 1:
66–84.

Sentilles, Sarah. 2017. "Colonial Postcards and Women as Props for War-
Making." *New Yorker*, Oct. 5. At https://www.newyorker.com/books/second
-read/colonial-postcards-and-women-as-props-for-war-making.

Sheth, Falguni A. [2009] 2022. "The Hijab and the Sari: The Strange and the Sexy
between Colonialism and Global Capitalism." In *Unruly Women: Race, Colonialism, and the Hijab*, edited by Falguni A. Sheth, 83–103. Oxford: Oxford
Univ. Press.

Stadler, Andreas. 2009. "It's Not about the Veil, It's about Us." Austrian Cultural
Forum, May. At https://www.acfny.org/fileadmin/useruploads/fdfx_image
/Press_Texts/Veil/Director_Andreas_Stadler_-_Catalog_Text.pdf.

Street Art NYC. 2013. "Interview with BR1." May 14. At https://streetartnyc.org
/blog/2013/05/14/speaking-with-br1/.

Warren, Rossalyn. 2014. "Two Artists Are Taking Hijab Selfies and Declaring
'Damn, I Look Good.'" BuzzFeed News, Oct. 23. At https://www.buzzfeed
.com/rossalynwarrenmuslim-women-are-taking-selfies-in-their-hijabs-and
-declarin?utm_term=.asK1X1KAJ8#.qiX5z58X29.

Wheeler, Kayla. 2019. "The Black Muslim Female Fashion Trailblazers Who
Came before Model Halima Aden." *Conversation*, May 10. At https://the
conversation.com/the-black-muslim-female-fashion-trailblazers-who-came
-before-model-halima-aden-116499.

Whitlock, Gillian. 2010. "The Skin of the Burka: Recent Life Narratives from
Afghanistan." In *Soft Weapons: Autobiography in Transit*, edited by Gillian
Whitlock, 45–68. Chicago: Univ. of Chicago Press.

Wooster Collective. 2009. "Interview with Princess Hijab." Good, Nov. 26. At
https://www.good.is/articles/putting-on-the-veil.

Zempi, Irene, and Neil Chakraborti. 2014. *Islamophobia, Victimization and the
Veil*. New York: Springer.

Contributor Biographies

Index

Contributor Biographies

Umme Al-wazedi is professor of postcolonial literature in the Department of English and dean of humanities at Augustana College. Her research and teaching interests encompass postcolonial literature, British literature, (Muslim) women writers of South Asia and the South Asian diaspora, Muslim feminism, and postcolonial disability studies. She has published in *South Asian Review, South Asian History and Culture,* and *Women's Studies: An Interdisciplinary Journal.* She is also the author of several book chapters. Her coedited book (with Madhurima Chakraborty) *Postcolonial Urban Outcasts: City Margins in South Asian Literature* was published in 2016.

Sahar Amer teaches at the University of Sydney. She is a specialist in comparative, cross-cultural relations between Arab and Muslim societies and Western cultures (Europe, France especially, and the United States) from the Middle Ages to now. She has published extensively on gender and sexuality in Arabic and French literature, Franco-Arab and Arab American postcolonial identities, and Muslim women's veiling practices. The main conceptual paradigm underlying her research is the notion of "borders" (cultural, linguistic, historical, and geographic), not as elements of separation and division but rather as fluid spaces of cultural exchange, adaptation, and collaboration.

Martine Antle teaches at the University of Sydney. As a specialist in twentieth-century French theater, contemporary writing, photography, and painting, she has published extensively on race and gender in twentieth- and twenty-first–century French and Francophone literature. Her scholarship spans the political, social, and cultural revolutions that shaped modernity from the turn of the twentieth century to the present. In *Cultures du surréalisme* (2001), she stages surrealism as a cultural crossroads characterized by its internationalism and its cultural plurality.

Joseph L. V. Donica is professor of English at the City University of New York's Bronx Community College. He writes about American literature and collective memory and how we use that memory to move us through collective crises, such as Hurricane Katrina, economic disasters, and the climate emergency. He has written for UK-based *Screenshot Magazine* and reviews plays and performances for *Thinking Theater NYC*. Most recently, he gave a talk on his coedited collection at the LBGT Center in New York and a talk titled "American Literature before, during, and after the Climate Emergency" at the Umbrella Arts Center in Concord, Massachusetts, which was sponsored by the Thoreau Society. His coedited collection *Queer: Then and Now* (with Debanuj Dasgupta and Margot Weiss) was published in 2023. He received the Carl Bode Award for his research on vice districts in nineteenth-century New Orleans. He has served on the elections committee of the Modern Language Association and the executive board of Rocky Mountain Modern Language Association, and he is currently a Wertheim Research Fellow at the New York Public Library. He is writing a scholarly trilogy titled *The Ends of Neoliberalism*. Book 1 is *Inequality's Subjects: American Literature after the Arab Spring and Occupy Wall Street*. He is also completing a fantasy series titled *The Secret History of Unicorns in the Bronx*. As a union activist, he devotes much of his work to returning the City University of New York to its founding vision as free for all New York City residents and reframing work in higher education as part of the global labor movement.

Nishat Haider is professor of English at Jamia Millia Islamia University, New Delhi. Recipient of the Meenakshi Mukherjee Prize in 2015, the C. D. Narasimhaiah Award in 2010, and the Isaac Sequeira Memorial Award in 2011, she has presented papers at numerous academic conferences, and her essays have been included in a variety of scholarly journals and books. She is the author of the book *Contemporary Indian Women's Poetry* (2010). Her research interests include postcolonial studies, popular culture, and gender studies.

Abdullah A. Hasan completed his PhD in the English Department at Ball State University in 2016. His main area of interest is North African feminist autobiographical writing in English, especially works representing the intersections of religion, linguistic heritage, and postcolonial national identity politics. His dissertation, "Trespassing Borderlines: Gender and the West in North African Literature," examines the limits of postcolonial cultural westernization in the North African feminist context and highlights the role of autobiographical gestures, both secular and Islamic, in mediating critical notions about the transferability of gendered Western ideologies into the North African scene. He presented his paper about the portrayal of the veil in Gillo Pontecorvo's film *The Battle of Algiers* (1966) at the Practical Criticism Midwest conference in 2014. He is currently a linguist in the medical field and an independent literary scholar.

Michael James Lundell is associate professor of English at Palomar College. He received his PhD in literature from the University of California, San Diego. He also has a BA in English literature from the University of California, Berkeley, and an MFA in creative writing from San Diego State University. He has published and has forthcoming publications in the fields of Victorian literature, *The 1001 Nights*, and postcolonial theory. He is currently working on a monograph titled *"The 1001 Nights": Paratexts of Empire.* This longer work studies the Victorian-era English translations of the *Nights*, in particular their redefinitions of that work and their subsequent and lasting influences, and critically reevaluates *The 1001 Nights* in the context of world literature. He also maintains the website the Journal of the 1001 Nights, an online resource for *Nights*-related news, scholarship, and information. He grew up in the United Arab Emirates and Kuwait and has traveled and studied in Syria, Jordan, the United Kingdom, Egypt, Cyprus, and Turkey.

Dallel Sarnou is professor of Anglophone literature, blended learning, human resources development, human resources management, digital humanities, and digital research methodologies in the English Department of Abdelhamid Ibn Badis University, Mostaganem (Algeria). She is also a poetess and an academic researcher interested in postcolonial studies, cultural studies, transnational literatures, border studies, orientalism, feminism, Islamic feminism, critical discourse analysis and discourse analysis, and writings by Arab women. She has published academic papers on contemporary Arab women writers and youth in Arab revolutions and has published a series of poems on websites. Now she is working on hyphenation, the perception of the diasporic consciousness in the works of Arab American women writers, and the specificity of the literary works of Anglophone Arab writers.

Cherie Taraghi is an independent scholar interested in issues related to popular culture, gender, media, and migration in the Middle East. Her various publications include, most recently, the essay "Muhteşem Yüzyil or Muhteşem Rezalet:

Controversy Surrounding the Television Series *Muhteşem Yüzyil* and the Crisis of Turkish Identity," published in *Contemporary Television Series: Narrative Structures and Audience Perception*, edited by Valentina Marinescu, Silvia Branea, and Bianca Mitu (2014).

Rachida Yassine is full professor of English and cultural studies at Ibn Zohr University, Morocco. She is also director of the PhD program in Race, Ethnicity, and Alterity in Literature and Culture and director of the research team Etudes féminines au Sud du Maroc at the Research Center of Ibn Zohr University. She has a PhD in critical theory and cultural studies from the University of Nottingham, an MA in linguistics and translation from the University of Bath, as well as an MA in English and American literature and a postgraduate diploma in comparative literature from the University of Essex. She is the author of *Rewriting the Canon: Aspects of Identity Reconstitution in Postcolonial Contexts* (2011). She has contributed chapters to collected volumes, including "Recasting Delacroix's *Femmes d'Alger dans leur appartement*: A Subversive Postcolonial/Feminist Counter-Representation," in *Min Fami: Feminist Reflections on Identity, Space, and Resistance*, edited by Ghadeer Malek and Ghaida Moussa (2014), and "Female Identity Reconstitution and Colonial Language: A Postcolonial Malaise in Assia Djebar's *L'amour, la fantasia*," in *Algeria Revisited: History, Culture and Identity, 1830 to the Present*, edited by Claire Eldridge and Raba Aissaoui (2017). She has also participated in a research program in the Institute of World Literature at Harvard University and in many international conferences in the United Kingdom, Ireland, France, and the United Arab Emirates. She has published several articles on colonial and postcolonial literatures, postcolonial feminism, writings by Arab women, and cultural studies.

Afrin Zeenat is professor of English at Dallas College, Dallas, Texas. She specializes in nineteenth-century American literature and rhetoric and composition. She is also interested in eighteenth-century British literature, postcolonial literature, and Bollywood. She has presented numerous conference papers. Her articles have been published in various journals, including *Studies in American Culture*, *South Asian Review*, *Spectrum*, and *Literary Paritantra*.

Index

Printed in the USA
CPSIA information can be obtained
at www.ICGtesting.com
CBHW020430260324
5881CB00001B/1

9 780815 638414